Testimonials for
Women and the Leadership Q

"Inspiring and easily readable. This book provides the key to unlocking the leader in each of us—no matter what profession or avocation. An outstanding game plan for success."
JoAnn Heffernan Heisen, Chief Information Officer and Member, Executive Committee, Johnson & Johnson

"Awareness of the variety of leadership styles was a career-altering event! It has provided me with a strategic advantage in many career—and even personal—situations. Shoya has written a creative and innovative way to understand not just our own leadership style but those around us."
Kathleen O'Hare, Partner, Deloitte & Touche

"The most concise, illuminating insight into personality differences, how they work and how you can *best* work with them. An eye-opener and shortcut to success!"
Eleanor T. Schmidt, Senior Vice President, Fiduciary Trust International

"A breakthrough book! Shoya Zichy has scored a bull's eye by showing women business leaders how to understand their strengths and use them to work and manage more effectively.."
Peter Tanous, President, Lynx Investment Advisors and author, *Investment Gurus and Wealth Equation*

"What a find! Zichy has made traditional "personality typing" easy to understand and use in daily interactions with peers, bosses and subordinates. I consider this book to be an invaluable element in the career toolkit of anyone who wants to be a highly effective leader."
Edwina D. Woodbury, President, The Chapel Hill Press (former Executive Vice President & CFO Avon Products Inc.)

"The Digital economy is changing all the rules—leadership is no exception. Use this book to understand your leadership style, gain insights from existing leaders and to create your personal template for leading diverse individuals in evolving situations."
Ruth Ellen H. Simmonds, President, The Associated Blind

"Among the books on leadership crammed onto bookshelves, *Women and the Leadership Q* clearly stands out. It reads well, is concise, provocative, and intriguing. The women profiled are an eclectic and fascinating group; the leadership quiz provides sharp insights for the reader's own character as well as those of colleagues."

NANCY R. EICHORN, Managing Director,
The NASDAQ Stock Market

"A fun and practical approach to identifying and improving leadership style. It will become your personal guide for self analysis and an amazing resource for understanding others."

MARY LOU GIUSTINI, Managing Director,
Merrill Lynch & Co., Inc.

"This book departs from the 'one size fits all' approach that has dominated the field of management in the last decade—it should be in all business collections."

HEIDI L. SCHNEIDER, Executive Vice President and Member,
Executive Committee,
Neuberger Berman

"Crisp, entertaining and informative. A must read for all women (and men!) in leadership."

ARNOLD R. BLUMENFELD, Managing Director,
First Union Securities

"You cannot read this book without learning about yourself and about the colleagues with whom you work. Shoya Zichy approaches leadership within each of our personalities. While her book is certainly a guide for self analysis, it is also a guide to understanding the styles of co-workers. I recommend it enthusiastically."

JOAN SHAPIRO GREEN, President,
BT Brokerage Corporation

"Leadership is about bringing out the best in people or an organization—and making them more effective. This cannot be accomplished in a vacuum. This book provides a unique framework, combining business experience and psychological insight."

ELAINE LAROCHE, Managing Director,
Morgan Stanley
and CEO,
China International Capital Corporation

"Women leaders have taken many roads to success. Shoya has mapped their routes and color-coded them so that we can see the role that personality style has played in their journeys—and in our own."

JUDITH GRIFFIN, President,
Griffen Associates

WOMEN AND THE LEADERSHIP Q

*The Breakthrough System
for Achieving Power and Influence*

SHOYA ZICHY

*With special contribution by
Bonnie Kellen, Ph.D.*

MCGRAW-HILL

New York San Francisco Washington, D.C. Auckland Bogotá
Caracas Lisbon London Madrid Mexico City Milan
Montreal New Delhi San Juan Singapore
Sydney Tokyo Toronto

Library of Congress Cataloging-in-Publication Data

Zichy, Shoya.

  Women and the leadership Q : the breakthrough system for achieving power and influence / Shoya Zichy ; with special contribution by Bonnie Kellen.

    p. cm.

  Includes bibliographical references and index.

  ISBN 0-07-135216-3 (cloth)

    1. Women executives. I. Kellen, Bonnie. II. Title.

HD6054.3.Z53 2000

658.4'09'082—dc21   00-055427

McGraw-Hill

A Division of The *McGraw·Hill* Companies

  3 4 5 6 7 8 9 0   AGM/AGM   0 9 8 7 6

ISBN 0-07-135216-3

This book was set in Bembo by Tina Thompson.
Printed and bound by Quebecor World/Martinsburg.

McGraw-Hill books are available at special quantity discounts to use as premiums and sales promotions, or for use in corporate training programs. For more information, please write to the Director of Special Sales, Professional Publishing, McGraw-Hill, Two Penn Plaza, New York, NY 10121-2298. Or contact your local bookstore.

 This book is printed on recycled, acid-free paper containing a minimum of 50% recycled, de-inked fiber.

To Mother, Sheila, Charles, and Fiona
My own living color laboratory
And
To the brilliant men who have served as lifelong mentor and coach
Disque D. Deane and James G. Squyres

CONTENTS

FOREWORD

Today's rapidly evolving marketplace demands that smart companies work hard at attracting, developing, and retaining a diverse workforce. Talented and innovative executives such as Jean Hamilton, who directs Prudential institutional businesses and is profiled in this book, are a business necessity. They provide companies with a path to fresh ideas and new ways of thinking that are critical in a global economy.

Hopefully, the advice and insights shared by the women in this book *Women and the Leadership* Q which is so skillfully presented by Shoya Zichy, it will help to inspire and guide both employees and employers alike.

Arthur F. Ryan, Chairman and Chief Executive Officer,
The Prudential Insurance Company of America

INTRODUCTION

WHERE IT ALL BEGAN

On a muggy night in the early 1980s I sat stranded in an Asian airport. Imelda Marcos had comandeered my plane to escort her jet-set companions to a party in Malaysia. Only the sweepers punctuated the late night desolation. It was the end of a long, overscheduled business trip, one of the many I took every year to search for new banking clients. In the middle of large pile of debris I noticed a book. Dog-eared and well used, it caught my attention. I picked it up, and from that moment on my view of the world was altered forever.

"If a man does not keep pace with others, perhaps it is because he hears a different drummer," it began, using the oft quoted statement by Henry David Thoreau. The book, an obscure and out-of-print interpretation of Jungian thought, outlined the seemingly obvious differences in the ways people take in information and make decisions. Some of this I knew intuitively, yet the information hinted at a new framework for dealing with clients and associates. Returning to Hong Kong, I set out to organize all my customers by personality type, with a color-coded file for each type. Each file contained brief instructions for support staff to follow in the event of my absence: "When Gold comes in, make sure all statements are up to date and organized in date-sequential order. If Blue makes an appointment, call our investment guys in New York and get three new ideas." And so it continued, outlining a strategy for each of four color groups. It proved uncannily effective. Almost overnight our new business increased by 60 percent, but there was more. I began to enjoy my clients more, my stress level went down, and in time, relationships with others began to improve.

For some 10 years, I continued to use the model. The bank sent me back to the United States, and the clients grew more diverse—white-robed sheiks in Abu Dhabi, shipping magnates in Athens, aristocratic landowners in Spain—with the same color-coding instructions dotting their files:"If Gold comes in, make sure their statements are...."

In that decade I never met another individual who spoke of Jung—at least not in terms of his marketing wisdom. Neither did I. After all, this was the domain of high finance, and pop psychology was not the subject of our Monday morning meetings. Most of us toiled in a world governed mostly by greed and fear, not human connectedness. Then, in 1990, I joined some friends in Maine. It was an escape from burnout and institutional reorganization; I needed to rethink my career. The small Port Clyde Inn sparkled in the crisp October sunlight, and on the front porch sat a lanky dark-haired man reading a book. We began to chat and he spoke of the author, Isabel Myers, and her new applications of the work of Carl Jung. It was the conversation I had been looking for.

That moment was a turning point, a seemingly accidental event that steered my life in a new direction. Over the next few years I would discover a hidden universe. There were books, seminars, tapes, and associations involving hundreds of people around the world dedicated to exploring the same personality-coding system that had intrigued me for years. Compared with others, I knew little, but I knew I had a new commitment and a strong sense of internal direction. I knew that this material would prove to be an organizing force that would weave a tapestry of experiences culled from several careers over the years. Suddenly, assistance came out of nowhere and things just began to happen. The right people and events began to materialize. Jung would have chuckled. He would have called it synchronicity.

It would be a couple of years before I could undertake my own research, applying these concepts to areas of personal interests such as investment behavior and leadership. The material that follows is the result of this research on leadership. It sums up the information provided by the over 1000 participants in my seminars. It is also based on the written works of "personality type" experts who for the last two decades have laid the intellectual groundwork that serves as the basis of this book. I have pulled their principles together, viewed them through the lens of my own experience, and tested them through the lenses of others. For the sake of simplicity, I have returned to my own color-coding system of earlier times. "When you meet a Gold, make sure that. . . ." It served me well for many years. I hope it will work for you!

PURPOSE, SCOPE, AND METHODOLOGY

There are many systems for understanding people. This is the one I have found the most profound, the one that probes most deeply into the recesses of human behavior. It shows that one size does not fit all; that there are many styles of leading; that those styles are natural, observable, and predictable; and that each one can be effective. Once mastered, this model provides practical tools and techniques to maximize natural leadership talent. It is not the answer to all management problems. It is not a shortcut to maturity and wisdom. Most of all, it is not a labeling system that denies the individuality of each person.

Many people share the fantasy that with just a little more effort they can do anything and be anyone. This is an illusion that blocks real development. Growth does not require significant change or the emulation of others. It requires that we understand and accept the dynamics of our style—its unique strengths and weaknesses—and in time soften some of the blind spots. It also demands that we appreciate the styles of others and willingly make use of qualities that complement our own.

The framework does not claim to offer a complete description of any person. There are billions of unique people on this planet and only eight leadership styles.

The framework is not gender-specific: It works equally for male and female leaders. Both men and women are found in each style, though in some groups the percentages differ. My focus on women came out of the access to large groups of female executives provided by membership in the Financial Women's Association of New York and affiliated organizations. The participation of these of women in seminars and surveys provided valuable data and an opportunity to retest the conclusions.

In time it also became clear that there was a need for a book that would showcase a wide range of natural styles through the personal stories and views of women who have achieved success by embracing their individuality.

Thus the format was conceived. I created Leadership Q a self-scoring questionnaire (Chap. 1) and asked each woman to fill it out and consent to be interviewed about issues related to her style of leading. Individuals were chosen because they were recognized by the press or their peers as significant leaders in their field or avocation. The interview questions included what they perceived to be their strengths and weaknesses and the activities they found energizing, stressful, or boring. I also explored their failures and turning points, the impact of family, role models, and their advice to young women pursuing ambitious goals.

For the most part these leaders were dissimilar; there was no common external pattern to their success. Some came from tenements, and others from mansions. Only a few were firstborns, not all had college degrees, and many had advanced degrees. Some were aggressive; others were more self-contained or collaborative. A number dressed elegantly; others paid less attention to personal appearance. They represented a broad range of fields: corporate work, politics, broadcasting, entrepreneurship, the arts, social activism and philanthropy. Most had had parents with high expectations, but a small minority did not. Thirty-six were Americans by birth or residence, and two were based in Europe. In age they ranged from 38 to 80.

Their managerial styles were noticably different, but all acknowledged the validity and truth of the color-coded leadership characteristics presented during the interviews. They spoke with authenticity. Their words reflected the particular values, their priorities, and the communication texture of each individual style. Their quotes have not been altered.

EVOLUTION OF THE MODEL

In reality, while people are unique, professionals have been coding them for over 25 centuries. Even Hippocrates got into the act in

450 B.C., and a host of renowned sages, including Plato, followed suit. Today's sophisticated brain imaging continues the tradition, validating many of the earlier theories by showing how chemicals and activities in different parts of the brain affect behavior. While each person is unique, there is a part of everyone—a core if you will—that is solid and predictable.

The personality model which follows is based on the work of a several important twentieth century thinkers. First, the groundwork was developed over 70 years ago by the famed Swiss psychiatrist Carl Gustav Jung, who spent most of his life studying people's similarities and differences. He concluded that many behavior traits are due to certain preferences which are inborn or emerge early in life to become the core of what people like and dislike in other people, activities, tasks, careers, and so on. Jung outlined his ideas in the book *Psychological Types* in 1921.

Jung, however, was very abstract. Fortunately, a mother–daughter team would provide a practical key to unlocking his work. These two American women, Isabel Myers and Katharine Briggs, individually and together, would spend the next 40 years testing Jung's ideas by observing the people around them. They quantified their observations and then rigorously tested and validated them. Ultimately, they produced the Myers-Briggs Type Indicator® (MBTI®)[1], a personality-coding questionnaire that identifies 16 personality types on the basis of four sets of preferences. Today the MBTI is the most widely used psychological instrument in the world. It has been administered to more than 15 million people worldwide and is the only psychological instrument that has its own membership organization and research center.

In the 1950s Dr. David Keirsey did work that overlaid the four-part framework begun by Hippocrates and culminated in the Jungian/Myers-Briggs types. In his book *Please Understand Me,* he outlined four temperament groups correlated to the 16 types. These two models combined serve as the basis of the four color groups and the eight leadership styles presented in this book.

Today the work is being continued by another family group, Peter and Katharine Myers, coguardians of the MBTI. Katharine D. Myers,

whose work with the instrument began in 1942, was one of the
founding board members of CAPT, the research laboratory and
resource center in Gainesville, Florida. In 1979 she became the first
president of the Association for Psychological Type (APT), the leading membership organization of the "type" community.

Twenty years later her strong sense of stewardship is still in evidence. Myers is a mentor to those seeking new insights and applications. Leadership is an area of evolving interest. "The Jungian model
for growth is an excellent nonthreatening tool for developing leadership," she said in a recently telephone interview. "A good leader
understands herself well—her strengths and weaknesses. She also
understands the styles of others—their motivations, priorities, and
communication styles. This enables her to consult and work with
those whose strengths complement her weaknesses. It took me many
years to own and understand my way of leading. I never wanted to
head anything; I wanted a voice in decision making on matters
important to me. I am a good catalyst. I scan for possibilities, and
when I see something that seems really important to do, then I will
work to make it happen." Myers is a Green Advocate, as defined Chap.
16. And like many in her group, she excels at identifying the common
denominator in a discussion and summarizing the points of agreement to move the group forward in a constructive way.

On a hot humid morning in July she can be seen standing at the
entrance of an opulent ballroom that shortly will be filled with over
600 members of the type community. It is one of the many meetings
around the world she will attend each year. She is a self-contained
presence with considerable influence. Her brand of power—personal
as opposed to positional—is of particular interest since she does not
have any formal authority. She does not command a budget or
resources that enable her to hire, fire, or keep others from publishing
their work. Hers is a power that comes from within. Fueled by passion
and commitment, it projects its own brand of charisma and, in the
words of Otto Kroeger, incoming president of the association, "keeps
in front of us all the need to show respect for each other and the work
we do around the MBTI."

HOW TO USE THIS BOOK

Women and the Leadership Q is an interactive book. It is meant to be read with paper and pencil in hand. Your leadership style, as revealed by the self-scoring Leadership Q questionnaire, is meant to be shared with your partner, associates, and family. This system is not intended to label you! It is designed to explain how personality differences affect the way you lead and relate to others. Optimally, you will revisit it over and over again.

Here is what you will find in the book:

- The Leadership Q self-scoring questionnaire.
- An explanation of what kinds of traits the Leadership Q examines to determine leadership styles, and a fuller picture of the four most basic leadership personalities: Gold, Red, Blue, and Green.
- A closer look at each leadership personality, including lists of the traits typical of that personality, most typical careers for that personality, and well-known leaders of the same leadership with that personality.
- Descriptions of the two major leadership styles of each leadership personality: Gold Trustees and Gold Conservators, Red Tacticians and Red Realists, Blue Strategists and Blue Innovators, and Green Mentors and Green Advocates.
- Each leadership style is highlighted in a separate chapter, with overviews of leadership style; optimal and least preferred working environments; other attributes relevant to a working environment, such as contribution to a team, decision-making style, and potential blind spots; and even suggestions for the best ways to persuade colleagues with that leadership type.
- Since even the strongest leaders have blind spots, each chapter on leadership style also includes style-specific strategies for increasing leadership effectiveness and development exercises specific to that style's typical blind spots.
- Finally, each chapter provides leadership profiles of successful

women and sketches out of their leadership history, their strengths and weaknesses, and their advice to young women hoping to succeed.

Even the most talented women may find that they have not maximized their potential. Dr. Bonnie Kellen, a practicing psychologist, has provided a chapter on the "sag" factors that can limit otherwise strong leaders, including a self-test to diagnose your susceptibility to those factors.

For readers who need a few extra pointers to determine their leadership personality and style, Appendix A, "When You Have Close Scores," features additional self-assesment questions designed to help you pinpoint your profile.

Leadership and work have changed tremendously since the days when our grandmothers faced their own leadership challenges. For readers who want more information on how great those changes have been and how they have affected the jobs of today's leaders, Dr. Kellen has written on "Leadership, Revisited" (Appendix B).

Finally, for the most scrupulous readers; and for those who want to learn more, there are notes and resources listed at the back of the book.

How you use the book, however, is entirely up to you.

If you are the kind of person who likes to explore new ideas with others, fill out the Leadership Q questionnaire, read profiles in your color group, and share the results with someone else. I guarantee a lively discussion!

If you are the type who needs to reflect on what you have learned, by all means take some quiet time, study it by yourself, and then share it with others.

If you are organized and goal-oriented, pencil in a block of time, say 20 to 30 minutes, in your calendar for daily sessions with this material. Let material sink in rationally and predictably before charging ahead to new sections.

If you hate planning and prefer to do things on the spur of the moment, leave the book by your favorite reading chair and pick it up whenever you can. Don't worry if in a couple of months it turns up again with the pile you are taking on vacation. You will already have begun to apply whatever you have read to your daily life. If it takes you 5 years to finish it, so what!

However, you are one of these people who love anything to do with psychology, then go for it. Stay up all night and read it. Analyze all your bosses, subordinates, competitors, clients, donors, family members, and friends. Take note of the bibliography. Order other resource materials. Arrange for an MBTI specialist to come in and run training sessions for your group. Just remember that not everyone wants to hear your latest analysis at every meal.

As you can see, there are many legitimate ways to approach new material. That is the thesis of this book Each way is valid, and each works for a different type of individual.

Enjoy your journey!

Shoya Zichy

ACKNOWLEDGMENTS

A book—particularly one that involves 38 profiles of powerful and very busy people—is a collaboration of many individuals. Helping to convince these women to be interviewed and to lend themselves to personality interpretation was truly a mark of support. I wish to express my special appreciation to: Lily Blake, Sheila Birnbaum, Tabor Butler, Kitty Cushing, Judith Griffin, Mina Knoll, Eric Rahe, Brenda Schofield, Elysia Stobbe, Candace Straight, and Peter Tanous who put their own credibility on the line to provide the introductions.

The personality categories have been shaped by seminar participants and the collective research from the Myers-Briggs community. I am particularly indebted to:

David Keirsey, Ph.D. who books *Please Understand Me* and *Please Understand Me II* serve as the intellectual basis for the Leadership Q color model. Without his groundbreaking work, the temperament model, as we understand it today, would not exist.

Katharine D. Myers for serving as a sounding board to my ongoing stream of ideas.

Linda V. Berens Ph.D., Director of the Temperament Research Institute whose writings include *Understanding Yourself and Others* and *Dynamics of Personality Types*. Our conversations have deepened my understanding of temperaments.

Those who have generously shared their insights and experiences, most particularly Otto Kroeger, Leona Haas, Catherine Fitzgerald, Elizabeth Treher, Alan Brownsword, Sandra Hirsh, Martine Robards, and Jamie Johnson of CAPT.

Heidi Fiske who over the years has provided priceless support and opportunities to address the sophisticated audiences of the *Institutional Investor Institute*.

The over four hundred members of the FWA who have participated in seminars and surveys and who provided the initial inspiration for the book.

A book also requires high quality editing, production, and marketing and for these I am indebted to:

My agent, Jan Miller who was the first to believe in the project.

My editors, Mary E. Glenn and Yedida Soloff for their editing savvy and support.

The efficient team of Paul Sobel and Elizabeth Strange for their editorial and production supervision.

The publicity group of Claudia Riemer-Boutote and Elizabeth Aviles for their creativity and enthusiam.

Ann Bidou whose clarity and insights have benefited every chapter in this book.

Laura Clift and Rebecca Rand for taking time out of their graduate studies to transcribe interview tapes and help finalize the manuscript.

Marantha Dawkins for being the best listener in the world.

Arthur Ryan and Mike Hanretta of the Prudential Insurance Company of America for contributing the Foreword.

Ongoing advice was provided by my strategic advisory board: Debra Flanz, Barbara Reno, Fali Rubinstein, Linda Seale, Josie Sentner, Ruth-Ellen Simmonds, Sally Strachan Davia Temin, Wina Woodbury and Sarabeth Wizen; by the marketing pros who served on the "launch committee" Joan Green, Gail Miner, Kathi Lenrow, Norma Niehoff, Nancy Sellar, Rose Marcotte, Patricia Schuetz, Ivy Dodes, Maria Foffe and Kimberly Quinones and by those who provided positioning ideas and contacts: Paulina Rogawski, Starlin Leitner, Judith Robinson, Jenene Karamon, Eunice Salton and Fabianne Gershon.

And last, but certainly not least, to Fiona Nemes whose youthful enthusiasm is a constant reminded of the potential of our upcoming generation of leaders.

PART

1 Foundation of the Model

1 What Is Your Leadership Style?

LEADERSHIP Q

- Choose the statement from the left or right column that best describes you at least 51 percent of the time.
- If both apply, choose the one that applies under *ideal circumstances of your own choosing* as opposed to being required of you at work or home. Your first impulse is usually right.
- Mark a heavy X in the left or right column corresponding to your choice.
- Answer *all* the questions.
- To get the most accurate results, put yourself in a relaxed frame of mind and work quickly.
- At the end, total each column, counting 1 for each box. The eight slots should total 38. If they do not, check back to make sure you answered all the items.

A	1	☐	ee	LEFT COLUMN	RIGHT COLUMN	ii	▽	2	B
				Value accuracy more	Value insights more				
				Are more of a concrete thinker	Are more of an abstract thinker				
				Prefer people who speak plainly	Prefer unusual forms of expression				
				Tend to be competitive	Tend to be collaborative				
				Prefer to be fair	Prefer to be compassionate				
				More often skeptical at first	More often accepting at first				
				Persuaded by objective reasoning	Persuaded by passionate conviction				
				Meet deadlines early	Meet deadlines at the last minute				
				Dislike surprises	Like surprises				
				Make plans before you start	Handle problems as they arise				
				Move to closure as soon as possible	Keep options open as long as possible				
				Usually remember many details	Usually vague about details				
				Like talking about practical issues	Prefer discussing ideas and concepts				
				Are seen as rooted in present reality	Are seen as more oriented to the future				
				Value ability to analyze logically	Value ability to empathize with others				
				Try to ignore emotional aspects	Look for emotional aspects				
				Often don't take things personally	Often take things personally				
				Are always punctual and sometimes early	Tend to be leisurely				
				Want to have things settled in advance	Like to be spontaneous				
				Like order and structure	Like to go with the flow				
				Are more interested in concrete data	Focus on patterns and relationships				

A	1	□	ee	LEFT COLUMN	RIGHT COLUMN	ii	▷	2	B
				Like projects with tangible results	Like projects that test new ideas				
				Choose solutions that worked in past	Prefer trying new solutions				
				Are concerned about underlying principles	Are concerned about impact on people				
				See flaws and critique readily	Overlook flaws and support readily				
				Manage and deal firmly with others	Manage by relating sympathetically				
				Look for reason	Look for harmony				
				Most often feel settled	Most often feel restless				
				Like to be scheduled	Find schedules confining				
				Like to be systematic	Stay unplanned when possible				
				Have a tidy workplace	Have a workplace with many piles and papers				
				Like meetings that apply existing ideas	Like meetings that come up with new ideas				
				Are admired for common sense	Are admired for seeing new trends				
				Like face-to-face interaction	Prefer the written word or e-mail first				
				Tend to have lots of friends	Tend to have a few close friends				
				Speak first, then reflect	Reflect first, then speak				
				Like meeting new people	Postpone meeting new people				
				Are energized by people and activity	Need substantial blocks of time alone				
A	1	□	ee	TOTAL	TOTAL	ii	▷	2	B

SCORING INSTRUCTIONS

1. Total all eight columns; they should *add up to 38.* If they do not, go back and check that you have answered *all the questions.* Remember it is what *you would choose 51 percent of the time,* not all the time.

2. Start with the two outer columns, A and B. Find the larger number. Enter the letter of the column.   A or B _____

3. Compare the second set of columns, 1 and 2. Enter the number.   1 or 2 _____

4. Compare the third columns, □ and ∇. Enter the symbol.   □ or ∇ _____

5. Compare the inner set of columns, ee and ii. Find the larger number.   ee or ii _____

Find your code below and circle the appropriate box.

If you have chosen A, look at the top four boxes. If A is combined with 1, look at the two left-hand boxes; if it is combined with 2, check the two on the right.

If you have chosen B, look at the bottom four boxes. If B is combined with 1, look at the third row; if it is combined with 2, check the fourth row.

A 1 □ *GOLD TRUSTEE*	*A 2* □ *GOLD CONSERVATOR*
A 1 ∇ *RED TACTICIAN*	*A 2* ∇ *RED REALIST*
B 1 □ *BLUE STRATEGIST*	*B 1* ∇ *BLUE INNOVATOR*
B 2 □ *GREEN MENTOR*	*B 2* ∇ *GREEN ADVOCATE*

If you have chosen ee, your preference is for "extraversion." For example, you may be an extraverted Blue Strategist. Enter an E in the small box attached to the left of your box above.

If you have chosen ii, you preference is for "introversion." For example, you may be a Gold Trustee introvert. Enter an I in the small box attached to the left of your box above.

If you have close scores, such as 5/6, *read the next two chapters carefully.* Very often we frame questions according to the demands of our jobs and families. Only you can determine your "true type." If you still have difficulty, turn to Appendix A or read several profiles and see which ones resonate best. Determining your true type is very important. Do it now!

I am _____

2 Defining Leadership

In the bustling San Francisco hotel lobby an Armani-clad woman pushes a stroller. Fifty minutes ago she stood before a gathering of corporate executives who manage some $50 billion of pension assets. Her presentation on asset allocation drew spirited applause. At the moment, however, the focus is on finding her daughter's pacifier. "As an investment strategist, I travel frequently," she says, "and we all had to learn to roll with the punches." She grins, pointing to the toddler, her nanny, and her obliging spouse.

Today the workplace is abounding with ambitious and accomplished women, from chief executive officers (CEOs) to governors. Even the Barbie doll ads read, "Be your own hero." Some see the trend as a wave that will only superficially alter the texture of the shore. For others, such as Claire de Hedervary, it is a cultural revolution—profound, lasting, and with new sets of rules. Hedervary, president of Belgium's United Business Institutes and a high-ranking veteran of the Political Department of the United Nations, sees it happening all over the world, at a different pace and in different ways.

"It is an irreversible trend," she notes, "that foretells of radical changes in the governance of the world and in the nature of the private relationships between men and women."

Clearly, the models of leadership have changed. Only twenty years ago most successful women dressed and acted like men. They wore pinstriped suits and silk bow ties and were described as forceful, competitive, logical, and task-oriented. More recently, as the upcoming profiles vividly demonstrate, they have been freed to exhibit a wider range of operating styles and goals.

This book is designed to help you look at the dynamics of these different styles. It explores the theme through the lens of Howard Gardner's *Leading Minds,* which defines leadership as "the ability to influence—either directly or indirectly—the behavior, thoughts, and actions of a significant number of individuals."[2]

This definition includes women who command massive resources—human and financial—and those who exert influence through personal power, literary achievement, or the compelling force of an idea.

Significantly, the definition is not gender-specific. On the gender front, scientific research on the differences remains inconclusive. Deborah Blum in *Sex on the Brain* summarizes it best. It is widely accepted that there are small structural differences between the brains of men and women. It is also clear that their bodies are different in size and shape and that for the most part people have a strong sense of gender identity. Beyond that the waters are murky. There seem to be more behavioral differences within each sex than there are between the sexes. Furthermore, the interaction between genes, hormones, and the environment is complicated and fluid. The brain is plastic; we are influenced by it, and we influence it.[3] "The anatomy of gender is straightforward," Blum said in an e-mail interview. "The chemistry of gender is more complex. It is, I believe, a continuum on which we can each find a place on the wide band of what is considered 'normal.' What's more, we can change our place and the place where we direct our children."

Additionally, the Jungian-based personality model used in this book contributes new insights to the gender debate. One trait—the thinking/feeling decision-making process (Chap. 4)—goes some distance towards explaining why certain ways of leading do not fit the gender stereotypes. If one believes that this trait is inborn, and a growing number of people do, the argument becomes even more interesting.

For example, the Jungian model explains why not all women manage collaboratively. It explains why not all women are nurturing, consensus-driven, or interested in creating win-win environments. Some women are competitive, tough, analytical, and task-driven. They excel in math and science. They do not take criticism personally. They handle confrontation with ease. These are the women who share what Jung called a thinking decision-making preference. They base decisions primarily on objective criteria, emphasizing what is fair and reasonable. According to the latest research, these women make up about 35 percent of the female population.

The remaining 65 percent of women are known in Jungian terminology as feeling decision makers.[4] They make decisions by stressing personal values and the impact a decision will have on people. Their decisions are keyed more to the specific circumstances of the situation than to objective principles. Feeling deciders typically have a better sense of how to motivate others. They are more collaborative and sensitive to criticism and confrontation. Their communication style is vivid and colorful. They excel at mining the potential of the people around them.

As leaders, Thinkers congregate in certain industries: finance, law, accounting, technology, and some branches of medicine. They represent about 90 percent of the women executives on Wall Street. They also populate the senior ranks of large established organizations; they adapt to the traditional and hierarchical power structure without too much stress.

Thinkers have a zest for competition. As executive vice president of the Prudential Insurance Company of America and CEO of Prudential Institutional, Jean Hamilton has businesses reporting to her that have a Fortune 250 ranking. "Coming up with new business models and creating successful companies is about the most fun you can ever have," she says.

Feisty venture capitalist Darla Moore's recent donation of $25 million to a business school in South Carolina has given her plenty of clout in her home state. Now this Thinker wants to leverage her influence by substantially altering that state's political landscape. Her agenda includes reforming the legislature's way of tracking revenues to the overall system of education. For Hamilton and Moore, terms such as *aggressive* and *bold* have a positive connotation. They make no apologies and relish the prestige that these traits have helped them attain.

Feelers are also found in high positions. In large companies they frequently move up the corporate ladder through the sales or communication route. Or they may opt out of corporate America, creating parallel orbits of power outside the traditional centers. They are strongly represented in marketing, communications, entertainment, broadcasting, politics, and the arts.

Fox 2000 president Laura Ziskin recently chose to return to film production. "Power is not about being a studio head," she says, "It is about creating entertainment of value that will stimulate, provoke, and challenge people." Jolene Sykes, president of *Fortune* magazine, describes her leadership style as a "soft lead. I like to get everyone involved and on board with me." Journalist Diane Sawyer defines her strength as "finding that sweet spot, the point where the thing you care most about meets and joins with what matters to others."

Thinking/feeling decision-making differences, combined with three other personality traits, create the eight leadership styles outlined in this book. Each style has its own strengths and weaknesses. Each works best in a different environment, sets different kinds of goals, and relates differently to others. Each has a predictable path. Understanding the system allows you, the reader, to recognize and develop your own potential and lead others more effectively.

Differences apart, some striking similarities are found among the women profiled in the chapters that follow. First, they all have a high degree of intellectual energy. Their energy is focused rather than diffused. In the more outgoing women it shines forth bright and vigorous. In the more introverted ones it is self-contained, as in a silent owl staring at its target with steady intensity. In some women that energy is focused on a vision defined as something new, not yet in existence. In others the focus is on a concrete long-term goal. The rest downplay the need for goals, focusing instead on short-term objectives that shift as new opportunities present themselves. As Cathy Hughes, chair of Radio One, puts it, "I never had a five-year plan. I never had a five-week plan. My only plan was to take care of today, my payroll and my son."

These differences are innate, somewhat fixed, and more related to the core personality style than to gender, IQ, upbringing, corporate culture, or the nature of the specific goals themselves. They create very different styles of management.

Second, all the women profiled here have a sense of mission and commitment that borders on obsession. Their mission is a driving force that prompts them to take risks and step outside their comfort zone. It enables them to keep a positive can-do attitude regardless of setbacks. For Kathleen Kennedy Townsend the vision is about creating government initiatives that will inspire the citizens to improve their own communities, and she fights for her programs despite significant opposition.

Third, they all, without exception, put a positive spin on setbacks. Each interview, whether by phone or in person, left me believing individual effort can make a difference. Senator Kay Bailey Hutchison viewed two major setbacks, including the loss of a congressional race, as necessary stepping-stones to representing Texas in the U.S. Senate today. Governor Christie Whitman entered an impossible race with no funds or support from her party and parlayed it into a successful bid for the governorship. Lorna Wendt took her own divorce public and created the Center for Marital Equality, which aims to change the laws governing the division of marital assets.

Fourth, these leaders know how to put things into perspective. They understand the value of confidence without forgetting the need for humility and the need to improve themselves and their dreams.

Fifth, they understand the need to know and manage themselves. They understand that leadership is not something one masters all at once; it is an ongoing process of developing skills, talents, and insights. They understand the formula self-knowledge leads to self-management, which leads to self-confidence, which leads to accomplishment, which in turn produces self-esteem and ultimately the ability to lead and influence others. Master this formula. It will give you the tools to develop your own path to success.

BUILDING BLOCKS OF LEADERSHIP

Leadership

⇧

Self-Esteem

⇧

Accomplishment

⇧

Self-Confidence

⇧

Self-Management

⇧

Self-Knowledge

3 A Tour through Leaderville

To get a better idea how a person's leadership style is profiled, let's take a quick excursion through a mythical village known as Leaderville.

First of all, in Leaderville neighborhoods are not based on class, wealth, or ethnic background. The four neighborhoods are based on personality types. Second, the four neighborhoods are not equal in size; the size of each one reflects its percentage of that personality group in the United States as a whole. Third, these personality traits are innate. In Leaderville people are born and die in their own neighborhoods. While the residents operate best in their own communities, the township provides free and easy transportation to the other neighborhoods. Sometimes individuals will visit other neighborhoods several times a day. They may not always be comfortable doing that, but they respect the atmosphere and services and they have a certain affinity with the people who live there. Some neighborhoods they usually avoid. They may visit only a couple of times a year, say, at tax time or maybe to see clients. In these areas they are not comfortable. They do not share the same habits, sense of humor, activities, and interests with the residents, or they get irritated at the pace and approach those folks use to get things done.

Let us label these neighborhoods by color: Gold, Red, Blue, and Green. These colors have been chosen because they seem to express some basic characteristics of each group. Golds are solid and grounded, Reds are instinctive and adventurous, Blues are reasoning and strategic, and Greens are humanistic and diplomatic.

In each of these communities there are two boroughs where the inhabitants differ somewhat but still share many traits. In the Gold neighborhood, for example, there are Trustees and Conservators. In the Blue area there are the Strategists and Innovators. Among the Reds, one can find Tacticians and Realists, and among the Greens there are Mentors and Advocates.

As I describe each neighborhood, compare yourself to its residents. By the end of the chapter you should be able to determine which neighborhood seems most like "home." Then see if your choice reflects the results from your Leadership Q questionnaire. These two steps provide a double check to help you find your "true" color type. As was mentioned previously, results from the Leadership Q questionnaire may be skewed by how you framed the questions before choosing your answers. Reading about the neighborhoods will help you ascertain your true type. This is important if you are to get the greatest benefit from the leader profiles in this book.

Your neighborhood walk also will provide an overview of the system and show how each color group differs from its neighbors. This is a good opportunity to note where your friends, family members, and work associates "live." The color areas provide important clues about what motivates and drives them.

Remember, this is a mythical village where exaggerations are acceptable to illustrate pivotal points. Let us begin by taking a stroll.

THE GOLD NEIGHBORHOOD

The Gold neighborhood is strikingly well maintained. The houses are solid; some are made of brick, others of wood. Mostly they have a traditional style of architecture; there are few modern styles. The inhabitants seem to prefer what reflects traditional values and what was tried and found to work in the past. The bushes are neatly trimmed, falling into exact straight lines or graceful, well-balanced curves. Lawns are cut, and flowers are planted in predictable patterns.

In the center of the neighborhood you will find, proudly displayed, the village and country flags. Each evening these flags are respectfully lowered in the presence of officials. You also will note that people wait until the light changes before crossing the street. They respect authority and follow the rules. The neighborhood council is chosen annually, drawing from the many candidates who have volunteered for the various committees. Golds believe in governing by chain of command.

The children are well dressed, courteous, and punctual. They often can be seen doing chores, cutting the grass, and running errands for their parents. The essence of "Goldness" emerges early in life. Gold children want parents to be parents, not buddies. They expect well-run homes, with meals served on schedule and a steady supply of shoelaces. They prefer schools with rules, discipline, and a traditional curriculum. Young Golds do best with teachers who give clear directions and stick to the lesson plan. They respond well to objective tests, factual subject matter, and a dependable reward system.

Gold parents also live by rules. They maintain well-defined family roles and daily schedules that list all activities including fun and recreation. Marital partnerships are stable. A well-organized home is particularly valued, and Gold parents always know what should be done. Typically, they dislike change and surprises.

Commerce in this neighborhood is stable. Gold stores open and close on time and are well stocked. Salesmen wear suits, ties, and starched white shirts. Women wear simple tailored apparel. Butchers and grocers have clean white aprons; their work areas are immaculate. Services of all types are punctual. Tradespeople arrive when they are supposed to and deliver reliable services. They are usually much in demand throughout the entire village, and woe betide those who do not appreciate their exacting standards or, worse yet, keep them waiting at a prearranged appointment.

There are many individuals with professional titles, such as doctors, lawyers, and judges. Education, achievement, and financial prosperity are highly valued because they represent accomplishment. There also are bankers, managers, and military personnel. Mostly one finds folks working for large, well-established institutions that are financially secure and respected in the community.

Volunteerism is valued. Gold residents make up most of the boards in the village—religious, civic, and cultural—even on institutions in other neighborhoods. One might ask why they join and run so many committees. First, because they are asked to; everyone knows they get things done. Putting a project in the hands of a Gold means it's a done deal. Second, when asked, they accept, vaguely mistrustful that if they do not, the project will not be done properly.

Golds frequently attend the appropriate religious services and celebrate the major holidays. This is where the Fourth of July parade begins and where the largest Thanksgiving reunions take place. Holiday decorations are tasteful and are put on display way before other neighborhoods have begun to think about them. Golds value these icons because they represent stability, tradition, and a natural way to pass on cultural values to the next generation. In fact, Golds are known to sponsor the reading of oral histories of each celebration, choosing older citizens, who are honored to perform the readings.

Leaving the calm and order of Golddom, we head for the Red neighborhood, where the atmosphere is very different indeed.

THE RED NEIGHBORHOOD

In the Red neighborhood, the houses have many add-ons and there is much activity in each one. In fact, there is much activity everywhere. There are people on bicycles; others are jogging, taking part in a softball game, or heading for the sports complex in the center of the community. Other residents are bustling around to carry out their mostly entrepreneurial activities.

Visitors rarely find immaculate houses. The activities of the day are in full swing, and guests find that they must join in or be left behind.

Reds like to live well, though they are not necessarily the most affluent people in the village. Usually, however, they like expensive restaurants, wine cellars, and gadgets in general. Life is somewhat hectic. It is not regulated. The residents do not like schedules, rules, or rituals; they like to follow their impulses and do what seems best at the moment; rarely are they driven by guilt or duty. Their style is fraternal. They are good to friends and family members but hate being tied down to imposed routines.

Their view of the world is based on what they can see, touch, and observe for themselves. The general store here carries mystery stories, adventure books, travelog, the latest best-sellers and magazines about food, cars, and cigars. Theoretical books and publications on self-improvement gather dust for months, until they are purchased by a visitor from another area.

Many Reds are self-employed, choosing to be their own bosses and avoid corporate politics. Whereas Golds do well in hierarchical companies, Reds usually bomb out quickly. When employed by a company, they prefer to run independent activities or act as general troubleshooters. A fair number go into professional sports, and many are found in films, both as actors and as producers. This explains why there are so many theaters and professional sports arenas in this part of the village.

Also, this is where most of the fire trucks are housed and where the police are headquartered. When sirens sound, Reds want to know what's happening and how to help. Reds also shine in any area that requires negotiating skills. In fact, most of the town's wheeler-dealers live in this neighborhood.

We encounter a group returning from an African safari. Excitedly, they point to photographs of a newly discovered tribe, along with a close-up of an irate rhinoceros, and once again we marvel at the electric excitement generated by this group.

At home Reds are engaging mates whose motto, "Life is to be enjoyed," applies to work, play, athletics, hobbies, and sex. The garage is filled with whatever adult toys a person can afford. The latest in electronic and sports equipment is haphazardly displayed. The skis are in the hall closet, the jogging suit is on the hook of the kitchen door, and the remnants of last weekend's outing are still in the back of the car. Guests are welcome; Reds are often excellent cooks who, even when unprepared, respond warmly to drop-in visitors, sharing whatever is available.

As parents they are fun and responsive. Their live-and-let-live philosophy provides their offspring with an active, nonjudgmental, and spontaneous environment. They may neglect to focus on the child's future but respond well to immediate needs.

Red children are apt to be energetic and impulsive from babyhood on. They find playpens confining and are rough on toys. In the classroom they are equally restless. Their learning style is distinct and requires special consideration. They respond more to hands-on experience, gamelike competition, and experiential activities such as field trips and lab-type situations. Generally, young Reds finish their formal education as soon as possible, preferring to test themselves in the real world of work.

THE BLUE NEIGHBORHOOD

Continuing our stroll, we come upon another neighborhood with modern and futuristic houses. These houses have large open areas and well-stocked libraries. Learning is valued very highly in this neighborhood, which also has most of the town's bookstores, universities, and public libraries. The residents never feel they have enough knowledge. In contrast to the joviality of the previously visited section, people in this area are more intense, although they do have a jousting and sarcastic sense of humor.

The atmosphere is filled with challenge: Children challenge their parents, employees challenge their bosses, and spouses challenge each other. Visitors may find this group blunt and confrontational, at times even irritating. The residents, however, enjoy these exchanges. Only by challenging, they reason, can one come up with creative solutions and designs.

In the Blue neighborhood, a high value is placed on intellectual achievement. Coffeehouses proliferate where deep intellectual discussions run for hours, day and night. Comedy clubs feature the most clever and cutting-edge performers.

There is a marked absence of signs and directions: Blues tend to flout rules, rites, and accepted ways of doing things.

The Blue neighborhood was the first to access the Internet, and every household has at least one computer, usually more, as well as a small cache of electronic gadgets, palm ponds, laptops, and digital phones. Residents eagerly embrace the latest technology and are the first to master new equipment.

In the home Blues pay serious attention to the development of their offspring. They never stint on the intellectual development of the family but are far less willing than Reds to spend money on luxury and status items. Their children are precocious, independent, and fairly solemn from an early age. They talk, read, and interpret events sooner than other children do. At school they challenge authority and methods of study. Like their adult counterparts, young Blues do not try to please. When it comes to rules, the motto is "the fewer, the better."

In general, Blues have a hard time with emotional issues and usually avoid them. They are best known as agents of change who take risks, challenge existing systems, and create new ones. Among them we find many journalists, CEOs, strategic planners, professors, and computer specialists.

THE GREEN NEIGHBORHOOD

The Green neighborhood completes our tour. We stroll through a community with many flowers and interconnecting porches. Beds of organic foods proliferate in many gardens. There is much leaded and cut glass in windows, creating prisms of light that fall everywhere.

On many porches group meetings are in progress. One has a meeting to discuss ecological issues. A second serves as a meeting place for a support group for grieving spouses. On a third porch activists are organizing consumers to form food co-ops.

At the center of Greenville is a large community center where causes compete for a spot on the daily agenda. The neighborhood has an intense interest in spiritual, physical, cosmic, and self-development issues. The center's sports activities focus on noncompetitive activities such as swimming, skating, weight lifting, yoga, and dance. The volleyball players prefer keeping the ball in the air to scoring a point.

There is a free-exchange craft shop where artists periodically donate pieces of their work and in exchange take home any other pieces of their choice.

Commerce is of secondary interest. The clothing store features elegant and unusual handcrafted designs. There is a bookstore specializing in spiritual and psychic topics. Down the road a pyramid-shaped roof shelters a health and herb center, but beyond that there is not much in the way of retail.

The residents are more interested in improving the quality of life than in acquiring possessions. Many do very well financially because they are creative and highly gifted communicators. They are often found in marketing, public relations, and advertising, or they gravitate toward consultative sales in areas where they excel because of their innate ability to grasp the issues of concern to their clients. Others serve as TV anchors. Many work in psychological fields of all types. Many others are highly acclaimed writers and motivational speakers and gurus.

As parents Greens fantasize with their kids and provide nonjudgmental support. That support extends to other children as well, and family activities often include others in the community. The home will host puppet shows, historical dress-up evenings, and craft fairs. Green children respond enthusiastically to many activities—so many, in fact, that they often have trouble setting priorities.

Green schools give individual feedback rather than grades and stress cooperative team activity. Some of these teams have achieved national acclaim by producing plays, films, and even a special kids' TV show.

In general, the residents of Greenville dislike confrontation and look for appreciation from others. They strive to create a harmonious and collegial community that inspires its members to new levels of development. Power to Greens means the ability to influence, not to control.

WHERE DO YOU WANT TO LIVE?

Now it is time to consider which of these four neighborhoods is most attractive to live in. Most people will identify with parts of several, and so deciding on one area is often difficult. This is the case because the various roles and conditions of our lives demand that we draw on different functions in our brains. As you will learn in Chap. 4, however, we have preferred functions that enable us to function with more energy and better results. The bottom line is that while we visit all four neighborhoods, home is where we are happiest, most energized, and least obligated to the demands of others. Circle your neighborhood preference in the boxes below. These results will be validated by your results on the Leadership Q questionnaire on page 6.

| GOLD | BLUE | RED | GREEN |

THE FOUR NEIGHBORHOODS

GOLD	BLUE
Are grounded, responsible, and realistic	Are theoretical, challenging, and competitive
Maintain order and stability	See the big picture
Organize workflow efficiently	Enjoy solving complex problems
Respect tradition and rules	Embrace new theories
Have systems for everything	Are skeptical of accepted beliefs
Make quick decisions	Are brief, terse, and concise
Set up realistic schedules	See dimensions others do not grasp
Schedule most of life	Stress logical analysis
Dislike theory	Flout rules and rites
Pay attention to details	Demand strategic competence
Demand and offer accountability	Never feel they know enough

RED	GREEN
Are spontaneous, flexible, and action-oriented	Are empathetic, humanistic, and expressive
Look for immediate results	Need to affect the world
Are adaptable and spontaneous	Are tactful and diplomatic
Take risks	Are future-oriented
Dislike schedules and rules	Coach and encourage others
Get impatient with abstractions	Are articulate and persuasive
Need variety and action	Seek creative solutions
Get bored and restless easily	Overpersonalize criticism
Handle crises well	Get people to work together
Are fraternal and collegial	Require harmony
Change schedules easily	Enjoy being unique and authentic

4 Penetrating Your Personality Preferences

Now that you know where "home" is, let's learn more about why it feels homelike.

It is important to reiterate that there are many things these neighborhood types do not measure. They do not say anything about intelligence, mental health, education, maturity, stress level, physical health, or neurotic tendencies. This is simply where your mentally healthy self prefers to be in its most natural state.

These color types do measure how people see reality, judge that reality, and prefer to structure their daily lives to deal with that reality. A fourth dimension defines how people are energized and direct that energy to interact with the world.

Each color represents a combination of inborn preferences to do things in a certain way. It is somewhat like using the right or left hand. You are born with a preference for one over the other. You use both hands throughout the day, but instinctively you have a preference for one. You use it effortlessly and efficiently. You can switch hands but would find having to write with your nonpreferred hand awkward and uncomfortable. The color types function in much the same way.

THE CASE FOR SENSING VERSUS INTUITING

One inborn set of preferences involves how we take in information. One part of the brain takes in information through the five senses and is called the sensing function. The five senses collect data about things we can feel, smell, touch, taste, and hear. This information focuses on what is concrete, real, and in the present. It focuses on physical details and facts. A second part of the brain looks beyond the concrete and focuses on patterns and relationships. This is called intuiting. It relies on a sixth sense to determine not what is but what could be. It creates abstract concepts and relationships.

Everyone can both sense and intuit, but each person prefers one to the other. An individual uses the preferred part of the brain with greater facility and energy and with better results. The best available statistics suggest that 73 percent of the population prefers sensing, and 27 percent prefers intuiting.[5]

Jung was the first modern thinker to define these human preferences. He observed that Sensors use their intuition, but in a limited way and only after having built a solid base of facts. Having to rely on their intuition too early in the game is tiring for them. Sensors need to test their intuitive conclusions against what they see as reality and do not trust the intuitive perception of others. They are more interested in what actually exists than in what might be. They like to deal with things that can be documented and are measurable. They tend to be literal in describing people and events. They may interpret but tend not to go beyond the facts.

Individuals who prefer to focus on patterns, mental relationships, and abstract concepts are known as Intuitives. They take in information through the five senses but immediately begin to put it into a theoretical framework and relate it to other things. They read between the lines. They interpret and in so doing trust leaps that may go beyond the facts. They speak in a figurative way, often using metaphors or analogies. They can spend hours discussing ideas, models, paradigms, and future trends. When doing so, they become animated and energized. When speaking about literal subject matters, they quickly lose interest and move the conversation into other areas.

As for sensing versus intuiting, neither is better or worse. Neither indicates more intelligence or less. They are simply different. Each has its own natural strengths and blind spots. They do, however, produce fairly different behaviors.

If you ask a Sensor, for example, what she had for dinner last Wednesday, chances are that she will describe the exact components of the meal, the special spices, the physical consistency of the sauce on the pasta, and probably what her neighbors ate as well. She will describe the condition of the tablecloth, the style of the cutlery, and, if pushed, what everyone wore. Ask an Intuitor about the same dinner, and she will pause trying to remember what dinner, what week, what night, and where. Having finally pinpointed the event mentally, she will try very hard to remember what she ate and more often than not forget half the meal. She will remember that she had a pleasant time but beyond that will find the exercise boring and tiring.

For Sensors, facts are sacred; for Intuitors, facts are there to support the larger picture and approximate is usually good enough. Sarabeth, a high-powered executive on Wall Street, recalls her summer stint as an assistant in a jewelry story at age 17. One day she informed her supervisor that she thought a man was casing the store. The supervisor, who had been in the same store all day, dismissed her concerns, gently rebuking her for watching too much television. The next day the man came in, ordered all the employees facedown on the floor, and proceeded to rob the store. Later the police questioned all who were present. Having been paralyzed by fear, few even got his clothing right. Sarabeth, the only Sensor in the group, was able give a perfect description of his clothing, build, height, and general physical appearance, including the mole on his arm. On the basis of her description alone, the man was picked up a few hours later.

Here are statements and words associated with sensing and intuiting.

Sensing

Prefer concrete information

Focus on what is going on now

Intuiting

Prefer abstract information

Focus on what will happen in the future

Rely on past experiences	Look for new ways of doing things
Like ideas with practical value	Like new ideas for their own sake
Are literal in speech	Are figurative in speech; use analogies
Recall the past accurately	Are vague about the past and interested in the future
Are realistic and pragmatic	Are theoretical and imaginative

If you have opted for more choices in the Sensor column, chances are that you have a higher score in the A column of the questionnaire and have chosen either the Gold or the Red neighborhood. If you have chosen more items in the Intuitive column, you probably have found yourself drawn to either the Blue or the Green neighborhood and have a higher score in the B column.

Unfortunately, Sensors and Intuitors rarely appreciate each other's point of reference. Each side believes its way is more accurate and useful. Sensors think Intuitors are impractical, and Intuitors think Sensors never get beyond the obvious. This dimension is a major source of conflict in both professional and personal relationships. Furthermore, the more pronounced the preference is (i.e., the more items you have chosen in one column over the other), the greater is the potential for miscommunication with someone who is your opposite.

Now let's move on and describe a second set of preferences.

THE CASE FOR THINKING VERSUS FEELING

Thinking deciders rely on objective standards. They base decisions primarily on what is fair, consistent, and reasonable. They trust only what stands up to the scrutiny of the analytic process. They weigh the pros and cons carefully. They consider the logical consequences of their choice. They search for the flaws and inconsistencies. They critique well, usually being the first to highlight what is wrong with a situation or line of reasoning. They base judgments on impersonal logic.

Feeling deciders, by contrast, base decisions on subjective criteria, mostly their personal values. Before making judgments they take into account how others will be affected by the decision. They do look at the pros and con, but ultimately, the deciding factor is, what matters most. Feelers value harmony more than justice and compassion more than fairness. They tend to affirm and support when thinkers critique and analyze.

It is a mistake to link the thinking preference to reason and the feeling preference to emotion. Jung saw it differently. He went to great lengths to explain that these are simply two contrasting ways of making judgments and coming up with conclusions. They are both rational processes.

We use both preferences when making decisions. We do not, however, use them equally or equally efficiently. One is our preferred decision-making mode and produces better output. Usually people check in with both modes. If the two modes arrive at the same conclusion, the decision is easy. If the two, however, produce different results, people tend to fall back on their preferences.

Here are the statements associated with each mode. Check off the ones that apply to you.

Thinking Deciding	**Feeling Deciding**
Are direct	Are diplomatic
Analyze problems	Empathize with people
Stress competence	Stress relationships
Critique easily	Affirm easily
Enjoy playing devil's advocate	Avoid conflict and arguments
Appear cool and matter of fact	Often appear emotional and excited
Place a high value on monetary reward	Place a middle to low value on monetary reward
Are more thick-skinned	Are more sensitive
Use direct, even terse speech	Engage in small talk and social niceties
Project coolness initially	Project warmth immediately
Are interested in solving the problem	Are interested in putting people at ease first

Which are you? If you have chosen thinking, chances are that you had a higher score in column 1. If you have more items in the feeling column, you should have a higher score in column 2.

These two different ways of making decisions are actually highly complementary. Some, in fact, say they make the perfect decision. When they agree, we have the truth of wisdom. For example, a Thinker faced with asking employees to put in overtime to complete a project early will lay out the pros and cons and logical considerations. A Feeler will factor in how the employees will react and how to best ensure their buy-in. The combination creates a winning formula.

Too often, however, the two clash. Thinkers consider Feelers unpredictable, soft, and overly sensitive to criticism. Feelers, in turn, view Thinkers as cold, critical, and devoid of social skills.

Current research shows the thinking versus feeling preference to be gender-sensitive. More women prefer the feeling approach and more men prefer the thinking approach. The numbers, however, are not as lopsided as is normally assumed. The best estimates show that 65 to 70 percent of men prefer the thinking deciding mode and 70 percent of women prefer using their feeling preference.

Individuals who prefer thinking often are drawn to mathematics and science, while those who prefer feeling tend toward the arts and humanities. Again, this is not true in 100 percent of cases, but it is true of the majority. In a similar vein, thinker deciders find the greatest satisfaction in jobs that draw on their natural ability to work with figures and budgets, weigh the pros and cons, thrive in a competitive environment, and handle confrontation and tough negotiations. Feeler deciders are drawn to occupations that make best use of their interpersonal skills, emotional intelligence, and ability to understand the mind-set of clients and staff members. They excel in positioning issues and products for optimal results. The management style of Feelers tends to be more collaborative and inclusive, although under stress, these individuals often becomes dictatorial.

The following family interactions illustrate some of the differences. Joan is a Feeler with a 10-year-old thinking daughter, Meg, and a 12-year-old feeling son, John. Joan dislikes returning items to the store. She finally learned to have her daughter return the item. "After all," Meg says, "that is what the store tells you to do." Joan also knows that her children will respond differently when asked for their opinion of her outfit, hairdo, or whatever. Meg, the Thinker, usually looks at her intently and proceeds to tell it like it is. "I like your blue blouse better," she declares with typical bluntness. John, by contrast, smiles disarmingly and tells her how great she looks before diplomatically adding that he sort of prefers the other blouse.

THE CASE FOR JUDGING AND PERCEIVING

A third inborn preference defined mostly by Myers and Briggs has to do with the way people prefer to structure their daily lives. According to recent research, 55 percent of Americans prefer a day that is organized, goal-oriented, and orderly. The other 45 percent prefer a day that is flexible and full of surprises.

This preference is called judging or perceiving. It is important to note that judging does not mean "judgmental." It means a preference for having an organized, structured, and decisive lifestyle. Perceivers, by contrast, like to keep things as unplanned and open as possible, always confident in their ability to "wing it" and improvise any situation that comes up.

Judgers are punctual. They meet deadlines well ahead of the due date because they like to get things done and checked off the list. They typically prefer a neat working environment with as few piles as possible. They make decisions as quickly as possible whether they have considered sufficient options or not. Open-ended situations make them uncomfortable.

Perceivers like to collect information, keeping their options open until they have had a chance to consider many alternatives. They feel no need for closure. They find schedules confining. Going with the flow and seeing what happens from hour to hour are much more attractive. They are adaptable and able to turn on a dime. Commitments can be renegotiated if something better comes along. They rarely plan a strategy, knowing that they have the ability to handle problems as they arise. Their workplace usually consists of many piles through which only they seem to be able to navigate.

Judgers and Perceivers drive each other crazy. To a Perceiver, a judging boss or mate seems rigid and uptight. To a Judger, a Perceiver seems messy and irresponsible.

Here are some statements associated with each type. Which ones apply to you?

Judgers	Perceivers
Need to have everything settled in advance	Like to be spontaneous
Insist on having a tight schedule	Are easygoing about making changes to the schedule
Try to complete projects as soon as possible	Like to start projects and complete them at the last minute
Work out possible problems ahead of time	Adapt and solve problems as they arise
Like structure	Want things to be flexible
Have fun after work is done	Have fun while working
Work in a neat environment	Work in an environment that may appear chaotic to others
Dislike being interrupted	Are accommodating when interrupted
Usually finish to-do lists	Make to-do lists loosely

If you have chosen the Judgers column, you should also have a larger score in the □ column. If you have chosen the Perceivers column, your score should be higher in the ∇ column.

As with the other preferences, neither one is right or wrong. Consider the following scenario.

Mary and Ruth are partners in a public relations firm. They are an effective team with complementary skills and interests. Mary, the Perceiver, is always ready to meet the needs of a client. She gives out her home number and is open to being contacted at any time, day or night. Clients also appreciate her ability to solve a crisis better than most. Ruth, the Judger, ensures that work is delivered on time and within the budget. She maintains an organized database of press contacts and other resources that might be helpful to their clients. She plans the marketing strategy and tracks the firm's program on a weekly basis. She also keeps the billing system up to date. Mary and Ruth appreciate each other. The problem arises in their workspace. Since this is a new firm, space is limited and they share an office. Ruth works on one project at a time and then returns the file to its appropriate place. She goes through her incoming mail promptly and handles paperwork decisively. At the end of each day she has acted on the paperwork, filed it, or thrown it away. Her desk is clean, and rarely does she lose a name or phone number. Mary, in contrast, is surrounded by piles of newspapers and open files. She keeps files for weeks on end, always working on several projects simultaneously. Her file cabinet capacity is insufficient, and papers are piled on the desk, floor, and chair, rapidly encroaching on Ruth's side of the office. Despite the respect and affection Ruth has for her partner, the physical condition of their mutual workspace is making her very irritable. She finds that she cannot concentrate properly.

THE CASE FOR EXTRAVERSION VERSUS INTROVERSION

The fourth set of preferences and the one least stressed in this book is known as Extraversion/Introversion (note that Jung specifically spelled extraversion with an "a" as opposed to an "o").

This preference is *not* about being socially adept or shy. It defines the individual's principal source of energy.

Extraverts get their energy from being with people and participating in communal activities. Introverts get theirs from spending time alone to recharge their internal batteries. Even if they like being with people, which many Introverts do, too much interaction drains their energy.

We all live in both worlds, but not at the same time. Extraverts are more alive when they are with others. If they have to spend too much time alone or doing tasks that require solitude, they quickly become tired, bored, drained, and dispirited. If they are strong Extraverts, they even become irritable. More moderate Extraverts can do solitary activities for a limited amount of time without becoming too restless.

Extraverts tend to talk and think out loud. They then change their minds and express a new opinion. Introverts think and reflect before speaking. Once they have formulated an opinion, they rarely change their minds. Introverts are at their best when working alone. They prefer to be in a quiet environment without the noise of a television or radio. They become tired, drained, and irritable if they are forced to be with other people for extended periods.

The population divides about equally between Extraverts and Introverts.

The following traits describe the two groups.

Extraverts	Introverts
Think out loud	Think things through before speaking
Like action and activity	Concentrate on one thing at a time
Prefer interacting with others	Can spend long periods of time alone
Are talkative and easy to know	Are quiet and reserved
Enjoy a broad range of acquaintances	Enjoy one-to-one or small-group interaction

Which are you? Extaversion corresponds to the ee column and introversion to the ii column.

A relationship between an Introvert and Extravert is often tense. An Extravert who wants to talk and banter back and forth will find the quietness of an Introvert irritating. To an Introvert, an Extravert is pushy, noisy, intrusive, and loud. Since the two frequently are attracted to each other initially, many form relationships and continue to argue for years. This is the case because Western culture is highly geared to the Extravert, who is seen as more "with it."

Recap of the Preferences

- There are four sets of preferences.
- Each deals with a different aspect of the personality.
- People can and do perform all those behaviors but have a preference for one or the other.
- These preferences are inborn or developed early in life.
- Current research indicates a neurochemical basis for these preferences.
- Sensing and intuiting indicate a person's preference for taking in information. Sensors prefer dealing with concrete facts and realities. Intuitors prefer dealing with abstract concepts, patterns, and relationships.
- Thinking or feeling indicate a person's preferred way of making decisions. Thinkers base decisions on objective and logical criteria. Feelers base decisions on personal values and the impact of a decision on people.
- Judging and perceiving indicate a person's preferred lifestyle. Judgers like life to be organized, scheduled, and planned. Perceivers prefer life to be spontaneous and flexible.
- Extraversion and introversion point to a person's source of energy. Extraverts get their energy from people and activities. Introverts get theirs from time spent focusing on their inner resources.
- Together the four dimensions create a whole that is more powerful than the sum of its parts.

A final word before we move on to the different leadership styles. These styles are based on a combination of the preferences described above. Each combination is far more powerful than the sum of its individual parts, hence the emphasis on the four neighborhoods. It is the combination that explains what motivates and energizes each style and explains how people with these styles interact, run a business, raise their children, approach their investments, and choose their careers. It is the whole rather than the parts that makes this model insightful and powerful.

2 The Eight Leadership Styles

5 The Golds

"Let's do it right."

Representing 46 percent of the population,[6] Golds, also known as Sensor Judgers, are the backbone of many institutions: public, private, and corporate. They are the most grounded, realistic, and organized of the four groups. They need to be accountable. In the process, however, they also demand a great deal of themselves and others.

They have procedures and systems for everything from raising children to running companies. Golds tend to view the world in black and white and to fully uphold the rules and guidelines that govern behavior. More than any other type, they uphold the customs and traditions of their groups and societies. They want to know what is "appropriate" and, where possible, follow the guidelines.

They make detailed plans. First there is work. Then there is play, and play is scheduled in advance.

They have a highly evolved sense of time and of the amount of time required to finish any task. "Oh, I will have it done by 5:00 P.M.," said a Blue to his Gold spouse. "No, you won't," said the Gold. "You won't finish it until noon tomorrow." And so it came to pass. At noon the following day the Blue mate finished wrapping all the gifts for the upcoming holiday.

Summary of Core Characteristics

- Take life seriously
- Need to know and follow the rules
- Are responsible, concerned, and focused
- Plan and schedule most aspects of life
- Like to be useful
- Respect authority
- Repeat what has worked in the past
- Honor tradition and rituals
- See money as a proof of accomplishment
- Tend to be thrifty and buy good-quality items
- Value family and community
- Demand and offer accountability
- Value membership in different organizations
- Take excellent care of their possessions
- Aim for respect, status, and power
- Excel in decision making
- Use a practical, commonsense approach
- Like things to remain orderly

Well-Known Golds

General Colin Powell
Barbara Walters
Kay Bailey Hutchison
Harry Truman
George H. Bush
Mother Teresa
Queen Elizabeth II
George Washington
Elizabeth Dole
Dan Rather
Gerald Ford

MOST FULFILLING CAREERS

Golds are happiest in settings that are predictable and that have high levels of responsibility and a clear chain of command. They like to be rewarded for their accuracy, ability to get things accomplished, and dependability.

They are highly clustered in fields that provide professional respect, require high levels of competence, and contribute in a meaningful way to the key institutions of society. These fields include the following:

- Military service
- Appointed government positions
- Law
- Medicine and dentistry
- Manufacturing, banking, and finance
- Accounting
- Small product-based businesses such as stores and restaurants.
- Teaching (usually primary and middle school)
- Administration of all types (government, health care, business, social services)

They are, of course, also found in smaller numbers in other areas where they can shine by establishing a special niche. Examples include acting and psychotherapy.

CLUES TO RECOGNIZING GOLDS

Golds exhibit many, though not necessarily all, of the following behaviors.

Speak in a straightforward and fact-based fashion
Speak in a decisive tone
Back up their opinions with factual examples
Use short sentences, not compound ones
Use concrete words
Describe things in a literal fashion and give many details
Emphasize accountability

Usually belong to groups and volunteer their time

Are punctual

Are neat: desk, home, closets, spice cabinet

Always dress in an appropriate manner; are coordinated

Have neat, well-maintained hairdos

Do not purchase things on impulse; avoid debt

Do not like surprises; like to plan ahead of time

Buy carefully; insist on long-term quality

Are predictable

Get visibly disturbed when things do not run efficiently

Have good manners

Respect and follow authority and rules

Have conservative values

Do what they promise to do

Speak in a sequential way; do not jump from topic to topic

6 The Trustees

Trustees combine preferences for sensing, the information-gathering process that focuses on common sense, verifiable facts, practical data, and current events rather than future possibilities; thinking, the decision-making process that emphasizes an objective, impersonal, and analytic approach to decision making; and judging, the lifestyle preference that stresses goals, schedules, structure, planning ahead, and settling matters as quickly as possible.

OVERALL

Realistic, grounded, and responsible, Trustees are often pillars of their communities. They are seen by others as being able to get the job done. They value "the system," trust contracts, and organize their lives around procedures, providing security and stability for those in their care. They enjoy being in charge and frequently rise to positions of responsibility in their jobs and volunteer organizations. Belonging is a strong need, and service is a tangible expression of their commitment to the community.

They communicate in a style that is simple, clear, direct, and frank. Highly observant of details, they prefer working with real things and trusting their own experience as opposed to new theories. Inherently efficient, they are gifted at implementing policies and ensuring that things remain orderly and on track. They gravitate toward situations that allow them to plan ahead, set goals, and control the schedule.

Trustees tend to be traditional and conservative. They honor rituals and traditions. Holidays, birthdays, and religious and cultural events are celebrated with the proper fanfare; they are seen as symbols of continuity to be passed on to the next generation. Family is a central focus for a Trustee, who often is the first to trace her roots and family heritage.

Trustees are most irritated by people who are disloyal, unreliable, and disorganized and who miss their deadlines.

Trustees have a certain moral certitude and are not shy about letting others know what they see as right and wrong. They want their universe kept organized and orderly. Sloppiness, impracticality, and people who break the rules are particularly annoying to them. They have an acute sense of "appropriateness" and therefore little tolerance for those who dress or behave in unusual ways.

As economic realists, they excel as professionals and frequently become accountants, bankers, and administrators. They are also heavily represented as physicians, dentists, lawyers, military officers, teachers, pharmacists, and stockbrokers, along with working in other fields that provide professional respect and contribute in a meaningful way to the key institutions of society.

In relationships they are straightforward and loyal. They show affection by doing things for people rather than by expressing their feelings, true to their belief that actions speak louder than words.

Trustees like to focus on leisure activities that have purpose and a measurable outcome, such as sports that combine business with socializing. They also enjoy working on volunteer activities.

In the second half of life Trustees often begin to develop the more spontaneous, intuitive, and feeling side of their personality. The strict parent becomes the doting grandparent. The hard-driving executive devotes more time to her favorite volunteer activity. She may even leave a whole Saturday unplanned, exploring the city with a favorite friend.

Leadership Style

Excel at getting the right things to the right people, in the
right amounts, at the right time
Set and achieve clear, measurable goals
Respect the chain of command

Attend to the practical needs of the organization
Deliver in a reliable and consistent manner
Reward those who play by the rules
Are decisive
Draw on past experience to solve most problems
Manage others closely to ensure that things are done right

Optimal Working Environment

Is organized and efficient
Has clear rules and expectations
Includes dedicated people who pride themselves on doing
    things right
Is stable and well respected, with a predictable future
Rewards precision and dependability with progressively
    higher levels of responsibility
Involves concrete and practical projects and products
Is results-oriented
Has a well-defined hierarchy
Values loyalty

Least Preferred Working Environment

A loose organization without clear goals or timetables
Associates who are sensitive and emotional
A setting where intuition is valued more than hard data

Approach to Change

Resist it as long as possible
Let others try it first

Contribution to a Team

Are logical and accurate; do not let important details fall
    between the cracks
Keep the team on track and ensure that things get done on
    schedule
Act as a reality check: Can it be done and at what cost?

Ensure that needed resources are available

Get to the core of a problem quickly

Can make tough decisions

Decision-Making Style

Absorb and assess as much factual information as possible

Apply strictly logical criteria

Decide as quickly as possible

Potential Blind Spots

May prematurely dismiss new ideas

Decide too quickly without consulting other people or considering enough options

May become rigid in supporting established way of doing things

Notice only the flaws, with too little affirmation of the efforts of others

Overlook long-range implications in favor of immediate results

Adhere to the way things have always been done

How to Persuade a Trustee

Be factually accurate

Present things in a logical, sequential manner

Deliver on commitments

Be professional; avoid personal chitchat until you know her well

Follow procedures and respect the hierarchy

Point out practical uses

Be on time

Be straightforward

Stay on schedule

Strategies for Trustees to Increase Leadership Effectiveness

Be more tolerant of the ideas of people who challenge the status quo

Pay more attention to one's own intuition and that of others

Pay attention to the sensitivities of other people

Avoid overscheduling; use free time to go with the flow

Postpone making a decision and encourage others to present
alternative options

Express appreciation more frequently

Don't shoot down all the impractical ideas; support the ones
that have potential

Give subordinates independence to do things in their own way

TWO TYPES OF TRUSTEES: EXTRAVERTS AND INTROVERTS

Extraverted Trustees are friendly, outgoing, and highly energetic. They express their opinion readily whether it's solicited or not. They are joiners, seeking out like-minded people in clubs or volunteer or religious groups where they can take charge and manage.

Introverted Trustees are quiet and serious. They think things through before acting or speaking, rarely venture to give an opinion off the cuff, and are particularly adept at calmly handling high-stress situations. They are the most private of all the types.

A Note of Caution

Since type does not explain many aspects that are important in defining an individual (intelligence, education, mental health, and individual life experiences, among others), no overall profile can describe all the variants in a personality. Invariably, some of the traits described above will not ring true for you. If the majority do not ring true, however, it could mean that you belong to another group. In that case, go back and revisit your Leadership Q questionnaire. Check the columns where you have close scores. Try reading a profile that reflects the other combination of your close scores. Alternatively, show the profile detailed below to an individual who knows you well, such as a mate, boss, close friend, or team colleague, and ask for comments. If you are going through major life changes, try waiting until things have stabilized.

DEVELOPMENT EXERCISES FOR TRUSTEES

People who succeed instinctively or deliberately learn to develop their nonpreferences. This softens their blind spots and enables them to adapt to the demands of different people and situations.

Do the exercises below to be more effective.

Exercise 1. Handling Conflict

You are rational and fair. Well-developed leaders understand the need to factor in how people will react to decisions. This requires developing your feeling preference.

- Recall a recent conflict involving several people.
- Think about each person who was involved. Write the names of those individuals on a piece of paper.
- Set aside the consideration of who was right. Focus on the personal motivations and emotional issues surrounding the conflict and note them.
- Consider other ways in which the conflict might have been handled.

The point is that using both preferences reduces conflict.

Exercise 2. Creating Balance

You are goal-driven and outcome-oriented. These qualities have contributed to your success. Taken to an extreme, they make you rigid and controlling. They also undermine your creativity.

Think of three non-work-related activities that would improve your life. They can related to hobbies or family life. Write them down. Then resolve to fit each of them into your schedule over the next month. Finally, do them.

Exercise 3. Developing the Ability to Brainstorm

1. Identify a problem or project that requires fresh solutions (work issue, product-naming issue, etc.).
2. Sit down with a couple of colleagues or friends and a flipchart.
3. Ask them to list all the ideas that pop into their minds no matter how silly or impossible.
4. Do not pass judgment on the ideas for 10 minutes. Write them all down on the flipchart.
5. At the end of 10 minutes ask the group to choose the three most attractive ideas.
6. Allow 10 minutes for this process.
7. Choose the idea that was selected most often.
8. Write it at the top of a new sheet of paper
9. Ask everyone to list ways to accomplish the chosen idea. Do not pass judgment.
10. Repeat steps 5, 6, and 7. Continue until you have solved the problem to your satisfaction.

Exercise 4. Working with Other Types

You have been assigned to cohead a project with Meredith, a well-regarded manager who is considered to be on the fast track. She is a Blue Innovator. She differs from you in two major preferences. She is an Intuitor (abstract, change-driven) and a Perceiver (spontaneous and adaptable).

This assignment is important to your career. Her impression of you will determine future assignments.

Read the Blue Innovator personality profile summary. Write down some of the key differences below.

Meredith   **Me**

1.   1.

2.   2.

3.   3.

4.   4.

Read the section on how to persuade a Blue Innovator. Note the points below. Incorporate them into the presentation you will make at the initial meeting.

1.

2.

3.

Read through your blind spots. Note which of them will be most irritating to her. Devise a strategy.

My Blind Spot   **Strategy**

1.   1.

2.   2.

Now repeat this exercise with a real person you have to work with who is different from you. It can be a boss, colleague, or client. Look at the overall four color descriptions and the section on how to recognize each color group.

My Type _____   **His or Her Type** _____

How to Persuade:

Blind Spots   **Strategy**

Photocopy your comments and keep them someplace where they are easily accessible.

The point is that if you do this exercise often enough, you not only will be more effective with that person but will learn to appreciate what he or she brings to the table. Soon you will expand that understanding to other people and become known for your skills in managing people. This is the path to leadership.

Exercise 5. How to Be a Better Leader

- Turn back to your leadership style summary.
- Choose one strategy for increased leadership effectiveness.
- Write it on an index card and develop three specific steps to achieve that strategy.
- Place the card someplace where you will see it frequently. Read it several times a day.
- After several weeks repeat the process with another strategy.

KAY BAILEY HUTCHISON
U.S. Senator
Texas

She is Texas's first woman senator and a rising star in the Republican party. It is 8:30 A.M. on an early fall morning in Washington, and Kay Bailey Hutchison is greeting her constituents at the weekly coffee gathering in her Senate offices. Dressed in a bright red suit, she slowly works her way through the room, stopping to chat with each individual and small group. She is a poised, petite, blond presence yet is very much in charge. It is clear that she ascended the political ladder through gritty determination.

Raised in the small town of La Marque, Texas, Hutchison was the daughter of an insurance agent and a homemaker; she was a middle child with two brothers.

In high school she was a popular cheerleader and ponytailed prom queen. Life was good. She attended the University of Texas and, in an unusual move for the mid-1960s, enrolled in law school. At graduation from law school she was one of 5 women in a class of 500. After that her world collapsed. Despite her good law school record, no law firm would hire her. Simply put, the Texas white-shoe male establishment had no place for women lawyers.

This first setback remains a vivid memory: "I hit the brick wall of life. Not being able to get a job was my first big failure. I was devastated. I had to reach deep into myself and find a new way."

As with many of the women leaders portrayed in this book, however, setbacks are viewed through the lens of new opportunities, and Hutchison did just that. She took a job as a television news reporter and discovered that being a TV presence provided an opportunity to go into politics. She came to the attention of the Republican National Committee's co-chair, Anne Armstrong, who remains one of her key role models.

Hutchison did a brief stint as Armstrong's press secretary and then ran for office herself. At 29 she was the first Republican woman elected to the Texas House of Representatives. In 1976 Gerald Ford appointed her vice chairman of the National Transportation Safety Board.

Life was humming again, but then came another major setback: She ran and lost a race for Congress in 1982. "I never thought I would be in politics again," she recalls. Deciding to turn to business, Hutchison spent a decade working in a variety of enterprises, ultimately becoming the owner of a candy-manufacturing company. "This was an absolute turning point," she says today, "because suddenly I was asked to run for state treasurer, which I could not have done had I been in Congress. I was qualified for the treasury post because of my banking and business experience, and it gave me the statewide exposure needed ultimately to run for the U.S. Senate. Today, she adds "my real-world business experience helps me deal with the economic issues, making me a more effective senator."

Leadership Style

Perseverance, tenacity, going the extra mile, and never taking no for an answer are what Hutchison considers her special strengths. "The difference between success and failure is picking yourself up after you have lost and trying again. I believe every successful person has had setbacks; it is the way people use obstacles that determines their ultimate achievement."

Succeeding is also about identifying the key issue, she notes, and then getting others on board to solve it: "I try to make everyone part of a win."

Staffers talk about her discipline and energy. At 6:30 A.M. you can usually find her on a fast walk up the stairs of the Capitol.

Such traits are typical of this group. Trustees are quintessentially no-frills, hard-charging, responsible and logistically-oriented leaders. They pay attention to details. They build organizations that function effectively and hold themselves accountable for the issues and people under their care. They demand unusually high levels of productivity both from themselves and from others. They are loyal. Their management style is decisive, predictable, and focused on well-stated goals.

"In my life, I am happiest and most fulfilled when I have a goal," says Hutchison. "There have been a few times when I did not have a goal, and I did not do well."

Today she again is looking to new horizons. "I might run for something else," she states, "possibly governor of Texas or president of the United States. When the opportunity is there and the timing is right, I will look at it."

Unlike women of other types, dealing with confrontation does not seem to be a problem. It rarely is for female Trustees, or if so only in the early years of life. "You watch others in the arena of influence," she says pragmatically, "and you see that everyone gets knocked down; it is not personal. This is true for any walk of life. If you take things personally, you will never be effective. You cannot go through life having everyone agree with you." This, she believes, is critical for young women who want to achieve influence and power, along with learning when to fight and when to quit, when to be aggressive and when to back off.

Advice to Others

"Get as much education as possible and pay your dues," says Hutchinson. Work hard and accept your knocks: "If you don't take any chances, you won't lose, but neither will you win." Her favorite poem provides inspiration:

> I'd rather be a "has been"
> Than a "might have been" by far.
> For a "might have been" has never been
> But a "has" was once an "are".

SONIA SOTOMAYOR
Judge
U.S. Court of Appeals

On November 6, 1998, the U.S. Senate confirmed President Clinton's appointment of Judge Sonia Sotomayor to the U. S. Court of Appeals, making her the first Puerto Rican woman to reach the nation's second highest court.

It has been a long journey from life in a South Bronx housing project to success on the bench. Sotomayor recalls her experiences with the practical wisdom that is characteristic of the Gold Trustee. There were many turning points.

When she was 9, her father, a Puerto Rican tool and die maker, died. He spoke only Spanish, and as a result, Sotomayor's command of English was poor. After his death her mother was able to implement her own ideas. As a practical nurse she earned little, but she moved the family to a rent-controlled housing development and managed to send Sonia and her brother to Catholic schools.

Her mother also made the apartment a center where other project children could gather. There was always a big pot of rice and beans on the stove or bacon-and-egg sandwiches, Judge Sotomayor recalls. By welcoming and feeding the gang, her mother succeeded in keeping the kids out of the drug-infested stairwells.

There were many different types of poor people, she reminisces: "the working poor, the despairing poor, or the addicted poor, and you saw different kids making different choices." Today that understanding of poverty gives her a more complex understanding of human nature.

Sotomayor's choice was to study hard. Her English improved, she immersed herself in Nancy Drew books, watched *Perry Mason,* and initially dreamed of becoming a detective. Being diagnosed with juvenile diabetes, however, ruled out a physical career. One day, while watching *Perry Mason,* she realized that whenever he wanted to do something, he had to ask the judge for permission. "Suddenly the light bulb popped in my head," she recalls with a grin. "I realized that the judge was the most important character in the show. Somehow I made the connection, and at the age of 10 I decided that this would be my life path."

Several years later, through scholarships and the guidance of an older friend, she found herself at Princeton. Culturally she was a fish out of water, but she was hell-bent on success.

"First I found that my vocabulary and writing skills were poor and I didn't know anything about the classics," she recalls. "So during my college summers I retaught myself basic grammar, learned ten new words a day, and set up a program of reading all the books I had missed." The effort paid off. She graduated summa cum laude from Princeton and continued at Yale Law School, where she became an editor of the *Yale Law Journal.*

With those degrees in place, the dream of the 10-year-old was about to become reality. She joined the Manhattan district attorney's office and after five years as a prosecutor went to the law firm of Pavia & Harcourt to broaden her experience with commercial litigation. Eight years later, in 1992, she was appointed a federal district judge.

Today, in the U.S. Court of Appeals, she spends a week on the bench and the balance of the month researching, writing, and thinking about the cases: "Most of my time is spent reviewing cases and the law and coming to decisions on how we are going to rule. The challenge is more intellectual. Many of the issues are difficult, and I have to test each premise until I narrow the choices and come up with a solution that makes sense."

While not all Trustees find this level of success, they are typically the most grounded, decisive, and results-oriented of all the types. They approach life in a practical fashion, with a strong work ethic and the belief that anyone can make it if she or he works hard enough. It is not unusual for young Trustees to set their goals at an early age.

Leadership Style

I meet Judge Sotomayor in her chambers in lower Manhattan. With dark hair framing a round face, she is intense and articulate. She projects self-confidence and the upbeat attitude that whatever she wants is hers to accomplish.

She describes her leadership strengths as first of all being highly organized: "I find the most direct and quickest route to accomplish things. I just look at someone doing something and immediately think of how it could be done more efficiently. Secondly, I am a good delegator. I look at my staff, figure out their strengths and weaknesses, and then pick projects that will challenge those strengths."

What do others say about her? "They perceive me as very hard-driving, aggressive, demanding, practical, and grounded. They say I get things done."

She attributes much of her success to perseverance and stubbornness. "Also," she says, "I pick my battles very carefully, and when I approach them, I try do so in the least confrontational way."

Of course, every style has its blind spots, and she readily admits to hers: "Sometimes I make decisions too quickly, or I may get caught up in the pure logic of the situation and forget to consider how others will react."

Overall the judge's comments reflect the leadership style of her color group. Trustees emphasize planning and prioritizing. They set clear, measurable goals and move along the most expedient route. With their assertive style, they usually persuade others to adopt their point of view.

Beyond that, however, the judge believes in other powers. "I have an extraordinary guardian angel," she states simply. "I have had people guide me in ways others don't. There are many who work hard but are not successful. Success is a combination of work and luck. I don't minimize my effort, but I am the first to say I am blessed."

Her main role model remains her mother, who was born in extreme poverty in Puerto Rico and was raised without parents. She pushed her children's education, moved the family to a safer environment, and at age 52 went to college to get a registered nursing degree. "I don't know anyone," says Sotomayor, "who accomplished as much, starting from so little."

Having, as she says, "skyrocketed to success," today she gears her goals to personal development. "I have achieved my lifelong dream 20 years early," she says, "and now I need to improve my physical and emotional well-being." Currently engaged to a consultant to architects and engineers, she plans to travel once a year, exercise every day, spend more time with friends and family members, expand her teaching schedule, and continue to remain involved in the activities of the Latino community. "Personal as opposed to professional development," she says ruefully, "may prove the biggest challenge of all."

Advice to Others

"Educate yourself at the best schools you can get into. Study hard and get the best grades you can get. Work the hardest at the beginning of any new job you get. Your first reputation is the most important thing and will stick with you throughout your work experience."

SHEILA KEOHANE
Principal
Barbizon Modeling School

It is 6 P.M. and 10-year-old Sheila Keohane is taking a quick break from her chores. Each evening she and her pet goat, Nancy, head up to the mountain in search of the fresh ivy that so delights the small animal. Sheila, like her friends in Cork, Ireland, has many responsibilities. She milks the cows, feeds the chickens, and helps her mother churn the butter. It is 1959, and despite its relative affluence, the 100-acre farm is far from town and does not have electricity. Only a battery-operated radio brings in news from the outside world. Sheila, however, is a happy child. She is a valued contributor to the family, a recognized member of the community, and an aspiring student at the local grammar school.

Though still in the early stages, Sheila's self-esteem is well in place. As a young Trustee she responds well to order, continuity, and the ability to serve and be accountable in her small universe.

In the 1970s Sheila visited the United States and fell in love with an aspiring entrepreneur. This was a major transition point. Trustees, particularly only children, do not leave their parents and home communities without considerable distress. Once committed, however, she threw herself into her new life with characteristic focus. She and her husband purchased a two-state franchise of the Barbizon Modeling School, whose mission is not only to prepare aspiring young models but also to improve the appearance and social skills of young people in general.

Leadership Style

Today her responsibilities include her family, her sales staff, and the young men and women who study in her program. By 10 A.M. she has called her daughter in college, given the instructions to the housekeeper, attended an exercise class, made several calls regarding her volunteer activities, and spoken with a contractor about household repairs. Now she is ready for an 8-hour workday in which she will manage, sell, and compete in business.

To other types such a schedule, day after day, would be stressful and exhausting. To a Trustee it is deeply satisfying. It meets her need to manage, control, be responsible, and have tangible accomplishments to show at the end of the day. Her prosperity ensures the respect of her Chicago-based community and it testifies to her organizational ability. When asked what she enjoys most about her work, she says, "Watching a young girl gain confidence by improving her posture and general appearance in a 6-month period." This statement is pure Gold; focused, specific, measurable, and grounded in reality.

Sheila is a former model, tall and energetic with a raucous sense of humor—outside the office, that is. Trustees are dead serious and rarely mix work and fun. She gets right to the heart of our interview. "People say I get things done," she says. "Running a company involves having a lot of irons in the fire, and you need to apply discipline to them all to keep the business on track. My strong suit is setting goals and sticking to them."

When asked what she finds energizing, she continues along the same track: "organizing, closing the door of the office, and accomplishing my day's objectives." The flipside, of course, is the stress points: "being interrupted and having other people not perform up to their abilities. "Leading," she continues, "is about showing by example, and I do that well, but it is also about stroking, and sometimes I am too harsh, too fast to criticize, and too slow to compliment."

Trustees typically do not think that average work merits a compliment. Of course, when employees perform exceptionally well, she responds with enthusiastic praise. Overall she describes her style as direct: "I explain what needs to be done, give them the tools to do it, and then expect them to, well, just do it."

Asked how she deals with confrontation, she responds, "Not well." The issue, however, is not her ability to handle a confrontation. "Actually, it does not bother me at all," she says. "The issue is more

about my response to the other person. I am too fast and too direct."
"Being diplomatic has better effects in the long run."

Overall Sheila exhibits many of the leadership traits of the Trustee. She is results-oriented and decisive and expects others to follow procedures without question. She manages herself and her staff in a task-oriented manner. Her formal and no-nonsense approach is motivated by a desire to achieve exceptional results. Her preferred work environment is structured, predictable, efficient, and staffed by hardworking people who focus on concrete goals. At their best, Trustees provide security and stability to those under their care.

Advice to Others

Her advice to young women is characteristically direct: "Once you have decided what your passion is going to be, try it and stay with it until all else fails. Figure out what the worst-case scenario is and decide whether you can live with that. How much are you going to lose? And if you lose it all, what can you do afterward? Most of all, do it while you are young enough to make the change."

ELLEN CHESLER
Senior Fellow and Program Director
Open Society Institute

She is a senior fellow and program director at the Open Society Institute, an international foundation started by the financier George Soros. The foundation provides her with $5 million a year to directly affect policies on women's health and reproductive rights. The monies also can leverage funds in other Soros programs, effectively translating into total foundation expenditures of some $500 million worldwide which ultimately affect virtually every woman's program around the world. When you are passionate about a cause, this is a powerful platform indeed.

Chesler is the middle child of three. Her father was a lawyer, and her mother a "very frustrated stay-at-home intellectual mom." She graduated from Vassar College and went on to earn a doctorate in history from Columbia University. In 1977 she left the university to manage Carol Bellamy's campaign for the office of president of the New York City Council. Bellamy was the first woman elected to citywide office in New York, and Chesler served as her chief of staff for seven years. Meanwhile, one foot lingered in academia as she converted her doctoral dissertation into a book. *Woman of Valor: Margaret Sanger and the Birth Control Movement in America* was published in 1992 to critical acclaim. Chesler was awarded the 1993 Martha Albrand citation for a distinguished first work of nonfiction from the American Center of PEN, the international writers' organization.

In between she married Matthew Mallow, a corporate lawyer, and they have two children, now 20 and 22 years old. "We had them close together," she says with a wry smile, "so as to amortize child care costs. But the most important thing is still to have a supportive spouse."

Leadership Style

She defines power as "the ability to control resources and ideas" and her style of leading as a combination of "the pulpit and the lectern." "The pulpit inspires," she says, "and the lectern convinces with sound preparation."

The Open Society Institute supports social policy change programs, and Chesler is widely recognized as one who gets results, "I like to think that I understand how to make things happen," she says. "I put resources in place, particularly when women's health movements have to reposition their issues to meet right-wing assaults."

She divides her time between grant making, and writing. Asked what she finds boring, she says, "I like practical work. I just don't like custodial or repetitive work." The foundation world remains of interest because ultimately it is about policy making. Some day Chesler would like to run a small foundation committed to helping advance women. "Despite a varied résumé," she says, "I am committed to women's rights." Like many Trustees, Chesler expresses a strong sense of belonging and commitment to her chosen community.

Advice to Others

"Education is important. Find out what you want to do in life as early as possible and stick with it. The women I see who are successful are specialists."

7 The Conservators

Conservators combine preferences for sensing, the informa-
tion-gathering process that focuses on common sense, verifi-
able facts, practical data, and current events rather than future
possibilities; feeling, the decision-making process that empha-
sizes personal values and the impact of a decision on others;
and judging, the lifestyle preference that stresses goals, sched-
ules, structure, planning ahead, and settling matters as quickly
as possible.

OVERALL

Warm, orderly, and conscientious, Conservators focus their energy on ensuring the welfare of those under their care, something they start doing early in life. Always curious about people, they are highly observant and quick to make others feel at ease. They are usually very affirming people.

They have a highly developed work ethic, viewing commitments and obligations with the utmost seriousness. They are involved in details, want everything organized, and excel at anticipating what needs to be done. They enjoy following through and mobilizing others to accomplish concrete goals.

Conservators respect authority, history, and tradition. The conservation of resources remains a high priority throughout their lives. They do not enjoy change, abstract concepts, and untested theories. In fact, when they start imagining things, they are usually sure the worst will happen. This can lead to gloom and doom and self-doubt.

As leaders, their contribution is significant, yet they remain modest. They strive to maintain a harmonious environment, always looking to stabilize the family, unit, or organization under their care. Focused on the here and now, they usually are not interested in change or future possibilities. Their warmth, people orientation, and sense of responsibility frequently direct them to careers and volunteer activities where they are of service to others.

In their communication they are straightforward and diplomatic. They are usually prepared and factually accurate. Highly observant of details, they prefer working with real things and trusting their experience as opposed to new ideas.

They are most irritated by people who are discourteous, unreliable, and unprepared.

Sales, insurance, interior design, fashion, customer service, real estate sales, dental care, teaching, dentistry, personal banking, and physical therapy are some of the fields favored by this group. These careers tap into their special ability to recognize and provide for the needs of others. They are also heavily represented in social work; as innkeepers, dietitians, and medical technologists; and in other areas that make use of their organizational and logistic abilities.

Conservators have strong "nesting" instincts and do their utmost to create an aesthetically pleasing home and work environment.

In relationships they are protective and warm, always ready to take care of other people. They are loyal and unfailingly attentive. Conflicts are considered a problem and typically are ignored as long as possible.

In their leisure time they enjoy entertaining and devoting time and energy to community organizations.

In the second half of life Conservators begin to relax their self-imposed need for perfection. They take up new hobbies and spend more time in leisure pursuits, frequently choosing those which develop more of their intuition and thinking preference.

Leadership Style

Have outstanding organizational skills: getting the right
   resources to the right people, at the right time
Welcome responsibility

Provide clear guidelines and instructions

Give and expect a high degree of loyalty; are impatient with those who question authority

Are accountable and prevent the misuse of key resources

Ensure that everyone is kept informed

Gain influence through personal concern for others

Follow the rules and uphold procedures

Manage productive teams

Optimal Working Environment

Stable, organized, and predictable

Has cooperative and hardworking people

Provides meaningful work relationships

Permits control over one's own projects

Has tangible products and/or provides an opportunity to see tangible results

Has clear rules and procedures and achievable expectations

Values and rewards factual accuracy and follow-through

Provides services that are of value to clients and staff members

Least Preferred Working Environment

A highly competitive and tension-filled environment

Impersonal work relationships

Dealing with products that take advantage of clients or staff members

Approach to Change

Need a great deal of time to get used to it

Approach it cautiously

Contribution to a Team

Factor in the practical needs of team members

Provide clear directions and practical systems

Keep the agenda on track; monitor the team's progress

Get things done on time and within the budget

Follow rules and procedures
Encourage others to express their viewpoints and ideas
Are cooperative

Decision-Making Style

Decide quickly about people but waver on major decisions
Rely heavily on concrete information and the experience
of others

Potential Blind Spots

Get too involved in the details; do not see the overview or
big picture
Assume their solutions are the best for everyone
Avoid conflict
Get discouraged if others do not express appreciation
Overreact to competition and political infighting
Emphasize established ways of doing things; this may stifle
innovation in others
Insist on procedure for its own sake

How to Persuade a Conservator

Establish the relationship first
Provide concrete and reliable information
Be the "expert"
Present things in a logical, sequential manner
Deliver on commitments
Follow procedures and respect the hierarchy
Point out practical uses
Be straightforward
Stay on schedule

Strategies for Conservators to
Increase Leadership Effectiveness

Find one or two opportunities each week to develop skills
in dealing with abstract or global ideas; for example, try
book clubs and strategic development teams

Deal with conflict as soon as possible

Communicate in a more concise manner

Welcome feedback as useful rather than critical information

Step back and consider logical reasons behind the behavior
of people and events

Learn to say no when you have too much on your plate

Avoid overscheduling; use free time to go with the flow

Do not shoot down all new ideas as impractical; support the
ones that have potential

TWO TYPES OF CONSERVATORS: EXTRAVERTS AND INTROVERTS

Extraverted Conservators are highly energetic and widely known for being gracious and effective in dealing with others. They are outgoing and talkative, placing a high value on having many friends and being involved in a myriad of activities.

Introverted Conservators tend to be more quiet and serious. They work behind the scenes, getting satisfaction from serving the needs of others. Dependable, calm, and consistent, they are always there when others need them. Privacy is highly valued. They have little need to control others.

A Note of Caution

Since type does not explain many aspects that are important in defining an individual (intelligence, education, mental health, and individual life experiences, among others), no overall profile can describe all the variants in a personality. Invariably, some of the traits described above will not ring true for you. If the majority do not ring true, however, it could mean that you belong to another group. In that case, go back and revisit your Leadership Q questionnaire. Check the columns where you have close scores. Try reading a profile that reflects the other combination of your close scores. Alternatively, show the profile detailed below to an individual who knows you well, such as a mate, boss, close friend, or team colleague, and ask for comments. If you are going through major life changes, try waiting until things have stabilized.

DEVELOPMENT EXERCISES FOR CONSERVATORS

People who succeed instinctively or deliberately learn to develop their nonpreferences. This softens their blind spots and enables them to adapt to the demands of different people and situations.

Do the exercises below to become more effective.

Exercise 1. Depersonalizing Criticism

Ask someone who is blunt (a Thinker) to critique something of value to you: a project, an idea, an outfit, a room decoration. Pay attention to your reactions to his or her comments. How do your intellect and feelings interact? What are your bodily reactions? Note them below. Can you sort out the facts you are hearing from your feelings about them?

- The critique:

- Facts:

- Feelings:

The point is that it is important to depersonalize criticism. It helps us grow and usually is not personal.

Exercise 2. Developing Spontaneity

You are goal-driven and outcome-oriented. These qualities have contributed to your success. Taken to an extreme, they make you rigid and controlling. They also undermine your creativity.

Follow someone around for a few hours. Just go with the flow. Do not suggest a schedule of activities. Observe and appreciate their rhythm. Note your reactions. At the end write down what you may have learned that you would not have learned under normal circumstances. Consider doing this once every couple of months.

The point is, spontaneity provides balance and stimulates creative thinking.

Exercise 3. Developing the Ability to Brainstorm

1. Identify a problem or project that requires fresh solutions (work issue, product-naming issue, etc.).
2. Sit down with a couple of friends or colleagues and a flipchart.
3. Ask them to list all the ideas that pop into their minds no matter how silly or impossible.
4. Do not pass judgment on the ideas for 10 minutes. Write them all down on the flipchart.
5. At the end of 10 minutes ask the group to choose the three most attractive ideas.
6. Allow 10 minutes for this process.
7. Choose the idea that was selected most often.
8. Write it at the top of a new sheet of paper.
9. Ask everyone to list ways to accomplish the chosen idea. Do not pass judgment.
10. Repeat steps 5, 6, and 7. Continue until you have solved the problem to your satisfaction.

Exercise 4. Working with Other Types

You have been assigned to cohead a project with Meredith, a well-regarded manager who is considered to be on the fast track. She is a

THE CONSERVATORS 69

Blue Innovator. She differs from you in several major preferences. She is an Intuitor (abstract, change driven), and a Perceiver (spontaneous and adaptable). She probably will drive you crazy.

This assignment is important to your career. Her impression of you will determine future assignments.

Read the Blue Innovator personality profile summary. Write down some of the key differences below.

Meredith	Me
1.	1.
2.	2.
3.	3.
4.	4.

Read the section on how to persuade a Blue Innovator. Note the points below. Incorporate them into the presentation you will make at your initial meeting.

1.

2.

3.

Read through your blind spots. Note which of them will be most irritating to her. Devise a strategy.

My Blind Spot	Strategy
1.	1.
2.	2.

Now repeat this exercise with a real person you have to work with who is different from you. It can be a boss, colleague, or client.

Look at the overall four color descriptions and the section on how to recognize each color group.

My Type _____   **His or Her Type** _____

How to Persuade:

Blind Spots   **Strategy**

Photocopy your comments and keep them someplace where they are easily accessible.

The point is that if you do this exercise often enough, you not only will be more effective with that person but will learn to appreciate what he or she brings to the table. Soon you will expand that understanding to other people and become known for your skills in managing people. This is the path to leadership.

Exercise 5. How to Be a Better Leader

- Turn back to your leadership style summary.
- Choose one strategy for increased leadership effectiveness.
- Write it on an index card and develop three specific steps to achieve that strategy.
- Place the card someplace where you will see it frequently. Read it several times a day.
- After several weeks repeat the process with another strategy.

LINDA CHAVEZ-THOMPSON
Executive Vice President
AFL-CIO

She was just 10 years old when she started working in the west Texas cotton fields. The third oldest of eight children born to dirt-poor share-croppers, she cried for two weeks when her father told her she could no longer go to school after the ninth grade. "I loved learning," she says, recalling the confusion of that day, "but he needed my earnings to make ends meet, and it was considered more important to educate the boys."

At age 16 she was elected by her siblings to present their father with an unusual demand—that he permit their exhausted mother to stop working and get some rest. Otherwise the kids would refuse to join him in the fields. She made her demand, and he capitulated, later boasting to his friends about his daughter's ability to drive a hard bargain.

She married at 19 and cleaned houses to add to her husband's income. As a second-generation Mexican American she was told repeatedly, that "the brown and poor" do not move into mainstream society. "That did it," she says. "I was determined to prove them wrong."

The union provided the way. Despite her lack of schooling, Chavez-Thompson was well read and self-educated. In 1967 she signed on as a bilingual secretary for a local group in Texas. Over the years she would advance through the ranks, forging a career as an organizer for the American Federation of State, County & Municipal Employees (AFSCME) while raising two children, one of whom is mentally challenged. Diminutive at 5 feet, 1 inch, she was tough, and fueled by memories of long days in sun-soaked cotton fields. Despite a lack of education, she pored over rule books, drafted grievances for workers, represented them at administrative hearings, and, in her words, "raised a little hell." She also knew how to enroll and persuade power brokers. The combination was her ticket to national prominence.[7]

Despite enormous opposition from within, in 1995 Chavez-

Thompson was elected executive vice president of the AFL-CIO, becoming the highest-ranking woman in a labor federation with 13 million members. Her election represented a deliberate effort by the president, John Sweeney, to break the glass ceiling regarding women and minorities. "I qualified on both counts," she says, "plus I had 30 years of experience in an organization that had grown 'male, pale, and stale.' I, on the other hand, am tan, female, and feisty."

Today her wall is filled with honors, including four honorary doctoral degrees. In September 1998 she completed a one-year appointment as a board member in the President's initiative on race. The high point was accompanying Clinton on Air Force One to kick off the race initiative in California. She even telephoned her mother. "For a poor girl from Texas," she says in a soft twang, "it was truly awesome."

Her mission today is threefold. First, she aims to tap new markets—women, minorities, and gays and lesbians—to increase membership. Second, she is coordinating the programs of 51 state federations and over 600 labor councils across the country. Third, she is building coalitions and partnerships with other advocacy groups, such as religious groups and environmentalists. This is a range of activities that draws well on her Conservator strengths.

Conservators are responsible, productive, and highly organized. More than any other group, they manage to balance the needs of people against the tasks to be accomplished. They know when to push, when to hold the line, when to back off, and when to schmooze. This makes them highly effective team leaders who, however, can become stressed when people do not live up to their expectations. They do best in occupations that provide services to others.

Leadership Style

Chavez-Thompson defines her strengths as energizing others to believe they can have an impact. "I have an ability to reach people where I think it makes a difference. I speak from the heart," she says. "I have had grown men come up to me, give me a hug, and tell me, 'I haven't cried in years. You made me cry tonight.'"

Other strengths include bringing a down-to-earth perspective to issues and (she hesitates before speaking further and then chuckles): "Okay, I might as well say it: a mother-earth-type quality to the overall effort."

As an extraverted Conservator, she most enjoys getting out among the members and learning about the issues of concern to them. That might mean going to rallies or becoming part of a lobbying group to affect the legislative process. She also enjoys being a liaison to the population at large—explaining what labor is trying to accomplish and why this would benefit all the members of the community, union and nonunion alike. In doing so she draws on her own passionate conviction and the considerable persuasive skills of her type.

Her blind spot, she admits, is impatience. "I want things done, and I want them done yesterday," she says with typical Conservator bluntness.

Asked what she finds boring, she points to piles of briefing materials that need to be read for upcoming meetings. "I just want to go in there and get things moving," she says wearily. Long meetings in particular are stressful to this action-oriented type.

Conservators in general have difficulty dealing with criticism and confrontation; that comes from having a preference for feeling. Over the years Chavez-Thompson has learned to deal with both issues. "I have developed a tough hide," she says. "I have been called many things; the one I like best is 'pushy broad.' It was my way of building up a defense against people hurting my feelings."

Advice to Others

"Know your goals and be persistent," she says. "Know that it is not going to be easy even today to enter into new fields, and sometimes you will suffer and have to sacrifice your dignity. So it is best to stop caring what others say and just get on with it." This is salient advice from one who took on the world on two fronts—gender and culture—and triumphed to tell others about it.

LORNA WENDT
Founder
The Institute for Equality in Marriage

Theirs was the classical story of marital success. They were high school sweethearts in tiny Rio, Wisconsin. He was the class president; she was a member of 4-H. They played in the high school band and went to church together. After attending the University of Wisconsin, they got married, packed a truck, and spent their honeymoon heading for the Harvard Business School. For two years he attended while she supported him by teaching music and typed his papers at night. After graduation, he joined a big company and skyrocketed to success. She ran a beautiful house, raised two well-behaved children, and hosted extravagant functions. She also supervised four relocations, catered to his every need, and glad-handed her way through scores of corporate events. Most of all, she played by the rules and never made waves.

Then, on a fateful night in 1995, just a week before their annual Christmas bash, Gary Wendt, CEO of General Electrical Capital, fired his unsuspecting wife. He offered her a severance package of $10 million. He thought she would be obliging and quietly tiptoe offstage. After all, other executive wives had done so, and often with less. Somehow he misread the cues.

Lorna was galvanized into action and played hardball in a way that took everyone by surprise. She hired a public relations agent, a writer, and a speech coach. Then she slammed a line drive by calling the press to announce she was taking him to court. Through *The Wall Street Journal*, she declared to the world, that she wanted half of the $100 million she estimated he was worth.

In the months that followed the soft-spoken and very proper housewife gave press conferences and interviews to most of the major publications and television shows: *The New York Times, 20/20, Nightline, Time,* and *U.S. News & World Report,* along with hosts of local papers. Her picture appeared on the cover of *Fortune* magazine. The story swirled with frenzied momentum, and at the center stood a transformed woman. In less than a year Lorna Jorgensen Wendt, daughter of a Midwestern minister, had become the lightning rod for a new movement: the cause of disenfranchised wives. "Marriage is an equal partnership," she declared to the world. "For 32 years I have given 100 percent of myself willingly and lovingly. Why should I walk away with only 10 percent of the assets? It is not about money; it is about fairness. I was 53, and he fired me."

The message was clear. The battle plan was drawn. Wendt wanted respect. She wanted to be acknowledged for the labors society often takes for granted; the unglamorous tasks of tending to a family's physical and emotional needs. Money was her way to make sure that happened.[8]

Ultimately the settlement was increased to $20 million. Now she is back in court for a second round to tap into her ex-husband's stock options and pension plan.

Today Lorna is hard at work heading up the Institute for Marital Equality, which she started and funded with a portion of her settlement. The institute is a nonprofit foundation. She is its spokesperson, the one who makes the speeches, raises money, and attracts the press. But other high-profile divorcees are joining the ranks, and the goals are ambitious.

We meet in their new offices. Dressed in a well-tailored St. John knit suit, her short blond hair in place, Lorna still looks very much the suburban housewife. She is focused, and her excitement is palpable.

"The issue of getting a fair share of marital assets affects women and men at all economic levels," she says. "Over the last two years we have found that the concept of marriage (and divorce) as an equal partnership resonates so deeply with Americans as to constitute a societal movement." The institute, she discloses, has hired a consultant to develop a strategic plan. In the coming months it will create a Web site and join with associates in other states. Ultimately the goal is to build a nationwide network that will lobby for new divorce laws across the United States and even worldwide. She ticks off the progression in logical steps. "The Institute," she concludes with startling intensity, "will promote a national dialogue on the meaning of equality in relationships."

In relationships Conservators are highly attuned to the needs of their mate. They bring warmth and efficiency to their homes and families. They are sociable and generous and normally do not upset the status quo. Tradition and rules are meant to be followed. A commitment is a bond forever. Although it is difficult for them to express their own needs, however, they resent those who take them for granted. If someone violates their sense of right and wrong, the retribution is swift and deadly.

Leadership Style

Interestingly, Lorna still does not think of herself as a leader, a refrain heard from many Conservators who view themselves through a very realistic lens. "I have certain strengths, of course," she adds quickly. "I am down to earth, and I always prided myself on doing things well," she is recalling the seamless management of her home, charitable, and corporate responsibilities. Beyond that, the awareness of her powers came late in life. Some of it she credits to her experiences with Outward Bound. "Outward Bound is about teamwork and facing physical challenges together," she says. "There people asked for my opinion and actually followed it. They valued my mind." After that eye-opener she began to assert herself. However, it was not until the divorce that she moved to center stage.

Conservators typically do not seek leadership positions but make distinct contributions when they hold such positions. They have strong opinions that are based on values and are willing to put a great deal of energy into the things in which they believe. Most of all, they can be counted on to follow through on their commitments faithfully.

Conservators have a clear, direct communication style; they tell it like it is. They like things to be organized and predictable, preferring projects with tangible results. It is particularly important for them that their work have a direct and positive effect on people.

They are also in a hurry and dislike ambiguity. They are not inherently future- or change-oriented. "Of course it is overwhelming," she says. "There is so much to do. The issue is big, and we can't get there fast enough. People suggest many things, but we have to find a way to narrow ideas down until we find our niche." The complexity of actually changing the legal system does stress her out, she admits: "I have always been very organized. If someone in my home owned it, I knew where it was, but this is different. This is a groundswell. We are creating something new. I am pulled in many directions, and we don't have a definite plan yet." That is, of course, distressing to her type, but she adds with characteristic determination: "Someone had to start it, and somehow I found myself the catalyst for this movement."

Advice to Others

Not surprisingly, her advice to young women is to "be true to yourself. Find out who you are and don't give up your dreams and hopes for anyone." This is appropriate advice from one who took more than three decades to come to terms with her own strengths.

MARLENE JUPITER

Author, *Savvy Investing for Women; Strategies from a Self-Made Wall Street Millionaire*
Former Senior Vice President,
Donaldson Lufkin & Jenrette

A diminutive and briskly attractive Marlene Jupiter stands up to exhort the women gathered for the book signing in midtown New York. "It is time," she tells them, "to take charge of your investment life, not to be frightened of it but to make it enjoyable and fun."

This is sound advice from one who knows. As a Wall Street professional and self-made millionaire, she recalls the many painful years it took to achieve the balance and confidence she exudes today.

Most of her 17-year career was spent at major Wall Street brokerage firms. She started as a secretary after graduating from Cornell University. Originally she wanted to be a doctor but was scared off by the prospect of spending years paying back the medical school debt.

Conservators abhor debt. They avoid it whenever possible, even accepted forms of debt such as school loans and mortgages.

Besides ambition, however, Jupiter had superior mathematical skills. Once she decided to throw her lot in with the financial community, she worked her way up from secretary to senior vice president. It is noteworthy that most of this 16-year achievement took place in a trading room, the highly lucrative center of brokerage houses where financial instruments are bought and sold for clients and the firm's own account. In hers, the ratio was 195 men to 5 women, which was about average in the late 1980s. She does not elaborate on the working conditions. (From my earlier days as a reporter walking into a trading room, I have vivid memories of an afternoon "free-for-all." In one corner there was a stripper brought in to celebrate a birthday; in another, 30 testosterone-spiked guys were throwing shredded pork and fried noodles at each other across desks, screens, and client files.) A trading room is the closest thing to a locker room permitted in the staid halls of business.

Jupiter survived because she brought in large, lucrative accounts and made money for her clients and the firm. "I liked my customers," she says. "I always did the right thing for them and was meticulous about follow-through and servicing their accounts." Because of the nature of her product, a highly complicated financial instrument known as a derivative, her clients were few but very large. More often than not, "some baboon," as she refers to her former colleagues, "would try to take my accounts away from me, but they never managed to."

Conservators enjoy meeting and serving people. They gather detailed information and turn it to good use for their clients. For Jupiter, this translated into client loyalty. Conservators also have a strong sense of responsibility and prefer to work with other well-organized people under conditions that are stable and predictable (hardly the atmosphere in a trading room).

For the first ten years she withstood the internal battles by focusing on what she did best: analyzing trends and capitalizing on the anomalies of the markets. Her mathematical skills enabled her to call the investment shots consistently.

Then, in her thirties, she had a major turning point. An investment colleague said to her, "Marlene, just get this. Perception is 90 percent of reality. Markets are moved by people. Markets don't move themselves. They don't move because of income statements. They move because of what people think is going to happen." Suddenly, she says, "the light went on in my head. There was an art as well as a science to the markets. Overnight, the creative part of me kicked in." She fine-tuned her investment strategy and soon became a high-powered investor.

She managed the stress of the job by turning to kindred souls: networks of women. Through her alma mater, she became part of the President's Council of Cornell Women, a group of accomplished individuals who provided moral support and advice. "So now, when someone said the only reason I was on Wall Street was because I was ugly and couldn't get married, I could laugh it off," she recalls. Even more important, however, the support of her new friends enabled her to go out and take more risks. This translated into superior performance. Within two years she rose to the rank of senior vice president.

However, it had become a road to burnout. The revelation came one day when a customer said to her, "Marlene, you don't sniff up the baboon enough, and you will never last. The baboon will drive you out. This is the way they behave in the animal kingdom."

Soon after that she made the decision to leave the company and summarize her experiences in a book that would empower other women to handle investments. Today the book is in paperback, and Jupiter is consulting and managing money on her own for selected clients. In the near future she plans to write a screenplay and teach.

Leadership Style

She describes her leadership style as that of "letting people grow, hopefully, to the point of going beyond me." Like many Conservators, Jupiter sees leading more as a process of teaching, and developing. This style lends itself to influencing in a personal way rather than controlling large organizations.

The toll of continuous confrontation, however, is not something Conservators handle well in the long run. For individuals with a preference for feeling, it is a gut-wrenching experience day after day.

Many years ago she shared her type's sensitivity to criticism and confrontation. Today she knows how to take it in stride. Dealing with hardball politics, she admits, is still stressful and something she will avoid in the future. Another blind spot of Conservators is being too meticulous and structured, which Jupiter readily acknowledges was a problem in the freewheeling world of investment banking.

Advice to Others

Her advice to young women today is to find an organization whose values are in sync with one's own. "If I were graduating from college today," she adds, "I would go through annual reports carefully. I would read the letter from the president, check out the company's culture, see whether there are any women on the board and how many hold important positions. If not, I would ask why. Life is too short to be constantly battling your environment."

She also advises looking at the growth fields, which she believes will be more gender-neutral. Money is important, she notes, but it is best to work someplace where they appreciate what you bring to the table rather than trying to turn you into someone you are not. "If you keep your integrity," she concludes, "God will open the necessary doors for you."

8 The Blues

"Let's change it."

Representing 10 percent of the population, Blues, also known as Intuitive Thinkers, are theoretical, competitive, and driven to acquire more knowledge and competence.[9] They are without equal in dealing with complex issues, designing new systems, and challenging old ones. Compelled to understand what makes the world function, they seek knowledge for its own sake and challenge and test authority. They have little interest in routine and established procedures.

Blues are natural skeptics whose first reaction is to criticize and set their own benchmarks against which to test everything and everyone, including themselves. Only after that process will the solution be acceptable.

Blues are very precise in thought and language. They usually value brief and even terse communication. At times, however, they get so involved in complex issues that others do not understand them even though the Blues think they are being clear and precise.

They are future-oriented, trusting only logic, not the rules and procedures of the past. Blues may resist authority and flaunt their disregard for rules, regulations, and what they see as trite rituals.

Blues often impress others as being serious and sometimes elitist. However, regardless of their level of intellectual achievement, they often do not feel competent enough. Self-doubt plagues them for many years.

In dealing with other people, they tend to apply the same rules of logic and analysis. This works less well in human relations. Others resent their critiques and lack of empathy.

Blues are usually sticklers for accuracy. They check their work and consult references, expecting others to do so as well. They have little tolerance for errors and no patience with those who err.

Blues are individualistic and have little concern about whether others approve of them. They respect people with intelligence and competence. They welcome new ideas regardless of a person's rank or position.

Summary of Core Characteristics

- Are challenging and questioning
- Try to understand things and events through logical, impersonal analysis
- Are frequently plagued by self-doubt
- Demand strategic intelligence and competence of themselves and others
- Value brief and precise language
- Enjoy solving complex problems
- Are oriented to the future
- Flout traditions and regulations
- Live in an abstract, theoretical world
- Ignore the approval of others (except like-minded people)
- Need autonomy
- Seek a global perspective
- Embrace change
- Want to be right even in small things
- Like to manage and be boss
- Avoid dealing with details and follow-up

- Compete on many fronts
- Yearn for ongoing education
- Value calm, reason, achievement, and power

Well-Known Blues

Nancy Snyderman
Bill Gates
Hillary Clinton
Abraham Lincoln
Thomas Jefferson
Lady Margaret Thatcher
Madeleine Albright
Louis Gerstener of IBM
Walt Disney
William Buckley
Kathleen Kennedy Townsend
George Soros
Douglas MacArthur
Dwight Eisenhower

MOST FULFILLING CAREERS

Blues are most productive in an environment that values intellectual energy and achievement. They enjoy solving complex problems and mastering new technologies. They do well when improving ideas and systems and less well with routine and repeated tasks.

They are highly clustered in fields that provide challenges, autonomy, and the opportunity to work with people they respect. These fields include the following:

- Professions (medicine, law)
- Computer programming
- Business management
- Higher education, teaching, history
- Technical, analytic, and scientific fields
- Engineering

- Architecture
- Inventing
- Researcher of all types
- Strategic planning
- Journalism
- Entrepreneurship
- Any field that allows the individual to work at a conceptual, abstract level, exercising logical analysis and independent thinking.

They are, of course, also found in smaller numbers in other areas more populated by other types, where they can shine by establishing their own niches. Examples including accounting and psychotherapy.

CLUES TO RECOGNIZING BLUES

Blues exhibit many, though not necessarily all, of the following behaviors.

Speak in compound sentences
Have a sophisticated vocabulary; use metaphors and puns
Speak nonsequentially; jump around from topic to topic
Are interested in topics that involve the future
Read a great deal
Have advanced degrees; are interested in new things
Are skeptical
Question the motivation of others
Are confrontational; challenge everything
Have a jousting, sarcastic wit
Are very concerned about doing things well
Have original ideas
Use abstract and figurative rather than literal terms
Flout rules and accepted ways of doing things
Have a strong need to contribute original work to the
    existing body of knowledge
Are intense and serious despite their sarcastic wit

Get bored easily; do not like routine
Read many books about future trends
Have a desk with many piles, some neat and others messy
Seem self-assured and sometimes arrogant
Are argumentative; will play the devil's advocate
Will overanalyze
May engage in one-upmanship and power plays
May be negative and pessimistic
Go for intellectually challenging hobbies
Focus on the big picture and neglect the details

9 The Strategists

Strategists combine preferences for intuition, the information-gathering process that favors abstract ideas, future possibilities, and connecting unrelated ideas to create new patterns; thinking, the decision-making process that emphasizes an objective, impersonal, logical, and analytic approach to decision making; and judging, the lifestyle preference that stresses goals, schedules, planning ahead, and settling matters as quickly as possible.

OVERALL

Independent, complex, intuitive, and focused, strategists create visions, devise strategies, establish plans and contingency plans, and then act decisively. In pursuing their goals they often disregard the advice of the skeptics around them. Strategists have faith in their own insights.

They gravitate to the world of theories, future possibilities, and bold new designs. Always competitive, they challenge existing systems and assumptions and drive themselves and others, sometimes to a degree that colleagues may find uncomfortable. Associates, however, usually recognize their unique abilities to create long-range plans that incorporate dimensions others cannot grasp. They enjoy the process of solving complex problems and are adept at mobilizing the resources needed to achieve their goals.

Their communication style is clear and direct. Above all, Strategists dislike repetition and the need to state the obvious. They persuade others through clear thinking and thoughtful debate.

They are most irritated by people who lack competence and commitment.

Insatiably curious, they remain lifelong learners and feel they never have enough knowledge. They see themselves as sharp, resourceful, and effective at making things happen.

Strategists excel in a broad range of fields, particularly those which tap into their finely honed logical and executive abilities. They are frequently found as lawyers, judges, management consultants, architects, business owners, strategic planners, and executives in corporate and government organizations. Computer fields and technology are also areas in which they are heavily represented.

In relationships they value loyalty and tolerance, though it may take them a while to establish intimacy. Intellectual compatibility is a priority.

They approach leisure activities with the same need for purpose and intellectual challenge. Activities that combine business with pleasure, such as engaging sports with clients, are particularly attractive, as are activities designed to improve the mind or body. Rarely do they sit around doing nothing.

In the second half of life well-developed Strategists find new ways to develop the feeling and spontaneous side of their personalities. They find satisfaction from involvement in volunteer activities and from spending more time with their close friends, children, and grandchildren.

Leadership Style

Create and communicate a vision

Focus on the future

Have an intuitive understanding of the inner dynamics of an organization and its subdivisions

Recognize the potential of a new idea

Find and make connections among seemingly unrelated facts and ideas

Have a flair for global issues

Can make tough decisions

Continuously challenge themselves and others

Implement and make things happen

Optimal Working Environment

Involves working with independent people who deliver their contributions in a timely fashion

Compensates people for being decisive, original, and results-oriented

Is in the process of change

Is headed by a highly competent and professional boss who permits autonomous work

Has a minimum of procedures, bureaucracy, and paperwork

Provides a competitive and challenging environment

Provides an opportunity to do strategic analysis and long-range planning

Focuses on complex issues

Least Preferred Working Environment

Has too many rules and procedures

Has associates who lack initiative and/or waste time

Responsible for too much detail

Approach to Change

Usually welcome it as an opportunity to improve things

Like to be involved in the grand design

Contribution to a Team

Look at the big picture

Cut to the core of complex problems

Move the group to timely action and results

Set high standards

Willing to consider untried solutions

Avoid wasting time and resources

Decision-Making Style

Generate numerous logical options

Decide quickly (sometimes too quickly)

Are willing to review decisions when new information becomes available

Potential Blind Spots

Decide too rapidly and overlook practical obstacles

Pay insufficient attention to human needs and concerns

Are impatient, dogmatic, or bitingly sarcastic

Manipulate others to achieve goals

Ignore details and implementation

Split hairs

How to Persuade a Strategist

Provide an executive summary

Know the material in depth

Stress the uniqueness of an idea or solution

Accept that you will be challenged and critiqued; take it as a positive sign

Speak about comparable studies

Be logical; avoid emotional appeals

Be professional; limit personal chitchat

Speak about future implications; show how they will contribute to long-term strategies

Be brief and concise; use a sophisticated vocabulary

Never be glib

Strategies for Strategists to Increase Leadership Effectiveness

Solicit feedback and involve others in decisions that affect them

Criticize less and encourage more; openly acknowledge the contribution of associates

Simplify ideas before expressing them to others

Have patience with both people and details; acknowledge that others work differently

Do a reality check on available resources before pushing a new project

Create a balance between work and personal life

Develop empathy for the issues and concerns of others

Do not try to control everything

TWO TYPES OF STRATEGISTS: EXTRAVERTS AND INTROVERTS

Extraverted Strategists tend to be overtly energetic, vivid, authoritative, and expressive about their opinions. They are action-oriented and exude a high level of confidence. They like to be in charge.

Introverted Strategists tend to think before speaking, have a great deal of inner energy, appear to have an air of critical detachment, and are usually intense and deliberate in their communications. They like to be independent.

A Note of Caution

Since type does not explain many aspects that are important in defining an individual (intelligence, education, mental health, and individual life experiences, among others), no overall profile can describe all the variants in a personality. Invariably, some of the traits described above will not ring true for you. If the majority do not ring true, however, it could mean that you belong to another group. In that case, go back and revisit your Leadership Q questionnaire. Check the columns where you have close scores. Try reading a profile that reflects the other combination of your close scores. Alternatively, show the profile detailed below to an individual who knows you well such as a mate, boss, close friend, or team colleague, and ask for comments. If you are going through major life changes, try waiting until things have stabilized.

DEVELOPMENT EXERCISES FOR STRATEGISTS

We may appear different in different situations. Over time we also grow and progress, but our basic preferences do not change. This has been proved by the large number of people who have retaken the Myers-Briggs Type Indicator in different periods of their lives and repeatedly come out with the same preferences. Thus, an abstract intuitive Thinker never really becomes a concrete sensing Thinker. A structured Judger never really becomes a flexible, go-with-the-flow Perceiver. A Blue Strategist never becomes a dyed-in-the-wool Gold Conservator.

People who succeed, however, instinctively or deliberately learn to develop their nonpreferences. This softens their blind spots and enables them to adapt to the demands of different people and situations. Listed below are exercises that will help you develop your non-preferences. Jung referred to this process as individuation.

Exercise 1. Giving Instructions

The strong intuitive mind-set of the Strategist often results in instructions that are vague and impressionistic. These instructions do not work well with Sensors (over 70 percent of the population), who need specific guidelines and a concrete plan of action. Poor instructions often lead to frustration, wasted time, and significant misunderstandings in the workplace.

Write your instructions or plan of action on a piece of paper. Check that the following conditions have been met.

- You have worked out the details in advance. Ask yourself when, where, what, how, and why.
- You are brief and specific about what needs to be done.
- You have demonstrated why the project makes sense, why it is needed, and what the practical applications are.
- If action is needed, give specific instructions; do not assume that others will read between the lines. For example, "Materials need to go out before the end of the week," not "We should think about sending materials."

The point is that other people take in information differently than you do. They cannot be productive unless that difference is honored.

Exercise 2. Handling Conflict

You are rational and fair. Well-developed leaders understand the need to factor in how people will react to decisions. This requires developing your feeling preference.

- Recall a recent conflict involving several people.
- Think about each person who was involved. Write the names of those individuals on a piece of paper.
- Set aside the consideration of who was right. Focus on the personal motivations and emotional issues surrounding the conflict and note them.
- Consider other ways in which the conflict might have been handled.

The point is that using both preferences reduces conflict.

Exercise 3. Creating Balance

You are goal-driven and outcome-oriented. These qualities have contributed to your success. Taken to an extreme, they make you rigid and controlling. They also undermine your creativity.

Think of three non–work-related activities that would improve your life. They can related to hobbies or family life. Write them down. Then, resolve to fit each of them into your schedule over the next month. Finally, do them.

Exercise 4. Working with Other Types

You have been assigned to cohead a project with Judith, a well-regarded manager, considered to be on the fast track. She is a Red Tactician. She differs from you in two major preferences. She is a Sensor (concrete, fact-driven and sequential) and a Perceiver (spontaneous and adaptable).

This assignment is important to your career. Her impression of you will determine future assignments.

Read the Red Tactician personality profile summary. Write down some of the key differences below.

Judith	Me
1.	1.
2.	2.
3.	3.
4.	4.

Read the section on how to persuade a Red Tactician. Note the points below. Incorporate them into the presentation you will make at the initial meeting.

1.

2.

3.

Read through your blind spots. Note which of them will be most irritating to her. Devise a strategy.

My Blind Spot	Strategy
1.	1.
2.	2.

Now repeat this exercise with a real person you have to work with who is different from you. It can be a boss, colleague, or client. Look at the overall four color descriptions and the section on how to recognize each color group.

My Type _____   **His or Her Type** _____

How to Persuade:

Blind Spots   **Strategy**

Photocopy your comments and keep them someplace where they are easily accessible.

The point is that if you do this exercise often enough, you not only will be more effective with that person but will learn to appreciate what he or she brings to the table. Soon you will expand that understanding to other people and become known for your skills in managing people. This is the path to leadership.

Exercise 5. How to Be a Better Leader

- Turn back to your leadership style summary.
- Choose one strategy for increased leadership effectiveness.
- Write it on an index card and develop three specific steps to achieve that strategy.
- Place the card someplace where you will see it frequently. Read it several times a day.
- After several weeks repeat the process with another strategy.

NANCY SNYDERMAN, M.D.

Surgeon
Medical Correspondent, ABC

She divides her time between sterile operating rooms and hectic television studios in Manhattan. Television is the intellectual challenge, medicine the spiritual one. It is a life of contrasts, and Dr. Nancy Snyderman is energized by all of it.

It is 8 A.M. She has dropped off her three children at school and gone horseback riding for exercise. Now she is ready to put in a full day at the hospital. There will be new patients to see and sick ones to check on, perhaps surgery to perform. At 6 P.M. she will be home to fix dinner and help the kids with homework. This is the schedule—at least Monday through Thursday. On Friday she will be in New York, ready for a 5 A.M. wake-up call for a medical report on *Good Morning America*.

She is the oldest of four children. Her father was a surgeon, and her mother an artist-homemaker. Snyderman knew she wanted to go into medicine by the third grade. Blue Strategists are focused even as children and frequently set detailed goals early in life.

After completing medical school at the University of Nebraska Medical Center, she chose a medical residency in pediatrics in Pittsburgh but quickly realized that was not her field. By chance she fell into ear, nose, and throat surgery—the same field as her father—and later focused on head and neck cancer surgery, her specialty today.

During her medical residency in Pittsburgh she got her first taste of television. One of the stations was doing a story on tonsillectomies and came into her operating room. After the operation they interviewed her. Several days later they called back to ask her to appear occasionally on evening news programs to discuss medical issues. In 1983 her residency ended. She took a position as a surgeon at the University of Arkansas School for Medical Sciences and decided to turn her early media experience into a second career.

In 1987 she signed a contract with ABC; today she is one of the top medical correspondents on television. Of course, this means frequent travel, a grueling schedule, and having to read constantly to stay abreast of areas outside her specialty.

Then there is the inevitable question of whether she will give up her medical practice. She quickly nixes that suggestion. "I love being in the operating room," she says, "and can't in my wildest dreams imagine giving it up." There is another advantage. "If I call another doctor for information, he returns my call the same day. He probably would not do that for a reporter. And he even gives me inside information."[10]

Leadership Style

"I have the luxury of a bully pulpit, which I do use," she says, speaking about her influence. "I can tell people what they are supposed to do and bully them into making lifestyle changes."

In her medical practice and daily life, however, it is more about leading by example and force of personality. "I am very much a run-of-the-mill person when it comes to talent," she says, "but I do know how to set priorities and budget time." Every night her secretary leaves her work to do. By the morning the desk is clean. "It is a deal I have with myself," she says, "that things will be neat and orderly and will get done. I do not procrastinate." Each day starts with a fresh list that will be reprioritized during the course of the day.

Like many Strategists, Snyderman is decisive. She understands both the strengths and the pitfalls of that quality. "It inspires confidence, but at some level it also intimidates certain people," she says, "and I have been known to lead people in the wrong direction." she sheepishly describes a session at a leadership seminar. Each team was supposed to collaborate to put together the pieces of a puzzle into a square. Her team had some high-powered types—heads of endowments and PhDs—who all capitulated to her demand that a rectangle be considered a square to meet the time deadlines of the exercise. "We were videotaped," she notes, "and I couldn't believe that I had talked all these intelligent people into accepting something that was clearly wrong."

Strategists are competitive and driven. They have a strong need to take charge and ensure that goals are achieved on schedule. They dislike inefficiency and indecisiveness and are tough on those who fall short of their expectations.

Over the years Snyderman's strong personality traits have softened somewhat. "In my twenties," she says, "I had blinders on, and all I could focus on was getting through medical school and being a superstar resident. I was focused beyond focus. In my thirties I had to deal with self-esteem issues; who I am and why I am doing what I am doing. Then, in my forties, I finally found my voice."

Today much of Snyderman's energy is directed toward balancing the demands of being a good parent with the requirements of her dual-career lifestyle. It helps to have a very supportive husband and good professional support, but mostly it is about putting those fabled organizational skills to work. At the beginning of each year she checks with the school for special events such as field trips and plans her schedule around them. Her husband fills in at other events. She also frequently makes overnight trips to New York to avoid being away more than one night at a time. "People wonder how I do it all," she says. "What they don't realize is that I don't do it all. Leadership is about having the freedom to march to your own drummer and choose your own priorities."

Advice to Others

Synderman advises ambitious women to listen to their gut and get away from naysayers: "Be passionate about what you do. I am always amazed at people who say they have committed time to a particular field and can't take the risk of changing to another area. If getting up in the morning and going to work isn't a kick, then you should get out of there."

JEAN HAMILTON

Executive Vice President
The Prudential Insurance Company of America
and CEO, Prudential Institutional

It does not take much skill to interview a Blue Strategist. All you have to do is insert a tape and press the record button on your machine, then sit back and let the interviewee take over. Jean Hamilton is a typical Blue Strategist. We meet for breakfast in small Upper East Side hotel that is well known to power brokers of Manhattan. Her questions are placed neatly next to the bowl of oatmeal and fruit. She has thought her answers through and expresses them with the clarity that is the hallmark of Strategists. My machine does not fail me.

Leadership style strategists are passionate about leading, and it is the depth of their conviction that brings color and immediacy to their views. "Leading always came naturally to me," she says. "Even when I was young, I ended up being the one who was responsible, the one in charge. As I matured, however, I learned the importance of enrolling others."

"Today," she continues, "I get the very best person for each job. So I usually have a group of people whom I trust and who trust each other. Then I have to make sure they all see the same vision and want to be a part of it. Determining how to explain that vision and generating their enthusiasm and feeling that this is something they want to be a part of and that is beneficial to them—that is truly exciting."

That is one part of her leadership style. The other is to see the big picture and hone in on what works. "There are a million good ideas out there," she says intently. "It is executing well that creates a sustained win. I don't want just a quick flash; I want results that last and make a difference."

"Jean is player for the long run," says the management consultant Judith Griffin. "She has climbed carefully to the top, where she appreciates the view and is more dedicated than ever, remaining warmly— ever rationally—human."

Hamilton is responsible for the Prudential Insurance Company of America's institutional unit, which coordinates the manufacturing and distribution of specific products, including group insurance, retirement services, and real estate/relocation services. The businesses that report to Hamilton, taken together, represent a company that approaches a Fortune 250 ranking. About 5,500 people report to her.

Her professional background includes time spent in asset management at Prudential and lending at First National Bank of Chicago. These experiences, along with an undergraduate degree in journalism which included a number of business courses and an MBA from the University of Chicago, are the building blocks of her career.

The part of her job she finds most energizing is creating successful companies. "I love understanding what a company is all about," she says. "That might involve fixing ones that are not working well or creating new ones. Coming up with new business models is about the most fun you can ever have." As an example she cites current efforts to develop a business model that will wrap around institutional businesses and improve the provision of human resource benefits products at both the institutional and individual customer levels. "This challenge is just incredible," she says. "The wonderful thing is to take all these different pieces and pull them together into a new whole that is of benefit to everyone."

To understand the dynamics of those companies, Hamilton taps into all her background experiences in lending to, investing in, and marketing to companies. To that she adds an attitude of ownership: "You take responsibility for the company as if you owned it."

More than any other group, Blue Strategists enjoy complex problem solving and are happy to run as much of the organization as they can. They are results-oriented, independent managers with a passion for action. They have an almost religious reverence for logical analysis, undisguised truth, and efficiency. They expect their subordinates to be autonomous and to implement broadly defined goals and strategies independently.

I ask about her strengths and stress points. "The creation of a vision is a very artistic processes," she reflects. "You need to link the intuitive and analytic process." Being able to do that is a gift, admits Hamilton. It also involves a positive "can do" attitude and the ability to draw intriguing ideas from others. The next step is knock those ideas around until they have been dissected, refined, and made ready for implementation.

Her stress points include lack of change and excessive emphasis on details. "I have a high need for change," she says. "If I have done something, I don't like doing it a million times. As for details, if something is not working, then I will get involved in the details, but otherwise I prefer to delegate those things to others."

Strategists frequently get irritated by bureaucratic details and people who beat around the bush or fail to live up to their responsibilities. "I get absolutely sick when I see a business that is being mismanaged," she says, sharing the outrage typical of her type, "because that means people and assets are being wasted."

Dealing with confrontation is a major issue for many women leaders; this is less of an issue for Strategists, who have a preference for the Jungian thinking rather than feeling preference. "I don't take it personally," she says. "I put myself out there in the open and try to understand where the other person is coming from. I try to find the common ground and sweep away the things that are getting in the way."

Blind spots include the need to move quickly whether others are ready or not. "This is something I have to watch," she admits, "that I don't short-circuit the process."

As for role models, she does not point to any in particular. Her process is to set a goal and then look around and see who does it well—how those people do it and what personal qualities are needed. "I scan the universe," she says, "and keep mental checklists, constantly comparing myself against them." Sometimes this involves people she knows well, and at other times it may be someone in a history book or profiled in *Fortune* magazine.

Advice to Others

Her advice to young women is to interact frequently with as many segments of society as possible: men, people from other cultures, and individuals at different economic and social levels. "The world is coming together very rapidly," she says, "and it is important from a business point of view to understand what drives all those groups and to move comfortably between them all."

Second, it is important to affiliate with other women who are strong and have self-confidence. This is especially true in the teen years, when social acceptance determines self-esteem. Associating with other young girls who share similar aspirations can provide support. Finally, it is important, to develop technical skills such as computer competence and engineering, she advises, because those skills open up different paths to getting to the top.

Hamilton stresses that in today's dynamic work environment, an academic degree or specific skill set cannot ensure lasting success. The best and most rewarding careers are those in which one can skillfully weave a tapestry of rich experiences and lasting relationships.

BARBARA MUNDER
Senior Vice President
The McGraw-Hill Companies

Her title is senior vice president for new initiatives. Her responsibility is to develop an electronic commerce strategy for the operating units of The McGraw-Hill Companies. It is an objective perfectly suited to a Blue Strategist, and Barbara Munder approaches it with passion and zest.

She was the oldest of four girls. Her father had his own construction company and had no sons; he pushed his daughters to compete and excel. He expected them to do well academically and to be actively involved in sports. During high school they all worked in his company. Her mother was a traditional stay-at-home mom who provided the milk and cookies. "But I knew who was the boss in the house," says Munder, "and subconsciously I made the decision early on that when I grew up, I would not be asking for money to buy a dress."

She studied political science and in 1969 joined *Institutional Investor* magazine as a journalist. Seven years later McGraw-Hill recruited her to start a conference group that would create a different delivery platform for the company's various magazines and newsletters. Later she moved to *Business Week* to head its business development effort.

In 1991 Munder was tapped to be the executive assistant to the chairman, Joe Dionne, with the mission to retool the company's brand image. McGraw-Hill had become a diversified company, encompassing not only education but also financial services and special markets such as aviation, construction, and energy. However, in the public mind, it was still considered mainly an educational publisher. It was her job to develop a new brand that would reflect the new realities. This ultimately involved changing the logo, company name, stationery, and advertising. It also meant communicating the changes to the company's 16,000 employees. Thus began her involvement with the electronic universe. She developed both the company's Internet sites and its Intranet, the internal communication system that would serve not only to provide information but also to be a tool to allow people from different parts of the company to work together to achieve team goals.

Today she applies that knowledge to her new objective: developing the company's electronic commerce strategy. Creating e-commerce goes beyond simply creating a Web site that features the company's products and services, she explains: "It means adding services that enable our customers to do their jobs better." There are two parts, she explains: "There is the part where you give information, and that is important. But there is also the part where you provide tools that help people accomplish their goals, and this is the added value. When our clients get up in the morning and immediately go to our site because they can't do their job without it, we have succeeded."

Munder is the mother of one child. Balancing motherhood and a demanding job has been a challenge. It helps to have a husband who does not expect you to cook every day. It also helps to have had excellent child care for 13 years. "I could not have done it without those two things," she says. "I came home each night in time to put her to bed, and that would be our time when we talked about her day and concerns. On the weekends we would do everything together, and that kept me involved in her life."

Leadership Style

She is most energized when she creates vision and pulls the team together to execute it. "I am excited and passionate about it," she says, "and that lets me sell others on what we have to accomplish. I motivate people to move forward and become involved." Working with a group of highly charged people to create something new is the ideal working environment for Strategists, and Munder is no exception.

Formerly she managed a staff of 30 but admits to not enjoying the people management side very much. "I like working on a team," she says, "but I prefer not to spend my time developing the individuals."

Being impatient with people is a blind spot, she admits, "but I am, particularly when they need constant guidance and reassurance."

Strategists enjoy being trailblazers. They focus on policy and goals and are usually adept at marshaling institutional resources to achieve their objectives.

Advice to Others

"If you have a vision, determine the best way to implement it and then go out and do it—the earlier, the better!"

SHERRY BARRAT
President and CEO
Northern Trust Bank of California, N.A.

Sherry Barrat never envisioned going into business. She wanted to be a stay-at-home mom. She married at age 17, had a child, divorced, and only then got a job as a clerk at an old savings and loan institution in Miami. At night she went to school to get a college degree. Her 6-year-old daughter used to sit in the library with her while Sherry did her work.

She was the older of two girls. Her parents were an eclectic combination: a self-made businessman and a debutante from New York. Her father was a very liberated man for his time, she notes. "He raised me kind of like a son. He wanted me to have choices so that I could do what I wanted." But it would be several years and two marriages later before those choices would come to be.

Today she runs Northern Trust Bank of California, a wholly owned subsidiary of The Northern Trust Company. Her responsibilities, such as geographic outreach, are broad and varied. Eleven offices report to her, with new locations opening each year. Northern Trust provides private banking, trust, and investment management services to individuals, companies, and not-for-profit organizations. I interview her at a conference in California. She has just arrived from the Florida bank to take over the California subsidiary. The troops are still eyeing her warily, but she works the crowd with ease, confident of her skills and ability to win them over.

Leadership Style

Barrat is most energized by working with new clients and new business development. "I love courting prospective clients, getting to know them, solving their problems, and then bringing them in as a new account," she says with enthusiasm. "It is the thrill of the win."

She also enjoys managing a team of high performers. "It is like a stable of thoroughbreds," she says. "It is worth putting up with a high-strung group when you respect what they accomplish. I'm a good synthesizer of ideas. I gather ideas and listen to what others have to say, but ultimately I drive the final decision." She adds, "I am not really looking for solutions that make the most people happy."

A number of qualities are valued in an institution such as Northern Trust, she notes. One has to understand how to position the institution and how to run a profitable division. Beyond that, it is a question of hiring the right people and leading them well. "At some level, " she notes disarmingly, "I really enjoy making people happy. That may mean bringing the bacon home for the company in terms of a fantastic bottom line. Or it may mean helping someone become a million-dollar-a-year producer."

Asked about her blind spots, she admits to being impatient, saying, "I expect people to either help me or get out of my way." Like other Strategists, she deals fairly easily with confrontation. "When it is between two other people," she notes, "I am skilled at defusing the conflict. When it involves me, I don't like the conflict, but I tend to deal with it head on."

Of course conflict is different from disagreement, she is quick to add. It is very important for leaders to build enough trust that others can disagree with them: "Perhaps that is the quality that distinguishes wise leaders from dictators."

Strategists, as it has been noted in previous profiles, like to be in charge. They enjoy the opportunity to map out what needs to be done and to assign the right people to do it. However, those people better be up to the challenge, because Strategists have little patience for inefficiency.

Strategists value intelligence, perceptive insights, and originality. They are annoyed by clichés, shallow thinking, and those who insist on sticking to traditional ways of solving a problem. Problems invigorate them, and they excel in positions that demand innovative solutions.

Advice to Others

"You have to be a shining star at whatever you do. Concentrate on what you are doing today and don't worry too much about long-term goals." "A second thing," she adds fervently. "Remember that what goes around comes around. Build your relationships and know when to take a backseat and let others shine."

LISA EGBUONU-DAVIS, M.D.
Vice President
Global Outcomes Research
and Medical Services,
Pfizer Pharmaceuticals Group

By the age of 30, Lisa Egbuonu-Davis had a BA in biology from MIT, an MPH and MD from Johns Hopkins, and an MBA in health care management from Wharton. Motivated? I'd say so. Currently, she is a vice president of global outcomes research and medical services for Pfizer Pharmaceuticals Group, managing a staff of 100 and a budget of $50 million. Her group conducts clinical and health economic research on Pfizer's pharmaceutical products and services worldwide.

She is also a mother and wife. Managing it all often requires getting up at four in the morning to get a jump start on the day. "I take fairly frequent vacations," she says with a grin. "It's the only way to stay sane and healthy."

Leadership Style

We meet in her office in mid-Manhattan. Like many Strategists, she has analyzed herself with the same objectivity she brings to business issues. "I try to lead charismatically," she says. "I enroll others, but ultimately I drive the process. I see the patterns earlier and faster than others, and I am also willing to address problems before others are ready to deal with them." Egbuonu-Davis's ease in dealing with the politics of the organization reflects the innate political savvy of this personality group. "My vision," she says, "is to be a facilitative leader who catalyzes positive change in organizations, environments, and communities."

What keeps her going? She is energized by creating new ideas, analyzing trends, developing strategies, and bouncing ideas around with other creative people.

As an example, she cites her work on a public-private partnership campaign for healthy babies. Her task was to bridge two different communities: business and public health. "They each operate in different ways," she says. "I had to get them to collaborate and understand each other. This involved converting the public health reports into a business plan and then selling the plan to the business community that had the money and power to make it happen."

Asked about her blind spots, she admits to sometimes stepping on the toes of others (more of a problem in her earlier days) and occasionally not following through when things get boring. She also readily acknowledges her impatience: "I can try to persuade people and break things down for them, but in the end, if they don't get it, I am not very patient. Though I have learned that sometimes organizations are not ready to hear things; then you have to wait."

Levi Watkins, the first black person to ever go through the cardiac surgery pyramid at Johns Hopkins, is one of her chief role models: "He played the game on their court and by their rules and won, then made them change some of the rules."

Strategists take charge with confidence. As a result, others willingly follow. They usually have a high degree of sensitivity to the inner dynamics of the organization and will be team players if that is what it takes to accomplish their goal. They prefer working with autonomous people who do not need constant guidance to do their job. They trust logical reasoning above all and are usually quite persuasive in communicating their point of view to others.

Egbuonu-Davis is the oldest of three children. Her father, an industrial engineer and member of the Ibo tribe in Africa, arrived in the United States from Nigeria at age 17: "The Ibos are known for being fairly clannish, and for their business and professional achievements." Egbuonu-Davis jokes about her visit to the ancestral tribe before going to business school. She said they all shared a good laugh because "everyone in Nnewi [the village] gets all these professional degrees and then ultimately ends up going into business."

Her U.S.-born mother was a classical musician who gave up her career when she got married. Her husband did not think it was a useful profession. Ultimately she went into real estate and teaching. "She taught us not to give anything up," says Lisa recalling her mother's regret at giving up her music.

In her twenties, Egbuonu-Davis recalls being "more direct, abrasive, and blunt, and less sensitive to the emotional climate." As a result, her medical residency was a "humbling experience." "When I went back to school [after residency]," she says, "I went with a more mature sense that sometimes you win, sometimes you don't. I was softer and more sensitive to people." It was the turning point that needs to be acknowledged by every Strategist, particularly women who want to rise to positions of power.

Today Egbuonu-Davis makes good use of professional women's groups. She finds them useful for exchanging views on how to manage career choices and survive today's hectic lifestyles.

Advice to Others

"First I would develop unique skills—whatever they are—because you have to bring something of value to the table to be considered a 'player.' Then I think it's important to fine-tune those skills by using them in different settings. Finally, I would recommend studying others and analyzing what makes them successful or not successful in different environments."

HILLARY CLINTON
First Lady of the United States

Who is Hillary Clinton, and what makes her one of the most interesting women of our time? The question is relevant because her future success will depend on the extent to which voters feel they know her.

My request to interview her was turned down. I had had a brief encounter with her several years earlier when, at the request of a friend, I produced a pencil portrait sketch that was presented to her at a fund-raiser in New York. I am glad I met her, because she is much more interesting in person than her image indicates. She is engaging and charismatic.

Therefore, I decided to go ahead and write this profile, the only one not based on a direct interview. Extensive research and candid conversations with journalists and friends revealed some tantalizing clues.

Hillary Clinton disdains the cloak of subdued femininity which other First Ladies have used for their own ends. Rather, she comes across as assertive, purposeful, and determined. Her issues have always been global, connecting the concerns of American women and children to struggles in the third world. She speaks of genital mutilation in Africa and forced abortions in China. She knows the issues in depth and expresses them in her trademark style, clause after clause after clause, each with its own verb and noun tacked firmly into place.

All of the above points to a take-charge Strategist who, like the other women profiled in this chapter, is forceful, focused, and global in outlook. She leans toward abstract concepts and is well known for her use of compound sentences to express them.

Hillary was born in Chicago and grew up in Park Ridge, Illinois. She has two brothers and is the oldest of the three. Her youth provides further clues to her personality type. She was a National Merit

Scholar and a high achiever in college and law school, showing the kind of academic drive typically demonstrated by Blues in general. In her early days, according to her mother, she took charge of the boys in the neighborhood, and they allowed her to. She organized the special athletic and social events for the kids in the area.[11] Her teachers considered her an exceptional student who took in information and argued a point thoroughly but would change her mind when new input demanded it. In her senior year in high school she was voted most likely to succeed.

At Wellesley she was an activist and student body president. She went on to law school at Yale, where she specialized in children's rights. After graduation from Yale, she became part of the impeachment inquiry staff investigating Richard Nixon. This, by all accounts, was a solemn group. She worked tirelessly dawn to midnight, seven days a week. Hillary is remembered as "determined and dutiful, grinding away in a mildewed office overlooking an alleyway"[12]

These traits again point to a Strategist working tirelessly on a problem of interest and functioning without undue stress in a negative and tense environment.

Over that summer she fretted over her relationship with William Jefferson Clinton. She joined him in Arkansas to direct his campaign for a congressional seat. She tangled with his campaign manager, Paul Fray, who later granted her grudging respect. "She was hard-nosed, and she would cuss," he would later say, "but she was an organizational genius."[13]

Hillary and Bill married. The match between these two provides one of the more interesting pairings in presidential history. Personality type dynamics go a long way toward explaining why the marriage took place, why it endured, and why, barring further high-profile mistakes, it will continue to last.

The personality type of Bill Clinton has been a debated issue in the Myers-Briggs community, but according to Dr. David Keirsey, a noted temperament specialist, he clearly falls into the category of the Red Realist because of "his love of contest, delight in risk, joy in performing, in being 'on stage,' and need for people contact."

Their 24-year marriage is a complex dance of two opposite styles. They complement each other. He loves politics; she prefers making policy. He is a quick study; she has depth and focus. He looks for ways to compromise; she weighs alternative strategies. He forgives and forgets; she remembers and keeps score. They are both outgoing and energetic, but there is a difference. He dives into a crowd with abandonment; she reaches out but always remains at a cool distance. They are both very bright, but their intelligence differs. He works from the gut; she is guided by logical analysis. He thrives on risk; she circles it cautiously. The relationship is complex, and tension will always be part of the dynamics.[14]

Each of the four color groups has a different type of intelligence, which Keirsey has defined as "the ability to do well under varying circumstances." Bill Clinton's is known as "tactical intelligence." It is described as the ability to see and make use of the opportunity of the moment. This includes swaying the crowds, making use of popular ideas, and producing a quick and immediate impact. It also means not being tied to any particular political agenda. Rather, he focuses on what works at the moment.[15]

Hillary as a Strategist has made different contributions to the marriage. She is the one who is able to draw and clarify the battle lines. She is not concerned about stepping on toes. Her goals (the legal rights of children and health care reform) are long-term, strategic, and fairly abstract.

Together they make a powerful team. Cynical observers say it is a marriage of convenience, but friends see it as an attraction of opposites. She speaks with admiration of his political skills. "We have a deep connection that transcends whatever happens," she has said to friends. He seems deeply attracted to her strength and resolve, her ability to speak her mind regardless of the effects.[16]

Not long ago Hillary's running for office would have seemed very far-fetched. Today, with a single-minded focus she is poised to carve out her own place in history. She is alive. Her thinking is fresh. She creates a buzz. The energy is focused. She could be an author or an ambassador, serve on corporate boards, or run a foundation. Money is clearly not what motivates her career choices; what she wants is her own voice and the ability to set her own agenda.[17]

Hillary Rodham Clinton is doing what comes naturally to all Strategists: taking charge.

Advice to Others

In a recent TV interview she stated, "I would hope that young women—women of all ages—understand how important it is to live your own life according to your own values and not be constantly looking over your shoulder to think what anybody else is thinking about you or saying about you, because ultimately, at the end of the day, you have to live with yourself."

10 The Innovators

Innovators combine preferences for intuition, the information-gathering process that favors abstract ideas, future possibilities, and connecting unrelated ideas to create new patterns; thinking, the decision-making process that emphasizes an objective, impersonal, logical, and analytic approach to decision making; and perceiving, the lifestyle preference that stresses adaptability, flexibility, and keeping options open as long as possible.

OVERALL

Inventive, insightful, and mentally stimulating, Innovators constantly scan the universe for new and unusual ideas.

Characterized by intellectual energy and a compelling interest in everything around them, they are usually alert and responsive to new opportunities. Independent and highly resourceful, they are not afraid to take controversial positions. Sometimes, in fact, they enjoy debating issues from both sides.

Diversity is high on their priority list. They are most at home in a flexible environment which allows them to critique, redesign, and improve any project that has caught their interest. Whether others agree, understand, or support them is not important. They look for difficult problems, always confident in their ability to improvise as needed. Following through once a project has been launched, however, is of less interest.

Their unusual insights make them at times almost psychic about future developments. These qualities serve them well in a variety of entrepreneurial activities.

They communicate in clever and sophisticated language and persuade others through clear thinking and thoughtful debate.

They are most irritated by people who refuse to consider new ideas or are overly emotional and apply faulty logic.

In relationships they express affection through humor, play, and surprises. Their deepest feelings, however, usually are revealed only to a small circle of very close friends.

Many occupations are attractive to Innovators. They express satisfaction working as entrepreneurs, inventors, marketers, real estate developers, university professors, journalists, financial planners, advertising directors, research and development specialists, and investment bankers, as well as in other fields that make good use of their flexibility and ability to analyze matters logically and come up with unusual solutions.

In their leisure time they pursue mental activities such as bridge, chess, and travel.

In the second half of life well-developed Innovators learn to better balance the thinking and feeling functions. They find new joy in their relationships and their ability to work with others in voluntary or other types of socially useful projects.

Leadership Style

Generate high-quality ideas

Have well-developed problem-solving skills

Set high standards and push others to exceed goals and targets

Take the initiative and are comfortable with risk

Find ways to get around problems and limitations

Understand and appreciate global issues

Can make tough decisions

Are flexible and adapt quickly to changing conditions

Support the intellectual development of others

Optimal Working Environment

Provides an unstructured environment with a minimum of rules and procedures

Provides the opportunity to develop cutting-edge systems and solutions without having to worry about how they will be carried out

Has powerful and highly competent people

Has a nonemotional, logical workplace culture that rewards creativity and competence

Rewards people for taking risks

Includes an informal network of bright, independent, and motivated associates

Supplies strong administrative support that will handle the details and follow-through for projects

Emphasizes the start-up phase of projects rather than maintenance

Least Preferred Working Environment

Being responsible for routine, predictable, and detailed work

Being controlled and micromanaged

Coworkers who lack initiative and imagination

Approach to Change

Usually welcome it

Are not very interested in practical implementation

Contribution to a Team

Set high standards and encourage team members to go the extra mile

Provide a clear critical analysis of issues

Generate many options and see unique ways of solving problems

Encourage strategic and long-range thinking

Ask imaginative questions

Are quick to notice flaws and inconsistencies

Decision-Making Style

Evaluate factors in a logical and analytic manner

Generate many options

Change a decision easily if a more appropriate one comes along

Potential Blind Spots

Are irresponsible about deadlines

May not meet commitments

Initiate too many projects that cannot be completed

Intimidate those who are less quick witted

Are overly critical and opinionated

Change plans and strategies too frequently

How to Persuade an Innovator

Provide an executive summary

Know the material in depth

Stress the uniqueness of an idea or solution

Accept the fact that you will be challenged and critiqued; take it as a positive sign

Speak about comparable studies

Be logical; avoid emotional appeals

Speak of future implications; show how they will contribute to long-term strategies

Be brief and concise; use sophisticated vocabulary

Present options; be prepared to change directions and revisit a decision

Use humor; make it both serious and fun

Strategies for Innovators to Increase Leadership Effectiveness

Follow through on all commitments; set up systems to ensure their timely implementation

Request frequent feedback from associates

Prioritize on a daily basis; create time lines

Utilize and express appreciation for the skills of those who
value facts and accuracy

Accept the fact that other types of people need structure
and rules

Be more in tune with your feeling side; ensure the buy-in of
associates by factoring their feelings into your decisions

Develop time management techniques that work for your
way of operating

Develop patience and tolerance for others who operate
differently

TWO TYPES OF INNOVATORS: EXTRAVERTS AND INTROVERTS

Extraverted Innovators tend to respond with uninhibited energy and
enthusiasm and are forceful in persuading others to join them in the
project of the moment. They have a flair for the dramatic, an irreverent charm, and a disarming sense of humor that pokes fun at anything
that takes itself too seriously.

Introverted Innovators appear more reserved and detached until
they are ready to share their ideas, at which point they become
excited and persuasive. They see the irony around them and express
their mostly unconventional views with a small circle of close associates. Thinkers more than speakers, they work best with privacy and
quiet. They prefer to organize ideas rather than people.

A Note of Caution

Since type does not explain many aspects that are important in defining an individual, (intelligence, education, mental health, and individual life experiences, among others), no overall profile can describe all
the variants in a personality. Invariably, some of the traits described
above will not ring true for you. If the majority do not ring true,
however, it could mean that you belong to another group. In that case,
go back and revisit your Leadership Q questionnaire. Check the

columns where you have close scores. Try reading a profile that reflects the other combination of your close scores. Alternatively, you might show the profile detailed below to an individual who knows you well, such as a mate, boss, close friend, or team colleague, and ask for comments. If you are going through major life changes, try waiting until things have stabilized.

DEVELOPMENT EXERCISES FOR INNOVATORS

We may appear different in different situations. Over time we also grow and progress, but our basic preferences do not change. This has been proved by the large number of people who have retaken the Myers-Briggs Type Indicator in different periods of their lives and repeatedly come out with the same preferences. Thus, an abstract intuitive Thinker never really becomes a concrete sensing Thinker. A structured Judger never really becomes a flexible, go-with-the-flow Perceiver. A Blue Innovator never becomes a dyed-in-the wool-Gold Conservator.

People who succeed, however, instinctively or deliberately learn to develop their nonpreferences. This softens their blind spots and enables them to adapt to the demands of different people and situations. Listed below are exercises that will help you develop your nonpreferences. Jung referred to this process as individuation.

Exercise 1. Finishing Projects

Innovators are adaptable, flexible, open to new options, and process-oriented. They say things such as "I don't decide until I have to" and "I don't like to do the follow-up." As a result, their world is filled with unfinished projects and many frustrated associates. This openness is part of their flexibility. If taken to an extreme, this flexibility is counterproductive and probably is the most important reason why this type derails.

- Identify a couple of partially completed projects. Try to determine why you were constantly pulled away from them. Identify and note those impulses. Were they boredom, the need to get more information, or not having the appropriate materials around.

- Set aside a block of time, say, three hours, in the most productive period of your day. Make sure you have all the information and materials you need. If you are an Extravert, ask a detail person to work with you. Finish one or all projects in the time allotted. Note how satisfying it feels to have them out of the way. Savor the moment. Enjoy the feeling of control. File this feeling in your memory for future recall.
- From here on, when making a to-do list each day, circle with a color felt pen the one or two items that need to be completed no matter what.

The point is that in a short time you will find that (1) you have a greater sense of control in your life, (2) you have the respect of more structured types around you, and (3) you have eliminated a lot of the clutter in your life. This is called type development, which means softening your blind spots.

Exercise 2. Giving Instructions

The strong intuitive mind-set of the Innovator often results in instructions that are vague and impressionistic. These instructions do not work well with Sensors (over 70 percent of the population), who need specific guidelines and a concrete plan of action. Poor instructions often lead to frustration, wasted time, and significant misunderstandings in the workplace.

Write your instructions or plan of action on a piece of paper. Check that the following conditions are met.

- You have worked out the details in advance. Ask yourself when, where, what, how, and why.
- You are brief and specific about what needs to be done.
- You have demonstrated why the project makes sense, why it is needed, and what the practical applications are.
- If action is needed, give specific instructions; do not assume

that others will read between the lines. For example, write "Materials need to go out before the end of the week," not "We should think about sending materials."

The point is that other people take in information differently than you do. They cannot be productive unless that difference is honored.

Exercise 3. Handling Conflict

You are rational and fair. Well-developed leaders understand the need to factor in how people will react to decisions. This requires developing your feeling preference.

- Recall a recent conflict involving several people.
- Think about each person who was involved. Write the names of those individuals on a piece of paper.
- Set aside the consideration of who was right. Focus on the personal motivations and emotional issues surrounding the conflict and note them.
- Consider other ways in which the conflict might have been handled.

The point is that using both preferences reduces conflict.

Exercise 4. Working with Other Types

You have been assigned to cohead a project with Allison, a well-regarded manager who is considered to be on the fast track. She is a Gold Trustee. She differs from you in two major preferences. She is a Sensor (concrete, fact-driven, and sequential) and a Judger (structured and goal-driven).

This assignment is important to your career. Her impression of you will determine future assignments.

Read the Gold Trustee personality summary. Write down some of the key differences below.

Allison	Me
1.	1.
2.	2.
3.	3.
4.	4.

Read the section on how to persuade a Gold Trustee. Note the points below. Incorporate them into the presentation you will make at the initial meeting.

1.

2.

3.

Read through your blind spots. Note which of them will be most irritating to Allison. Devise a strategy.

My Blind Spot	Strategy
1.	1.
2.	2.

Now repeat this exercise with a real person you have to work with who is different from you. It can be a boss, colleague, or client. Look at the overall four color descriptions and the section on how to recognize each color group.

My Type _____   **His or Her Type** _____

How to Persuade:

Blind Spots   **Strategy**

Photocopy your comments and keep them someplace where they are easily accessible.

The point is that if you do this exercise often enough, you not only will be more effective with that person, you will learn to appreciate what he or she brings to the table. Soon you will expand that understanding to other people and become known for your skills in managing people. This is the path to leadership.

Exercise 5. How to Be a Better Leader

- Turn back to your leadership style summary.
- Choose one strategy for increased leadership effectiveness.
- Write it on an index card and develop three specific steps to achieve that strategy.
- Place the card someplace where you will see it frequently. Read it several times a day.
- After several weeks repeat the process with another strategy.

KATHLEEN KENNEDY TOWNSEND
Lieutenant Governor
Maryland

She is Robert Kennedy's oldest child, and there is a poignant resemblance in the mischievous smile and the expression around the eyes. Most of all, it lies in the gritty determination. Once she puts her mind to it, something will happen, no matter how much opposition she faces. She is the first Kennedy woman to have stood for office. Untainted by scandal, the mother of four, and married to the same man for more than 26 years, she is also, some say, the clan's most promising torchbearer.

Townsend (or KKT, as she is known) grew up the oldest of 11 children at Hickory Hill, a Georgian mansion on six and a half acres just outside Washington. Suited to her family's exuberant lifestyle, it housed a staff of more than eight and a menagerie that as she recalls included dogs, cats, ponies, ducks, iguanas, and for a brief period, a sea lion that kept lumbering over to neighborhood stores.

Guests speak of a constant stream of children who roamed through the rooms without restraint. "No door ever remained shut," recalls one former overnight guest, rolling her eyes. Apparently Bobby Kennedy encouraged the high-spirited behavior and added to it by allowing them to tackle him. "In fact, one night," she continues, "they were all playing a flag game, and the kids were leaping on and off roofs. I thought they were all going to kill themselves, but neither Ethel nor Bobby seemed concerned."

That energy extended beyond the house as well. Family lore also has it that after being sworn in as attorney general in 1961, her father descended to the first floor of the White House by sliding down the banister of the enormous curved staircase. He was followed by the 10-year-old Kathleen, whooping with glee.

All the children were expected to play football, sail, and memorize poems. At night they gathered around their parents' bed to pray and listen to excerpts from the Bible. The sibling rivalry was intense.

The experiences were similar for all, but the expectations were different. The girls were expected to grow up, have babies, and campaign for the men. The boys were expected to go out and accomplish things. The political legacy belonged to the males. It was embedded in the family's culture.

As Bobby's firstborn, Kathleen had a special bond with him. She was just 16 years old when he was assassinated. Among her special keepsakes is a letter he wrote to her two days after his brother, the President, was shot. It said, "As the oldest of the Kennedy grandchildren, you have special responsibilities now. Be kind to your family and work hard for your country. Love, Daddy." After his death she became a surrogate parent for many of her siblings, and he remains her most powerful role model.

In 1970 she went to Radcliffe, where she majored in literature and history. She also developed a crush on David Townsend, a lanky red-bearded graduate student who occasionally tutored her in American literature. He had a girlfriend, but that fazed Kathleen not one bit. They were reading *Huckleberry Finn*. She suggested that they build a raft and float down the Mississippi River, knowing her unsuspecting rival would have little interest in the journey. The plot, which would have warmed many an Innovator's heart, worked as planned. They married a year later.

The couple moved to Santa Fe, New Mexico. He taught. She had her first two children by natural childbirth at home, and following a southwestern ritual, they buried the placenta and planted a tree on that spot. In between she got a law degree and later entered politics through the well-paved Kennedy route—working on her Uncle Ted's 1982 Senate campaign.

In 1984 they moved to Maryland, her husband's home state. The plan was that he would obtain a flexible teaching schedule and take an active role in the household with his parents' help. Kathleen would do politics.

Her first attempt failed. In 1986 she campaigned for a seat in the U.S. Congress in tennis shoes with glasses and disheveled hair. Many saw her as a carpetbagger. Her staff was untrained. The district was heavily Republican. Her brother Joe, who was simultaneously running for Congress in Massachusetts, got most of the family support. The outcome was a small disaster.

She spent the next 8 years in appointed positions at the state and federal levels. During that time she instituted some of the programs she is most proud of today, including the nation's first mandatory student service program. This program requires high school students in Maryland to do 75 hours of community service work before graduating. The initiative was very controversial. Twenty-two out of 24 school systems opposed it, but Townsend persisted. She spent 6 years going from school to school to develop grassroots support. Finally, in 1992, the initiative was adopted.

Then, in 1994, she was the surprise addition to the Maryland gubernatorial ticket as lieutenant governor. The incumbent, Parris Glendening, was policy-oriented. He saw in Townsend the right mix of gender, pedigree, and connections. He later said he had found "his ideological soul mate." She accepted immediately, and the two have remained close.[18]

With a new hairdo, contact lenses, speech training, and a spiffy wardrobe, Townsend quickly became the most famous lieutenant governor in the country.

Behind the scenes she was a quick study. She now controls much of the state's crime agenda, with responsibility for a budget of over $1 billion and 15,000 employees. Her HotSpots program, which focuses on criminal justice resources and builds a community's ability to prevent and stop crime, and the ROTC-style Police Corps program for college students have won her nationwide praise. She understands the issues, and her disarmingly genuine desire for good government is attractive to many voters.

In the estimation of pundits, she is off and running. It is expected that she will run for governor in 2002; some say her goal may ultimately be the White House.

Of course, Townsend is the first to acknowledge that a supportive husband has made much of this possible. Two of her four children are already adults, which helps, but still there is strong practical as well as psychological support. When a child is sick, her husband often opts to stay home. KKT in turn avoids breakfast meetings. She drives one child to school and cooks breakfast for the other one. This gives her regular time with each child.

Blue Innovator females belong to the 35 percent of women who have a thinking preference. As such, they are often like fish swimming upstream. She is no exception. With her impatience and competitive spirit, Townsend challenges the stereotypes of women who are expected to be compliant and nurturing. In her early years her parents supported these traits; it was part of the Kennedy upbringing. Today they are further honed by the demands of the political process.

Meanwhile, she displays other characteristics of her color group. She is resourceful, is not afraid to take controversial positions, and tackles difficult problems, always confident in her ability to improvise as needed. She also generates high-quality ideas, has well-developed problem-solving skills, and sets high standards for herself and others. In contrast to Blue Strategists, Innovators are more opportunistic, and Townsend's ability to regroup and change course reflects the flexibility that is the hallmark of her type.

Leadership Style

I greet her in a Washington restaurant. She is wearing an electric blue suit. In the crisp November light it reflects her vibrant kinetic energy. "I like to give people a vision and then get them energized to figure out how they can best use their talents to reach that vision," she says, describing how she leads. "My special strength," she continues, "is to bring people together and persuade them to do things differently from what they have done before while making them feel they are part of something greater than themselves."

KKT is an extraverted Innovator and therefore is more exuberant than are those with a more introvertive bent. This personality type is flexible, engagingly irreverent, and masterful at finding new ways to solve problems. The world of these Innovators is filled with new possibilities and interests, and it is important that they prioritize and focus on their highest objectives. When they do, they become strong personalities with powerful insights.

Innovators are also visionaries and are unusually adept at mobilizing others to reach the stated goals. They have a keen understanding of the subtle networks of relationships within a group or between different groups. They also know how to pull a team together for as long as it takes to get a project moving.

As an example, she points to the HotSpots program targeted at high-risk areas in Maryland, the roughly 3 percent of neighborhoods where 50 percent of the crimes take place. "My belief," she says, "is that the government can't do it without engaging the residents of that neighborhood. You have to change their sense of responsibility. So now, before we commit additional resources, we require that they become part of the solution by doing things like identifying drug dealers, being willing to testify in court, joining community watch groups, and volunteering in after-school programs. The result is that crime in those areas has been reduced 20 percent, twice as fast as in the state as a whole."

Other programs of which she is particularly proud are the character education programs recently introduced into the Maryland school system to teach children right from wrong and the Police Corp program patterned after the ROTC, which provides scholarships for students who pledge to serve four years as law enforcement officers.

"I love politics," she says enthusiastically. "I love changing laws that will impact families and children, I love seeing my name on the bumper sticker of someone's car, I love working with a group that gets up at 5 A.M. to get ready for an event, and I love interpreting what people are saying and creating programs to meet their needs. I love all the parts of it."

Is there anything that stresses her out? I ask. "Not really," she says. "Maybe paperwork. But if it stresses me out, I ask someone else to do it, and I do what I enjoy and do best."

When asked how others evaluate her style, she is pensive: "They say I am a good listener, but I have had to work at it. They also say that I care deeply about the issues and that I am willing to get down in the trenches to make things happen."

Advice to Others

Not surprisingly, KKT's advice to young women is unusual. "Get involved in sports," she says. "When you are competing, you learn how to concentrate and galvanize all the parts of yourself to ensure the ultimate performance. And when you lose, you learn not to be disappointed because life is filled with loss and you have to avoid being defeated by it. Number two," she continues, ticking off what are obviously deep convictions, "get good at math and science. They are the language of power. People respect and listen to you when you understand economics. Finally, test yourself when you are young. Set goals and test yourself at whatever you can. If you want to be a leader, then *lead*." This is characteristic advice from a thinking female for whom analysis, competition, and confrontation are natural strengths.

I ask her about the future, and she flashes a wicked grin: "I am not putting any limits on myself." Without a doubt, Kathleen Kennedy Townsend is a force to watch out for.

COUNTESS ALBINA DU BOISROUVRAY
Founder
Association François-Xavier Bagnoud

She is a member of a glamorous royal family. She also inherited one of the world's major fortunes. Rarely, however, will you find her socializing with the rich and famous, unless it is to raise funds for the Assocation François-Xavier Bagnoud (AFXB), the organization founded after her beloved son, François-Xavier, crashed over the Sahara Desert in Mali on a cold night in 1986. He was just 24 years old, a luminous blond young man who spent his short adulthood flying rescue missions in the valleys of Switzerland. Today his mother circles the globe overseeing the association devoted to the causes he espoused.

Albina is the daughter of Count Guy du Boisrouvray of France and a close cousin of Prince Rainier of Monaco. On her mother's side she is the granddaughter of Simon Patino, the Bolivian "Tin King" who died in 1948 as one of the richest men in the world. Amusing, bright, and polished, she counts among her friends Baroness Lady Thatcher, the designer Karl Lagerfeld, and her cousin, Princess Caroline of Monaco. In an earlier era she was also a regular lunch companion of Jacqueline Kennedy Onassis. Now she devotes almost every waking moment to building AFXB into a global presence.

Her childhood was nomadic. She was born in Paris and moved to New York, then back to Paris, then to Morocco, where she was sent for five years with her nanny and retinue, then to Argentina, and eventually to boarding schools in England and France. Somehow she recalls her parents always seemed to be elsewhere. As a teenager she married the Swiss helicopter pilot Bruno Bagnoud. They had one son, François-Xavier.

After the brief marriage ended she attended the Sorbonne in Paris. It was the time of the 1968 student riots. "I wanted to change the world," she recalls, "and I thought you needed a revolution to do that." Later she briefly became involved in politics as a candidate for an ecological party but soon lost interest in the political process. "You were never free," she reminisces. "You had to shut your mouth, get the vote, sit through endless meetings, and listen to people who are a waste of time."

She branched out to filmmaking, ultimately producing 22 movies and being appointed vice president of the Cannes Film Festival jury in 1980.

Innovators like the Countess tend to challenge conventional wisdom, always with the belief that the impossible can be achieved. They have an interest in many fields and change careers and directions more frequently than other groups do. They can be successful in many areas as long as an activity does not involve too much routine. If it does, they become restless. They value adaptability and innovation and have little patience with those who insist on doing things the traditional way. Highly individualistic, they enjoy outwitting the system.

After her son's death, she sold off assets to start a foundation in his name. First she liquidated many of the real estate holdings inherited from her father, raising a total of some $50 million. Then, in a 2-day sale at Sotheby's in New York, she sold artworks and 66 lots of her mother's jewelry for another $55 million. Included were a Cartier necklace with 12 vast emeralds that went for approximately $2 million and a 287-diamond necklace that brought in $1.5 million. With proceeds of over $100 million, she started the foundation.[19]

Albina shuttles between fund-raising in Europe and the United States and fieldwork in third world countries. She spends 60 to 70 percent of her time traveling. Hers is a "can-do, make-it-happen" approach. She provides what is needed. That can mean touching and soothing the victims, or it can mean building new housing and providing economic incentives for those willing to adopt orphans. It also can mean bringing health care workers back to the United States for special training.

Innovators think broadly and strategically. They are always drawn to grand ideas and complex models. "I am always impressed by how intuitive her intelligence is," says Kitty Cushing, managing director of

Wainwright Investment Counsel. "She has an unusually deep understanding of global business trends."

Leadership Style

We meet in the muted lounge of an elegant Manhattan hotel, a far cry
from the smoldering plains of Africa and Thailand, where she usually
spends her time. Her accent is a combination of French, upper-class
English, and American. She speaks rapidly and with intensity, the passion evident in the large green eyes framed by dark billowing hair.
The appearance speaks of Latin America, the wry humor of France,
and the rapid movements of a longtime New York habitué. She is at
once all and none of these things. What she does have is the linguistic
and cultural adaptability to alternate between high-society events and
forays into steaming mud villages.

She lives, much as she did in childhood, out of a suitcase, lobbying
and encouraging everyone from heads of state to tiny AIDS orphans.
It is a constant balancing act, she admits, to do the small things that
make someone's life more comfortable and then to use her influence
in high places to raise money and change the way things are done.

Like others in her group, she is most energized by creating something new. "It is like solving a puzzle," she says. "We have limited
human and financial resources, so we have to be innovative with our
solutions."

She describes her leadership style as "democratically authoritative.
I consult and try to listen to what others have to say, always putting
into perspective who they are, where they come from, and what their
agendas are. I allow my views to be modified, but at the end I have to
follow my priorities and vision."

A clear vision and the passion to pursue it are two strengths she
values. "Also," she adds, "I am objective. I analyze situations logically,
and I deal with confrontation well. I face the truth. I don't overper-
sonalize criticism, and I don't push things under the rug."

Many female leaders find confrontation a problem. Innovators are
among the few who do not. "It is always better," she concludes, "to

have things out in the open and to solve them." Her blind spots, she admits, include getting impatient with people if things do not move fast enough. She also gets annoyed at rules and procedures and has little tolerance for error.

Another strength is "being relentless about battling obstacles." She cites the example of eight Burmese teenagers missing from a house of prostitution in Thailand. The girls were HIV-positive, and it was believed that they had been killed because of it. Albina and her coterie put pressure on both the Thai and Burmese governments to search for the girls. They never found them, but they did find 95 young prostitutes in another underground network. She pressured the government to raid the establishments and help her set up workshop centers to teach the girls new skills. The workshops are now part of a regular program in both countries to teach young women trades before they are pushed into prostitution. And how do the governments react? "They keep taking my visa away," she says with a grin. "Then they decide it is bad for their image, so they issue me a new one. It goes back and forth."

Today, like many maturing Innovators, she has learned to be less confrontational and more realistic about her expectations. "Fifteen years ago," she admits, "I thought you got what you wanted by fighting. Now I know you have to choose your battles carefully."

Her vision is to be an agent of deep change, especially for orphans with AIDS. "I need to change the mentality of people who are privileged or at a high corporate level. It may sound utopian, but if we did it about animals, we certainly should be able to do it about children."

Advice to Others

Her advice to young women is to "avoid being overly influenced by others—society, men, and bosses. Follow your convictions, and whatever the obstacles, never give up."

KIM POLESE
CEO and Cofounder
Marimba, Inc.

There is a lot of buzz around Kim Polese, but that is not surprising because she is one of the few successful female CEOs in the male-dominated Silicon Valley community. Most notably, she led a company from its beginnings to an initial public offering in the spring of 1999. In 1997, *Time* magazine named her one of the 25 most influential Americans, alongside Madeleine Albright and George Soros. She was just 35 years old at the time.

It all began when she and three associates at Microsystems began talking about starting their own venture. She was a product manager who had helped launch the company's Java programming language. The others were senior engineers. For seven days between Christmas and New Year's 1995, they met daily in a coffee shop to define product, pricing, and marketing strategy. Within a month, they had a business plan for their new company and the four cofounders were ready to jump ship. They each put up $15,000 to fund the initial costs. Their first office was a storage room in a now defunct stationery store in Palo Alto. Venture capital followed, and the company was on its way.

Three years later Polese heads a 198-person business that sold $31.1 million of software in 1999. That software helps systems managers deliver, over a network, regularly updated applications to office PCs, Web servers, and even Web appliances and devices. In other words, it is an Internet infrastructure company, working at a crossroad between software and "Internet.com."

Polese always wanted to be an entrepreneur in a science-related field. Her Italian father and Danish mother ran a machine and engineering shop in Berkeley, California, a university town populated by many professors. Polese was the younger of two children.

From junior high on, much of her life focused on competing in national science fairs. "Science always was fun for me," she says, speaking of her enthusiasm for the field. "It was about exploration and adventure." She went on to get a degree in biophysics from the University of California at Berkeley and continued with studies in computer science at the University of Washington. In 1985 her first job was as a technical support engineer at IntelliCorp, which developed artificial intelligence software. In 1989 she joined Sun Microsystems, where she named and led the launch of Java, the hot new programming language. In January 1996 she left Sun Microsystems, together with three other members of the Java team, to form Marimba, Inc.

Innovators are natural entrepreneurs. Being visionaries, they prefer to operate autonomously to achieve their goals. They are skilled at mobilizing others and usually head for areas where they can improvise and adapt as they go. In light of their need for constant change and excitement, the Internet is proving a fertile ground for this adventurous group. As Polese puts it, "It is a constant adrenaline rush every day."

Leadership Style

Her special strengths, as she sees them, are threefold: spotting trends, being a good communicator, and handling the multifaceted aspects of running a company.

"I love the diversity of my days," she says in typical Innovator fashion. "In particular, I enjoy driving the direction of the company and making rapid decisions on how to respond to changing markets." In the Internet world, "you have to have your ear to the ground," she continues, "constantly taking the pulse of the market to respond with the right products."

Internal communications is another area she emphasizes. Polese has implemented a number of programs to keep the staff informed. There is "Lunch with Kim," a monthly meeting for six to eight employees who join her at a nearby restaurant. At Marimba having lunch with the CEO is as simple as signing up on a list. Then there is the brown bag lunch, where ten or so employees sign up to join the entire executive team for a free-for-all discussion with no set agenda. Once a month there is the "All Hands" meeting, where executives get up and talk to the staff about what is going on in the company.

There are also bimonthly strategic brainstorming session where key players get in a room and stay for a day or more with a whiteboard. They discuss what is happening in the markets, what customers are saying, and where the company wants to be in 6 to 12 months.

Teamwork is obviously a high priority, and Polese traces much of the company's ability to get funding to her partnership with the three cofounders. They elected her CEO in part because she is an articulate spokesperson for the company who also draws a great deal of media attention but also because of her track record in successfully introducing important new technologies to the market, and her proven ability to lead teams.

I interview Polese by phone. Her intensity and excitement are palpable. She believes in her vision of the Internet and, like many Innovators, sees dimensions that others do not.

Innovators delight in coming up with new ways to grapple with complex issues. Ultimately, there is a steely pragmatism to their solutions, but the process of brainstorming to solve the problem is an enjoyable, open-ended process that usually brings out the creativity in others as well. They also have a relentless drive to be competent—to stretch, learn, and share with others.

Detail work is generally boring for this personality group, which prefers ideas to the details of execution. "I am not the type to dot every 'i' and cross every 't'," she says. "I do enjoy diving into a project and fitting the pieces of the puzzle together. For example, I lead a weekly operations review meeting where each product team reports on the status of every detail of its project, issues are raised and resolved, and action items are assigned."

Dealing with criticism is a skill that has been developed over the years and accelerated by the rush of media attention. Where there is a lot of press, there is also a backlash, and Polese has had a fair amount in the last few years. "I quickly realized," she said, "that it went hand in hand with being a young women building a company in a very visible environment. I had to rise to the occasion, and that included taking a lot of barbs."

Today her vision is "to make the Internet a common utility, so simple to use that it is like flipping on a light switch or turning on the water." Her company, Marimba, develops products to make her vision a reality.

Advice to Others

"Don't be afraid of what you don't know; go out and learn. Some of the most influential people in the industry are the most curious and are constantly asking questions. It does not scare them; instead, they seek out the information.

"Also, I stress the importance of connecting with other people and building your own 'network.' That means connecting with a wide range of smart people with diverse perspectives on the business you have chosen and sharing ideas on a regular basis. The most successful people in Silicon Valley are the ones who have built the strongest networks."

CANDACE STRAIGHT

Vice Chairman, New Jersey Sports and Exposition Authority
President, WISH List

Today she is a volunteer—most of the time. She sits on a couple of boards, such as mutual fund boards of Neuberger & Berman, a $50 billion investment management company. The rest of the time she pursues personal interests, a luxury made possible by several decades of hard work and astute investing.

Her vision is to help get a woman elected president of the United States. "I have the skills to work with that individual to help her achieve it," she says, referring to her involvement with the WISH List, a pro-choice Republican group that stands for Women in the Senate and House. "Politics is the toughest game in town," she notes. "It has the best barriers of entry of any business I have every seen." Fundraising is one barrier, networking is another, and Straight, like many other Innovators, excels in both. "I want to open up politics to more people," she says. "I think it would be good for the country."

"Power is the ability to get things done," she observes. "Success gives you the financial means to effect change. But it is important to not just do things for yourself. You have to give something to society as well."

Her interest in politics is long-standing, but for many years it took second place to a demanding career.

Straight graduated from college in 1969. She went to Bankers Trust hoping to get into its credit training program, only to be told it was not open to women. Instead, she became an assistant in the investment group, rising to vice president in eight years. In the meantime she got an MBA at night and became president of the Financial Women's Association of New York. It was a visible position that she parlayed into her next job as director of investments at the pharmaceutical company Merck. Straight was good at managing money but also found innovative ways to borrow and maximize profits in Puerto

Rico and Ireland. She did well at Merck and was wooed away only by the opportunity to become a limited partner in an investment boutique. The firm raised $50 million to acquire equity interests in 15 insurance companies, 3 of which ultimately went public. The partners earned an equity position in each of those firms, sharing 20 percent of the profits. Over the years this created a sizable portfolio, and at age 49, Straight was able to retire to pursue her other passions. That was in 1996. Life has been an adventure ever since.

Leadership Style

Straight is most energized by analyzing issues and coming up with a strategic plan. Over the years she has learned the importance of enrolling others. "In my twenties I was very impatient. In my thirties I learned that you have to bring people with you to reach your goals," she notes. "Today I feel you have to give the team enough rope to hang themselves or to succeed. You pray to God that they will succeed, because that means I will succeed as well."

Others note that she is generous in contributing to the causes she believes in. She served on Governor Whitman's first budget task force. Now she is strategizing about the horse-racing industry in New Jersey. People also note that when Straight is around, things get done.

Of course patience is still somewhat of an issue and, as with many Innovators, a blind spot that needs constant attention. "It is hard for me to understand," she says wryly, "that not everyone shares my agenda, that not everyone is going to follow me off a cliff. But I have learned to let them do it their way as long as they produce quality work."

Asked about her ability to deal with confrontation, she responds tersely. "You hit it head on. You try to listen to the other person to see if he or she is right, but regardless, you don't shy away." What about dealing with criticism? I ask her. "The critics may be helping me," she notes, "but even they are mean-spirited. You listen and figure tomorrow is another day. Just move forward."

Advice to Others

"Get the most and best education possible. An MBA may not seem necessary, but it opens a lot of doors if you are interested in business and finance. It is also important to understand the rules of the game you want to play. Find out what they are and then figure out what it will take to win. You can be the smartest person in the world, but if you play by a different set of rules, your chances of succeeding are not so great. Doing sports helps. It teaches you how to evaluate your opponent's weaknesses."

11 The Reds

"Let's do it now."

Reds represent 27 percent of the population. Also, known as Sensor Perceivers, they do not respond well to theories or abstract concepts, focusing instead on today's reality. Their view of the world is based on what they can see, touch, and observe for themselves.

They need freedom and hate to feel trapped in either work or relationships. Rarely are they ever driven by either guilt or responsibility.

Their style is egalitarian. They are loyal to friends and associates, but resent being restricted by other people's needs or schedules.

Reds thrive on the thrill of adventure, whether a safari or a business transaction. They trust their impulses and, more than any other type, want to enjoy every day to the fullest. Reds are proud of their daring. They know they can handle a crisis better than most. They are competitive and, as natural optimists, adopt a sportsman's attitude in everything they undertake.

When in good physical shape they enjoy and often excel in sports or performance arts.

Summary of Core Characteristics

- Are clever and bold
- Need variety and action with a minimum of rules
- Work best in a flexible and self-directed setting
- Want an immediate payoff
- Look for fun and adventure
- Need freedom and space
- Are spontaneous and impulsive
- Are best at verbal planning and short-range activities
- Are "now"-oriented, with little interest in past or future
- Negotiate skillfully
- Need constant excitement and stimulus
- Like and create fun
- Understand the "hot buttons" of others
- Are athletic
- Are often mechanically skilled
- Are adept at solving short-term problems
- Are challenged by a crisis; improvise well
- Are willing to take risks; are opportunistic

Well-Known Reds

Franklin D. Roosevelt
John F. Kennedy
J. Paul Getty
Donald Trump
Elvis Presley
Christine Whitman
Ernest Hemingway
Winston Churchill
Elizabeth Taylor

Most Fulfilling Careers

As excellent negotiators and troubleshooters, they are often attracted to careers that provide freedom, action, and variety. These careers include the following:

- Entrepreneurial businesses of all types
- Hotel and restaurant management
- Electoral politics
- Performance production in drama and music
- Law enforcement
- Investment banking and stock brokering
- Real estate brokers and land development
- Emergency services of all types (fire, police, crisis centers, etc.)
- Investigative work
- Computer game programming
- Professional sports
- Flying
- Promoting
- Physical therapy
- Athletic coaching
- Travel
- Cooking
- General contractor
- Risk management
- Health and safety

Other fields include those which provide variety and change. These are careers where each day is different; where the environment is flexible and relaxed without undue bureaucracy, and where people work with concrete things. They are, of course, also found in smaller numbers in other areas more populated by other types, where they shine by establishing their own niches. Examples include veterinary work and teaching.

CLUES TO RECOGNIZING REDS

Reds exhibit many, though not necessarily all, of the following behaviors.

> Dress casually or in a very dapper fashion
> Have a casual attitude and an easygoing style
> Have a sense of humor and frequently make jokes
> Find activity more fun than conversation
> Move constantly with restless energy
> Are often innately good at sports
> Eyes glaze over when there is a theoretical discussion
> Use down-to-earth, concrete words in short sentences
> Use sports metaphors
> Often do not have much formal education; prefer experience to learning
> Like to negotiate almost anything
> Are unpredictable
> Do not follow schedules
> Are usually late
> Ignore structure, hierarchies, and routine
> Avoid administrative work
> Are up-to-date on entertainment celebrities
> Pay compliments and go out of their way to charm people
> Need excitement; enjoy gambling, going to the races, and playing the stock market
> Like to take unusual trips
> Like good food and wine
> Need action and excitement
> Like adventure films
> Respect nature and respond well to animals
> Usually have messy piles everywhere: closet, desk, car
> Spend money easily and buy many gadgets

12 The Tacticians

Tacticians combine preferences for sensing, the information-gathering process that focuses on common sense, verifiable facts, practical data, and current events rather than future possibilities; thinking, the decision-making process that emphasizes an objective, impersonal, and analytic approach to decision making; and perceiving, the lifestyle preference that stresses adaptability, flexibility, spontaneity, and keeping options open as long as possible.

OVERALL

Unusually effective in times of crisis and change, Tacticians are active, resourceful, and independent, seeking the unexpected. When they are around, something usually happens. They function best in small collegial teams where hierarchy is secondary to getting the job done.

Realistic and pragmatic, they trust only what they know and have personally observed and have little interest in the long-term projects so important to Golds and the abstract ideas so dear to Blues. They excel at observing details and have a particularly acute visual memory.

Tacticians enjoy a variety of people and activities, often operating outside the norms followed by others.

Their communication style is blunt and direct. They want the facts, enjoy an anecdote or two, and respond best to practical solutions.

Although very attentive to what is being said or done, they have a short attention span and may resist closure, preferring to keep all their options open as long as possible.

Tacticians are highly independent. They trust their own instincts implicitly and are unusually adept at sizing up problems and moving in for the solution. They prefer immediate to long-term problems and are seen as gifted negotiators who can make logical and difficult decisions. Otherwise, they are adaptable individuals who speak clearly and do not have hidden agendas.

They are most annoyed by bossy people who insist on having things done their way and those whose emotionalism clouds the logic of an issue.

They live on the edge, seeking action, and are frequently found as athletes, show business types, promoters, small business owners, members of field rescue teams, negotiators, and troubleshooters of all types.

In business they tend to avoid managing large organizations, opting instead to sell or franchise while turning their attention to new interests. They rise to positions of high responsibility under crisis conditions or upheavals that benefit from their flexibility and ability to cut to the core of a problem. They are frequently found as entrepreneurs, real estate developers, stockbrokers, politicians, investigators, lawyers, management consultants, and emergency workers of all types.

Tacticians often seek high-risk avocations such as motorcycling, mountain climbing, racing, skydiving, deep-sea diving, surfing, and hunting. Highly sensitive to physical nuances, they understand and can minimize risks. They enjoy leisure activities that include competition and activity. Travel and entertainment are also of interest.

In the second half of life they continue to seek new challenges, but with more reflection between activities.

Leadership Style

Are realistic in their assessment of a problem and the
 expected outcome
Practice "get down in the trenches" management; are
 collegial and persuasive; get people to cooperate
Take charge and move expeditiously to get quick results
Use humor to ease tension when making difficult decisions
Are valued for being straightforward, fair, and decisive

Accurately identify and use the skills and strengths of staff
members and colleagues
Are comfortable with risk
Usually find a compromise to keep the negotiating process
going
Are driven to get bottom-line results

Optimal Working Environment

Is relaxed and informal with a minimum of rules,
paperwork, and supervision
Focuses on short-term problems
Involves working with real things and tangible products
Provides opportunities to use special troubleshooting skills
Includes variety and excitement, preferably with a crisis or two
Is aesthetically appealing
Allows them to handle the job in flexible ways
Includes associates who value fun and have practical
experience

Least Preferred Working Environment

Too many meetings, too much hierarchy, and too many
memos; being micromanaged
Emphasis on long-term projects
An overly serious environment that frowns on humor and play

Approach to Change

Welcome it and seldom dwell on the past or worry about
the future
Are highly confident in their ability to adapt and solve
problems as they come up

Contribution to a Team

Have realistic expectations of others and outcomes
Keep meetings brief and to the point
Make things happen

Focus on practical considerations
Negotiate a plan of action
Pay attention to facts

Decision-Making Style

Realistically evaluate known facts
Keep an open mind, make decisions, and change them as
   needed

Potential Blind Spots

Are too casual with the rules, authority, and procedures
   valued by others
Step on the feelings of associates
Do not follow through on commitments
Do not meet deadlines
Do not think beyond today
Are not prepared
Start new projects before finishing current ones

How to Persuade a Tactician

Get to the point; avoid complicated solutions
Be flexible about scheduling
Stress the immediacy of the solution
Offer a special deal
Offer an immediate payoff
Mix meetings with fun
Be lively; move around
Be open to interruptions and questions; offer many options
Bring a sample, demonstrate it, and let them try it;
   or use concrete examples
Use action verbs

Strategies for Tacticians to Increase Leadership Effectiveness

Check out how you are perceived by others; actively solicit
   feedback

Follow through on commitments; if you promise to do it, do it.

Prioritize every day; set a few long-term goals every week

Make a consistent effort to meet deadlines even for work
that is of lesser interest

Put some preparation into important meetings; it will
enhance your credibility

Recognize that others may need more structure and
guidelines to be efficient

Factor in the feelings of others when making decisions; it
will ensure their support

Avoid changing appointments and schedules unless it is very
important to do so

TWO TYPES OF TACTICIANS: EXTRAVERTS AND INTROVERTS

Extraverted Tacticians are outwardly energetic and amiable. People of action, they like being in the center of things or living on the edge, courting excitement and danger. They enjoy sports and adventure. They are noisy, fun-loving, and ready to make the most of any situation. They are the most heavily action-oriented of all the types.

Introverted Tacticians are generally more restrained and private. They do not share their views as readily as their extraverted counterparts. They prefer working alone to working in a group and can concentrate deeply if a project is of interest. Rather than engaging in constant activity, they prefer to conserve their energy until the right sport or activity engages them.

A Note of Caution

Since type does not explain many aspects that are important in defining an individual, (intelligence, education, mental health, and individual life experiences, among others), no overall profile can describe all the variants in a personality. Invariably, some of the traits described above will not ring true for you. If the majority do not ring true, however, it could mean that you belong to another group. In that case, go back and revisit your Leadership Q questionnaire. Check the columns where you have close scores. Try reading a profile that reflects the other combination of your close scores. Alternatively, show the profile detailed below to an individual who knows you well, such as a mate, boss, close friend, or team colleague, and ask for comments. If you are going through major life changes, try waiting until things have stabilized.

DEVELOPMENT EXERCISES FOR TACTICIANS

People who succeed have learned to travel to other neighborhoods. Do the exercises below to be more effective.

Exercise 1. Handling Conflict

You are rational and fair. Well-developed leaders understand the need to factor in how people will react to decisions. This requires developing your feeling preference.

- Recall a recent conflict involving several people.
- Think about each person who was involved. Write the names of those individuals on a piece of paper.
- Set aside the consideration of who was right. Focus on the personal motivations and emotional issues surrounding the conflict and note them.
- Consider other ways in which the conflict might have been handled.

The point is that it works best when you factor in the feelings of people.

Exercise 2. Finishing Projects

- Identify a couple of partially completed projects.
- Set aside a block of time, say, three hours, in the most productive period of your day. Make sure you have all the information and materials you need.
- Finish one or all projects in the time allotted. Note how

satisfying it feels to have them out of the way. Savor the moment. Enjoy the feeling of control. File this feeling in your memory for future recall.

- From here on, when making a to-do list each day, circle with a color felt pen the one or two items that need to be completed no matter what.

The point is that you will eliminate a lot of the clutter in your life. This gives you more time to have fun.

Exercise 3. Developing the Ability to Brainstorm

1. Identify a problem or project that requires fresh solutions (work issue, product-naming issue, etc.).
2. Sit down with a couple of friends or colleagues and a flip-chart.
3. Ask them to list all the ideas that pop into their heads no matter how silly or impossible.
4. Do not pass judgment on the ideas for 10 minutes. Write them all down on the flipchart.
5. At the end of 10 minutes, ask the group to choose the three most attractive ideas.
6. Allow 10 minutes for this process.
7. Choose the idea that was selected most often.
8. Write it at the top of a new sheet of paper.
9. Ask everyone to list ways to accomplish the chosen idea. Do not pass judgment.
10. Repeat steps 5, 6, and 7. Continue until you have solved the problem to your satisfaction.

Exercise 4. Working with Other Types

Choose a coworker with whom you have a conflict. It can be a boss, colleague, or client. Look at the overall four color descriptions and the section on how to recognize his or her color group.

My Type _____   **His or Her Type** _____

What are the Sources of Conflict?

How to Solve the Conflicts:

Photocopy your comments and keep them someplace where they are easily accessible.

The point is that if you do this exercise often enough, you will get along with that person better.

Exercise 5. How to Be a Better Leader

- Turn back to your leadership style summary.
- Choose one strategy for increased leadership effectiveness.
- Write it on an index card and develop three specific steps to achieve that strategy.
- Put the card someplace where you will see it frequently. Read it several times a day.
- After several weeks repeat the process with another strategy.

HELEN THOMAS
Journalist and Former White House Correspondent
United Press International

Q: *When you first started out, did you face obstacles as a woman that you might not have faced if you were a man?*

A: *Where did you come from, Mars?*

> —Helen Thomas, in an interview with
> the San Francisco Chronicle, *1995*

Former press secretary Marlin Fitzwater used to joke that the press corps parted slightly when Helen Thomas walked in, partly out of respect for her age, 79, and partly because they did not want to be embarrassed if she decided to push them out of the way. She was the "dean" of the White House corps whose "thank you" signaled the close of each briefing. It was one of the tightest unwritten rules, he recalls, that no press secretary ever walked away from a briefing without being excused by that famed line and survived to talk about it.[20]

Thomas and I sit knee to knee in her UPI booth, an enclosed cubicle about 7 feet wide and 9 feet long. The door is propped open with newspapers. There are two computers, telephones, bookshelves, and mounds of paper strewn around. Still, who can complain? This is prime real estate. It is the West Wing of the White House. Outside there is a narrow hallway that leads to the briefing room, the one with the movie-theater-style seats that always seems much bigger when you see it on television. Fifty feet in the other direction is the Oval Office, the seat of power of the United States of America. I am impressed and intimidated.

She was the seventh of nine children of Lebanese immigrants who could neither read nor write English. The family lived in depression-era Detroit, where her father owned a grocery store. All the children were urged to go to college, and all nine did. "Girls were not treated differently than the boys, and that was unusual at that time," she recalls. Thomas paid for her education by working in the library and her brother's gas station. After graduating from what is now Wayne State University in 1942 with a degree in journalism, she set off for Washington, D.C., to become a reporter.

She started as a copygirl at the *Washington Daily News* for $17.40 a week. Her job was to cut copies from the Teletype machine and get coffee for the editors. Unlike other women reporters who gave up their jobs to returning World War II veterans, she parlayed hers into a long stint as a radio news writer for UPI, covering the Department of Justice and other federal agencies.

In 1960 she was assigned to cover Kennedy's campaign. After his election there was an enormous demand for stories about his glamorous wife, and Thomas was assigned to the White House to cover the "women's beat": pieces on Mrs. Kennedy's clothes, children, and family life. Jacqueline was none too pleased. Once she recalls, she persuaded Secret Service agents to go after Thomas and another reporter, saying she was being followed by two suspicious foreigners. Today Thomas's comment on Jackie Kennedy is, "I am still getting the spit out of my eye."

JFK turned out to be a better fan of Thomas than his wife was. The two enjoyed exchanging good-natured barbs. In covering his administration she was automatically considered a member of the White House Correspondents Association, which sponsored an annual dinner, yet by the rules of the day Thomas and all other women were barred from the dinner. She raised hell with the press secretary, Pierre Salinger, who conveyed her anger to the President. Kennedy agreed to boycott the dinner if the rules were not changed. They were. Later Thomas became the association's first female president.

In 1974 she was named senior White House correspondent for UPI, the first woman to hold that post. Since then her tough questioning has earned her praise and criticism.

Persistence is her hallmark. Fitzwater recalls an incident in Saudia Arabia when Thomas, age 70, was following the activities of President Bush. She jumped off the military truck and in the 110-degree heat began to run toward the President, who was coming out of a bunker. The young marines watched her with disbelief, convinced she would drop dead, to hear Bush say, "Very interesting meeting."[21]

Colleague Al Spivak once said, "Presidents have thought of her as a cross between Lucrezia Borgia and Typhoid Mary." She sees it otherwise: "The office of the presidency should always be treated with the highest value and honor. I know that is asking the impossible of human beings, but whoever holds this office should have reverence for it, and I have not seen a lot of reverence through the years."

The remark is quintessential Thomas: outspoken, uncompromising, and populist. She happily interrupts photo opportunities with unwelcome questions. "If he wants his privacy," she once yelled at a Clinton aide, "then he should not be president." She scribbles on a small pad, seldom more than few words to a page. No one has ever deciphered those scribbles, which miraculously convert into full quotes accurate to the smallest detail.

She has a well-tuned ear for the great quote. In her recent book *Front Row at the White House* she remembers Jimmy Carter's mother saying to her, "Sometimes when I look at my children, I wish I'd remained a virgin."

At age 51 Thomas married a fellow journalist. A few years later he began battling Alzheimer's disease. She kept him as active as possible. In 1982 he passed away. Thomas does not discuss this part of her life.[22]

Her career spanned 56 years. Until her recent resignation the woman who "made" it in her field ahead of her time showed no signs of slowing down. In the words of best-selling author and longtime friend Peter J. Tanous, "The sight of Helen Thomas at 79 chasing after President Clinton, knowing that this is the eighth that she has covered, gave new meaning to the notion of work ethic."

Leadership Style

Red Tacticians tend not to be self-reflective, and Thomas is no exception. She is reluctant to discuss herself and shows far more interest in describing the leadership styles of the First Ladies she has covered.

The thing that energizes her most is "getting the news." Asked what she finds tedious and stressful, she responds tartly, "Not getting the news."

I try another avenue. What do other people say she does exceptionally well? "They don't tell me I do anything exceptionally well," she responds, glaring at me. "Well," she continues, softening somewhat, "they say I don't embellish anything. I just take the shortest distance between two points in a straight line. It is a very direct way of getting to the point."

For Thomas, leading is about doing, not talking. Her actions speak for themselves. She was the first to break into and eventually lead some of Washington's most prestigious male bastions: the White House press corps, the National Press Club, the Gridiron Club. It was her indomitable spirit that made her unstoppable.

Extraverted Red Tacticians are the ultimate "doers" who keep others on their toes and make life as exciting as possible. Their management style is highly action-oriented, and they excel in a crisis. "You only go around in life once" is their motto. Always objective and with a keen sense of reality, they are masters at getting to the heart of matters and spotting trouble early. Thomas is no exception. Her distinguished career says it louder than any words.

Advice to Others

"If you are interested in journalism," she says, "go for it. You will never be unhappy. It is an education every day. Very few professions give you the same sense of watching history unfold. The excitement is always there. Of course, news does not break on your time. So if you want a job where you can be organized and in control of your life, this is not the field to pursue."

"So why are you writing this book?" she asks turning the interview process around. Because I am interested in the psychology of leadership, I tell her. "Why?" she asks, looking at me quizzically. I find it a new way of looking at the subject, I tell her. "Oh, well, in that case, good luck," she says with a hint of a smile. "Now I've got to run; the President is briefing us on Kosovo."

DARLA MOORE
President
Rainwater, Inc.

Under clear skies and in soft Carolina breezes, an elegant Darla Moore clad in a lavender suit stands before 1,000 audience members who have gathered at the University of South Carolina to mark the renaming of the Darla Moore School of Business. It is March 1998, and the event follows a $25 million donation made by a 43-year-old Wall Street financier and investor whom *Fortune* magazine dubbed the "toughest babe in business."

"I am every inch a woman; I've suffered for that distinction" she says to her audience. "It has been an obstacle at times, but I have never apologized for it, never subsumed it, and I've always regarded it as a badge of honor. What I have learned from the obstacle is that you can either do things like everyone else and just do them better. Or you can learn to do things differently. I chose to do things differently. I am a Southerner, I am a woman, and I am a capitalist. And it is in the name of these three integral pieces of my identify that I am making this gift." She then promised to be both "irksome and involved" in her goal of boosting the business school to the top tier in the nation.

She grew up in the poor tobacco town of Lake City, South Carolina. Her mother, an administrator in the Methodist church, was she recalls, a strict disciplinarian with academic standards (no C's) and rules on clothing (nothing above the knee). Her father, an all-star athlete, had no sons and treated his little Darla Dee like a boy. He started her in basketball at age 3 and later timed her laps in the pool and took her fishing and hunting, further fueling her already competitive spirit. By age 8, she knew she wanted to go beyond the traditional female role. Most of all, she knew, she needed her independence.

Moore received a bachelor's degree in political science in 1975 from the university she later endowed and worked briefly as an intern for Senator Strom Thurmond. Soon disillusioned with the lack of stability in politics, she got an MBA and entered a training program with Chemical Bank in New York.

A mentor advised her to "find a niche and become the best at it. I saw bankruptcy as that opportunity because it had no status or rules. It was the heyday of the leveraged-buyout business, and it was off limits to the fairer sex. So I said, 'What is a girl to do?' I headed for bankruptcy, the knee-breaking, bill-collecting backwater of the financial landscape. I became the golden girl in a business dominated by balding, bespectacled men who were excluded from the mainstream establishment for their lack of pedigrees, their ethnicity, and their religion." Here she notes that performance and ability to deliver counted. When the leveraged buyouts tanked in the late 1980s, "I was there with the reputation and the experience to pick up the pieces." Before she left Chemical, Moore was earning $1 million a year. Her timing was impeccable.

She was, however, as she admits, "hell to work for. I was brutal and demanding. My whole group walked out on me one day—all six of them. I was not comfortable in my own skin. The bank labeled me a management problem. So I learned to relax. I got more confident, and by the time I left, people said I was exciting to work for." Of course, she was equally tough with clients, and the word got out, she says with a grin, "that you don't mess with Darla." At one client meeting she recalls opening the session with "Put on your rubber underwear, boys, it is going to be a long evening."

Moore's working style reflects that of Tacticians as a group. She is direct and assertive and moves along the most expedient route to find immediate results. When she is around, things happen. "She is a cutthroat killer," her friend Martha Stewart was overheard to say.

In 1991 Moore met Richard Rainwater, one of America's nimblest investors, who had advised both the Bass and Bush families. He found her brashness intensely attractive. She was not impressed. "You have too much money. You are going to ruin everything I worked for," she is reported to have said at their initial dinner.

They married, she took over his company's portfolio, and they tripled his net worth. Along the way she developed her tough-gal reputation by forcing famed corporate raider T. Boone Pickens out of Mesa Petroleum, which he had founded. Later, in a major corporate drama, she booted out CEO Richard Scott from Columbia/HCA after the company that Scott and her husband had cofounded became the target of a federal investigation. It was a strategy that she and Rainwater "clashed over." However, she won. "The difference between my wife and I," he recently said to a *Fortune* writer, is "I take a lot of time to solve a problem without hurting people's feelings. By the time I am ready to act, she will already have the job done." Still, he adores her and declares her the best investment he ever made.[23]

Today she is president of the sprawling private investment firm. Her time is divided between her family's farm in South Carolina—where she gardens, plays host at pig roasts, and eats fried gizzards at Allison's Truck Stop—and a plush office in New York City. We meet at her Park Avenue apartment, which is decorated with rare books and eighteenth-century French furniture.

Leadership Style

She describes her leadership style as the ability to create excitement and get to the core of an issue to achieve results. "I am a major troubleshooter. My strength is to see through the smoke and chaos and move in when everything is exploding. I have common sense, and I assess the landscape realistically," she says. "I also like so see the fruits of my labor quickly and persuade others to do things differently than they did them in the past. As a result, people want to be on my team. They want me to think highly of them."

Even at the bank she ran a very entrepreneurial shop. "I never aspired to senior management," she says. "I was too independent. Every time they reorganized and I would complain about my new reporting line, the higher-ups would say, 'Darla, everyone knows you never report to anybody anyway.' And that would shut me up—for a while at least."

Moore, like many Reds, emphasizes short-term rather than long-term goals. "They keep you on track," she notes, "and provide you with the near-term victories necessary to keep the interest of those you are trying to carry with you."

She also admits to an affinity for crisis situations: "It propels you. You don't have any choice but to move. And once you get through it, life is new and much bigger."

Activities she finds stressful include doing financial analysis and getting buried in details with no clear way to the get to the next step.

Like many successful career women, she has had plenty of turning points. They include leaving the Washington political scene and sorting out her position in the bureaucratic structure of Chemical Bank. Like others, she looks at them from a positive angle. "Every crisis," she notes, "landed me in a far better place." Not that it was easy, though. "There were horribly depressing and frightening periods," she recalls. "I never thought I would smile again, I was so unsettled. Then, somehow, I plopped through into another place." When asked how, she shakes her head: "If I could answer that, I could help a lot of people. It is a process and you cannot skip the steps. You've got to feel the pain, the uncertainty. You have to weep. You have to be open-minded and brutally honest. You have to figure out what you are really good at."

Dealing with confrontation, however, has been less of a problem than it is for women in other groups who do not have the thinking decision-making style. Early in her career she learned to "take the personal stuff," as she calls it, out of the debate. "I chose my fights carefully and articulated my points so that they impacted the business, not me personally." Recently Moore sent a note to a teary-eyed female state senator after a debate. The note said, "Always get to the bathroom before you start crying."

Today her spirited, risk-taking personality has found a new focus: the world of politics that so intrigues many Tacticians. "The business world has been exciting and fun," she says, "but I don't need a lot of repetition. Now I need to take my experience and reform my home state." Leveraging her recent $25 million donation, she is out to do nothing less than change the state's economic landscape without running for office.

When a Red is around, expect a spontaneous debate that leads the organization in a new direction. South Carolina got nothing less as Moore ripped the educational system apart in her address before the state senate. Calling it "borderline third world," she urged and persuaded the venerable members of the legislature to borrow $1 billion to fund reforms. "They had not borrowed money to build schools in 50 years, and the bill passed by one vote." she says with glee. The battle was intense. The room was filled to capacity. It was a historic moment, she recalls with excitement, "because I trashed very specific things and they did not want to hear it and certainly not from a girl. Afterwards, the president pro tempore came over and said, 'The Lord has sent ya.' Another guy outside was yelling, 'The Lord is going to punish you.' I mean, this is powerful stuff."

That was the just the beginning, she notes. Today she contributes 50 percent of her time to the affairs of South Carolina. "I have a whole agenda," she notes, "that includes everything from changing the way they forecast revenues, to funding the local districts, to how education is managed. I will take it one item at a time."

Eventually, maybe in her fifties, she notes, she may run for office. For the time being it is easier to be an icon that can tease and bully others into change. "I am smart," she says, "but not 'stump the stars' smart. I have experience, but most of all I speak to them in a way they understand. And they laugh and laugh and ultimately they do what I say."

Advice to Others

"The philosophy I have come to adopt more and more," she says, is "to never be attached to the outcome, personally or professionally." How does this square with the need to set goals? "You focus until the goal moves, and then you focus again. Otherwise this thing of goals will put you in a nuthouse. Do what you can and let it go where it goes. If it is your purpose in life, it is bigger than you and it will happen."

JESSICA M. BIBLIOWICZ
President and CEO
National Financial Partners

She was a star at several financial firms and is the daughter of one of Wall Street's top deal makers, Sanford I. Weill, cochairman of Citigroup. Bibliowicz always created a buzz but never more so than today, when, at the age of 40, she heads a financial conglomerate that is moving toward the biggest pasture yet.

In April of 1999 she signed on as chief executive of the newly formed National Financial Partners (NFP), a group designed to acquire investment advisory firms catering to high-net-worth individuals and corporations. Today the group owns 63 independent advisers and has another 250 deals in the pipeline. The goal is to create a $1 billion company before taking NFP public in five years.

Those who watched her grow up are not surprised. She was the younger of two and was always interested in the family business. She started working in the summer when she 14. Her job at the library of Shearson, the brokerage firm headed by her father, consisted of filing annual reports. She was paid $1 an hour. "I think they exploited me," she says with a grin, "but it paid for lunch." In later summers she worked in the back offices, on the trading desks, and in the branches, ultimately joining the brokers in the firm's "front offices."

She went on to Cornell, majoring in international relations with the goal of becoming a lawyer and ultimately a Supreme Court judge. However, she soon found she liked working more than studying. The plan after graduation was to join the workforce for a couple of years and then return for an advanced degree. She never did. It was 1982, she recalls, and there was a "cowboy-type environment that if you were in the right place, you could do something really cool. I was, and I did."

That year the firm launched the Shearson Equity Management product, which was controversial. It challenged the existing commission-based way of doing business by substituting fees. "There was no staff," she recalls with glee. "We did the marketing, the administration. We did everything, and we had to sell a new concept as well as a product. It was a lot of fun."

"I love the markets, and I like speaking to people about investments. In the early days," she says, "women did not like talking about money; they were afraid of it. I wasn't because I had grown up around the jargon, which others find intimidating."

She did not go to business school and regrets that decision today. Still she had by that time learned more from on-site experience than others had. Those summers in the "underbelly" (as the operation end was called) gave her a good sense of all the parts of the business. "This helped establish my credibility when I was 22 and trying to launch a new product," she recalls, savoring the excitement of those early years. "Also, I had been working with the brokers all those summers and that helped too. I was always straight with them. If I didn't think I could get something done, I would say so right up front."

Like other Red Tacticians, Bibliowicz is action-oriented and works best with lively, independent, and pragmatic people. Direct and assertive, she shares willingly, always finding ways to compromise and keep things moving. Also like most Tacticians, she prefers doing rather than studying. Learning is not undertaken for its own sake, but as a tool to achieve concrete goals.

After a few years Bibliowicz moved to Prudential Securities, rising to director of sales and marketing for Prudential Mutual Funds. Then, at the suggestion of, as she says, "you know who," she went to Smith Barney, where she became executive vice president of the mutual funds division. "You know who," of course was her father, who by then was chief executive of Travelers, which owned Smith Barney. The move was a double-edged sword. She enjoyed working with him (many say they are alike), but being the boss's daughter took its toll. "Like others," she says today, "sometimes I am guilty of having a good idea, and sometimes I have a bad one. I would constantly wonder if someone was being straight with me or treating me like Sandy's daughter." After three years she made a highly publicized exit and joined a John A. Levin, a New York investment management firm.

She has carved out a special niche for herself, and it appears that her timing could not be better. She seeks out other financial advisers with the pitch that they can become part of NFP while still remaining entrepreneurs. In return she pays the entrepreneurs up front, usually 50 percent cash and 50 percent in NFP stock. She also offers the advantage of being part of a larger group, which includes capital for acquisitions and Intranet-based products that connect them to other member firms.

Tacticians are naturally drawn to entrepreneurs and situations that reward entrepreneurial skills. They usually create work environments that are fun, offer variety, and have few constraints on risk taking. They are known for making quick connections with a variety of people. Mostly, however, they are superb negotiators for whom nothing is carved in stone. They anticipate the reactions of others by keenly observing small nonverbal cues. This enables them to grasp the motivation of colleagues and prospects quickly and stay several steps ahead of the pack in using that information to develop support for their objectives.

Today Bibliowicz is widely recognized for her ability to manage the many disparate parts of NFP. She also is an active parent of two boys. "Balancing home and office is a challenge," she admits. "Every stage of a child's life requires different things from you. When I am home, it is their lives that run the show." Of course, it helps to have a husband who is an independent architect and truly enjoys being a parent. "We really share this parenting 50-50," she says. "It also helps that we really enjoy our children's company, because outside of them we have no social life. Still, they give us an incredible perspective, and they also teach us a little more about negotiation and patience."

Leadership Style

"I like being in charge and I love the responsibility" she says. "Sometimes when you are making big investments and the technology is moving quickly, it can be tough. You have to be ready to make a couple of mistakes, then retract, go back, and fix them. Speed is really the big issue right now."

Being aware of her responsibility to the new shareholders is another issue: "They have taken their cash flow and converted it into our equity. If I didn't believe that we bring them added value, I would be a real louse for taking that money. But I do believe it, and I will live up to the responsibility. I did not always have this much confidence, but one day you wake up and realize you are in control. People want you to do it, and, well, you just do it."

Others view her as an inspirational manger, someone who listens to all sides of the issue, reducing tension whenever possible. Humor helps. Working with self-motivated people also helps. "I am not as good for people who need guidance all the time. They do not enjoy working for me," she says ruefully, "and they drive me crazy. I like to pull the team together and get things done as fast as possible."

People enjoy being associated with Red Tacticians, who are charming and energizing. As leaders they are comfortable with change and risk. Living on the edge is a great challenge that allows them to improvise and contribute their considerable troubleshooting skills.

Bibliowicz is most energized by doing new things and putting deals together. She also enjoys the public side of business: speaking with people, making presentations, and being the contact person for shareholders and investors.

Like most leaders who have a thinking preference, criticism does not bother her. Constructive confrontation is okay as well. "I force myself to be direct," she says. "It has taken me many years to learn to do that, but it is part of being in charge."

Activities she finds stressful include dealing with internal politics and hidden agendas. Some stress is important, she notes. It keeps you moving, but not stress related to turf fighting.

Advice to Others

Women should not be so hard on themselves, she says. "They should realize that there are times when things will go smoothly and times when nothing seems to work well. You have to be patient. A good partner and marriage help. Taking advantage of the Internet and its shopping and timesaving resources is another big help. You don't have to choose between a career and family anymore. Get your work done and go home. It is okay to go home."

In the workforce, she adds, it is wise to find the great potential career paths for women that are not as populated yet—areas such as money management and sales. Finally, it helps to get a mentor, develop a relationship with people who have been around a little and whom one can count on. It helps to have a protector.

SHEILA BIRNBAUM
Senior Partner
Skadden, Arps, Slate, Meagher, & Flom

Peers refer to her as "Madame Product Liability;" and many consider her the top female lawyer in the United States. Translated, this means that she settles high-end class-action lawsuits with multimillion-dollar and even billion-dollar settlements. The overwhelming majority of her cases culminate in a settlement. Her challenge is to be creative and avoid long drawn-out battles and litigation. For her outstanding work in this area, *Fortune* magazine has ranked her as one of the 50 most powerful women in American business.

Birnbaum is highly respected, but she is also liked. As one of her competitors admits, "Wherever Sheila goes, there is a party." Like many Reds, she is good-natured, fun, and generous with her time and resources, but as with other Tacticians, there is an essential toughness. Almost unconsciously they stay tuned to nonverbal and almost subliminal clues to what makes their opponents tick. It is all in the game, and they admire any opponent who plays the game as well as they do.

This is an individual who blazed her own trail by going into personal injury law when most female lawyers headed for trusts and estates.

The path began in the South Bronx of New York, where she grew up the oldest of three children. Money was tight, but it was a loving extended family. Her parents ran a grocery store and worked long hours.

Birnbaum was the first in her family to go to college. Although she always wanted to be a lawyer, at everyone's insistence she took a job as a fourth-grade teacher so that she would "not be more educated than her husband," she recalls with a grin. Two years later a not-so-happy teacher went ahead and enrolled in New York University (NYU) law school. The marriage did fall apart, but a childhood dream was about to come true.

It was still the dark ages for women lawyers, she remembers. There were no women clerking or on Wall Street. In the district attorney's office women did not try cases; they only did appeals. "When I applied for a job, people kept asking me, 'Is your husband going to let you work late?' Then they hired me at $1,000 less than a man, and they had the nerve to tell me that. Well, I never allowed anyone to hold me back, and in four years I was a partner," she recalls with satisfaction.[24]

Shortly afterward she began teaching and became the first tenured female professor at Fordham University in New York. In 1979 she moved from Fordham to her alma mater, NYU, which allowed its professors to become counsels to firms. She became counsel to Skadden while remaining a full professor and later an associate dean at NYU. In 1984 she finally left academia to join Skadden as a full-time partner. She recalls this as a major turning point in her life. "People said to me, 'You are giving up tenure at NYU. Are you out of your mind?' Not to mention," she says, "that I had been out of the business world for many years."

Today she heads the mass tort and insurance group (formerly known as the product liability department), managing 70 lawyers and 100 paralegals. With seven partners and a practice in excess of $30 million a year, it is a small institution within the institution. They represent major corporations in complex litigation and class-action suits.

Leadership Style

Birnbaum describes her leadership style as collaborative. It is leadership by example, by working with people to achieve a common goal. "Even in negotiations, when dealing with an adversary," she says, "we try to bring people into the fold so they have a stake in the outcome. I don't believe you can lead by dictating and coming down on people. Whether it is heading a committee or participating in the firm's administration, it is best to lead by creating a consensus."

She communicates in a style that is direct and does not have a hidden agenda. "I let people know what my opinion is and then back off if I can't convince my colleagues," she says. "I am not going to make any waves if I can't get people to reach a consensus."

The activities she finds the most energizing are getting new business and strategizing on how to resolve major suits. "Usually it is all-consuming," she says with relish. "You are dealing with government investigations, lawsuits in the courts, and media issues, and you have to respond on many fronts, often at the same time. It is around-the-clock crisis management."

Others see her as entrepreneurial, very competent, and a super rainmaker. Rainmakers are defined as those who brings in a lot of new business for their firm. "She gets to the heart of key issues and senses the right time to settle better than anyone I know," says a former adversary.

Tacticians are often referred to as the ultimate realists. Objective and flexible, they feel no need to fight the system unless it stops them from getting things done. They are the conciliators, the resourceful negotiators who move along the most expedient route, seeking immediate results. They usually manage to win others over to their point of view.

Also like many Tacticians, Birnbaum embraces risk and needs excitement. "The worst thing that can happen," she says, " is that the telephone doesn't ring all day. The more that is going on, the calmer I am and the more I handle."

Also like many Reds, she finds long-term goals of little importance. "I find long-term goals abstract," she says. "I never had a 5-, or 10-, or 15-year plan. I may not look for change, but I am ready for change all the time. I came to Skadden because I met someone at a cocktail party." She continues: "We never had a plan for the product liability practice. We just started it, it kept growing, and now it is the biggest group of its kind in the country."

She finds very little stressful. For the most part, Birnbaum finds high-stress situations energizing.

Dealing with details, however, is boring. She also considers her dislike of details a blind spot in her leadership style. "I hate reading agreements over and over again," she says, "or dealing with the nitty-gritty of the factual development of a case. I prefer to let someone else dig up the facts, and I come up with the solution. I enjoy enormously going to court, making an argument before a judge or appellate panel, and negotiating. Another blind spot is being too quick to accept people and then being disappointed when they do not meet expectations or are not as loyal as they should be.

Her attitude toward confrontation also reflects the prevailing attitude of her type. "In personal relationships," she says, "I don't like confrontation." In business, however, "it is something you have to deal with—with judges, with adversaries, and sometimes with people you have to fire. I am competitive but not aggressive. I rarely get angry, but you have to stand up for what you believe."

For Birnbaum work is highly satisfying: "When you are considered a top player, you converse with top players. And people in your field recognize that. Power is walking into a room and getting instant respect. Power is the ability to make things happen."

Advice to Others

"Follow your passion and don't worry about what others say."

13 The Realists

Realists combine preferences for sensing, the information-gathering process that focuses on common sense, verifiable facts, practical data, and current events rather than future possibilities; feeling, the decision-making process that favors an objective, impersonal, and analytic approach to decision making; and perceiving, the lifestyle preference that stresses adaptability, flexibility, spontaneity, and keeping options open as long as possible.

OVERALL

Resourceful, spontaneous, and adaptable, Realists are found where there is fun, stimulation, variety, and immediate tangible rewards. Members of the "now generation," they look for and find enjoyment in everything they do, pulling others in behind them.

Fun apart, they are realistic and down to earth, preferring to respond to things as they come up rather than plan ahead. They prize common sense and ability to solve immediate problems even though their approach is frequently unconventional.

Deeply observant, they collect a wealth of information about people and from an early age have an unusual understanding of the "hot buttons" of others.

Realists have diverse interests and a genuine and active love of animals, nature, and children.

They are most irritated by people who are disloyal and by intellectual snobs.

They avoid routine, need an exceptionally high degree of freedom and activity, and prefer to work harmoniously with others in an optimistic and humor-filled environment.

Long-term planning is of little interest to improvising Realists, who respond opportunistically to the challenges of the moment while keeping many balls in the air at the same time. They are frequently found as fund-raisers, occupational therapists, travel agents, social workers, designers, athletic coaches, performing artists, veterinarians, salespersons, and other careers where they can be of practical service to others.

Leadership Style

Collegial style; encourage grassroots participation
Move the group to action by focusing on the immediate
  issue
Excel in crisis management
Ease tension through humor and the ability to defuse
  conflict
Provide excitement
Are upbeat and optimistic
Have realistic expectations of people and outcomes
Create cooperative teams
Pay close attention to important facts and details
Adapt well to change

Optimal Working Environment

Is harmonious and aesthetically pleasing
Provides work that is concrete and tangible and produces
  short-term results
Offers much positive recognition
Provides opportunity to solve crises or mediate problems
Has minimal supervision
Permits humor and fun
Is flexible and action-oriented
Allows one to work on a variety of projects

Least Preferred Working Environment

Has a high degree of interpersonal conflict
Has many controls
Requires conformity to rules

Approach to Change

Welcome it and adapt well
Want flexibility to deal with it in their own way

Contribution to a Team

Usually are willing to give something a try
Accept people as they are and draw on their best qualities
Build morale
Excel at getting a team to work together
Define and move a group to achievable goals
Use humor to defuse tension

Decision-Making Style

Use common sense
May postpone difficult decisions
Usually are willing to change a decision

Potential Blind Spots

May find it difficult to confront poor performers
Can have trouble managing time
May be disorganized
May not finish what is started
May not prepare material ahead

How to Persuade a Realist

Stress WIIFT: what's in it for them
Have a sense of humor; be friendly
Expect her to resist closure; offer alternatives rather than a
    single solution
Stress the immediacy of the solution

Bring samples; demonstrate; let her try it

Use colorful visual aids or concrete examples

Take her on a site visit

Give her a special deal

Mix a meeting with a fun event

Be lively and move around

Strategies for Realists to Increase Leadership Effectiveness

Develop the ability to create a long-term strategy

Make and implement tough decisions when needed

Keep socializing and humor to appropriate limits in the workplace

Prioritize on a daily basis

Deliver what you have promised

Give negative feedback when appropriate

Plan ahead and develop contingency plans when managing a project

Spend more time considering logical criteria before making a decision

TWO TYPES OF REALISTS: EXTRAVERTS AND INTROVERTS

Extraverted Realists are active and fast-moving, often living on the edge of adventure at work, in a high-risk leisure activity, or with the thrill of a stock trade. They are playful and optimistic and can be quite persuasive in getting what they want.

Introverted Realists often are seen as calm and modest individuals who may appear cool and detached on the surface but operate through a web of a few strong personal relationships. Sensitive and artistic, they respond to the beauty around them and develop hobbies that involve various crafts. They function best in a harmonious and tension-free environment.

A Note of Caution

Since type does not explain many aspects that are important in defining an individual (intelligence, education, mental health, and individual life experiences, among others), no overall profile can describe all the variants in a personality. Invariably, some of the traits described above will not ring true for you. If the majority do not ring true, however, it could mean that you belong to another group. In that case, go back and revisit your Leadership Q questionnaire. Check the columns where you have close scores. Try reading a profile that reflects the other combination of your close scores. Alternatively, show the profile detailed below to an individual who knows you well, such as a mate, boss, close friend, or team colleague, and ask for comments. If you are going through major life changes, try waiting until things have stabilized.

DEVELOPMENT EXERCISES FOR REALISTS

People that succeed have learned to travel to other neighborhoods. Do the exercises below to be more effective.

Exercise 1. Handling Criticism

Ask someone who is blunt to critique something of value to you: a project, an idea, an outfit, or a room decoration. Pay attention to your reactions to his or her comments. How do your intellect and feelings interact? What are your bodily reactions? Note them below. Can you sort out the facts you are hearing from your feelings about them?

- The critique:

- Facts:

- Feelings:

The point is that criticism often is not personal.

Exercise 2. Finishing Projects

- Identify a couple of partially completed projects.
- Set aside a block of time, say, three hours, in the most productive period of your day. Make sure you have all the information and materials you need.
- Finish one or all projects in the time allotted. Note how satisfying it feels to have them out of the way. Savor the moment. Enjoy the feeling of control. File this feeling in your memory for future recall.
- From here on when making a to-do list each day, circle with a color felt pen the one or two items that need to be completed no matter what.

The point is that you will eliminate a lot of the clutter in your life. This gives you more time to have fun.

Exercise 3. Developing the Ability to Brainstorm

1. Identify a problem or project that requires a fresh solution. (work issue, product-naming issue, etc.).
2. Sit down with a couple of colleagues or friends and a flipchart.
3. Ask them to list all the ideas that pop into their heads no matter how silly or impossible.
4. Do not pass judgment on the ideas for 10 minutes. Write them all down on the flipchart.
5. At the end of 10 minutes, ask the group to choose the three most attractive ideas.
6. Allow 10 minutes for this process.
7. Choose the idea that was selected most often.

8. Write it at the top of a new sheet of paper
9. Ask everyone to list ways to accomplish the chosen idea. Do not pass judgment.
10. Repeat steps 5, 6, and 7. Continue until you have solved the problem to your satisfaction.

Exercise 4. Working with Other Types

Choose a coworker with whom you have a conflict. It can be a boss, colleague, or client. Look at the overall four color descriptions and the section on how to recognize his or her color group.

My Type _____   **His or Her Type** _____

What are the Sources of Conflict?

How to Solve the Conflicts:

Photocopy your comments and keep them someplace where they are easily accessible.

The point is that if you do this exercise often enough, you will get along with that person better.

Exercise 5. How to Be a Better Leader

- Turn back to your leadership style summary.
- Choose one strategy for increased leadership effectiveness.
- Write it on an index card and develop three specific steps to achieve that strategy.
- Put the card someplace where you will see it frequently. Read it several times a day.
- After several weeks repeat the process with another strategy.

CHRISTIE TODD WHITMAN
Governor of New Jersey

Neighbors remember bicyclists wending their way on a crisp November morning in 1993. It was Election Day, and the Republican candidate for governor and her husband were pedaling toward the polls to cast their votes. It would be the last time they would ride the public roads without state security behind them. In three short years Christie Whitman had catapulted from a position as a relatively unknown government appointee to the first woman governor of New Jersey.

Her ties to both the countryside and politics are deep and intertwined. She grew up on Pontefract, a 232-acre estate in the rolling hills of western New Jersey, where she still lives. It has a tennis court and a swimming pool, but it is also a working farm with cows, sheep, pigs, and chickens. It was the perfect home for a tomboy who loved to ride her horse, search for snakes, and go fishing.

At school she was stubborn and difficult, she remembers with a chuckle, always creating her own rules and testing the limits. According to family lore, at age 5 she brought a dead duck to her kindergarten classes, incensed that her brother had shot it. She carried it around with her all morning. At age 9 she amused a bored show-and-tell class by fabricating a tale about how her father had chased her mother around the dining room with a hatchet. More than anything else, she recalls with an easy laugh, she hated behaving like a girl and wearing a skirt.[25]

Her father, Webster B. Todd, was a contractor whose family firm built Rockefeller Center in New York and restored Williamsburg in Virginia. At 50 he retired and turned to his true passion, Republican politics, where he would shine as a kingmaker on the moderate side of the party. Her mother, Eleanor, known as "the Hurricane" for her unlimited energy, was equally active. She attended every Republican convention from 1940 to 1976 in an official capacity. In another era, Christie believes, she would have run for office.

Considerably younger than her three siblings, Christie grew up effectively as an only child. Politics surrounded her from an early age. At age 6 she and her young friend Steve Forbes presented Mrs. Nixon with dolls for Julie and Tricia. At age 9 she attended her first national political convention. While Eisenhower gave his acceptance speech, Christie stood under the podium and later presented him with a gift she had made herself: a leather pouch for his golf balls. At age 10 she did her own fund-raising by selling lemonade. The $10 in proceeds were forwarded to the Republican National Committee.

Christie attended private schools and went on to Wheaton College in Massachusetts, where she graduated in 1968. To no one's surprise, her marriage came about because of politics. She needed a date for Nixon's inaugural ball in 1973 and invited a banker, John Whitman, whose grandfather once had been governor of New York. They married a year later, and today her husband quips that their marriage vows should have said "in sickness and in health and in politics."

It would be eight years, however, before she would move into the political arena. She agreed to stay at home with the children until her husband got a firm footing in business. Then he stepped back and let her do what he has said "she was born to do."

In 1982 she ran for the Somerset County Board of Chosen Freeholders, the governing body of a county with 230,000 residents and an annual budget of $44 million. Later Governor Thomas Kean appointed her president of the Board of Public Utilities, where she served until 1989.

In 1990 she plunged into the limelight by running against Democratic Senator Bill Bradley, a move that lower-risk types would have considered sheer folly. Bradley was an all-American Rhodes scholar, a former star forward of the New York Knicks, and a formidable fundraiser. Her party did not support her, figuring she was going to lose. He outspent her $12 million to $1 million. "I knew it was a long shot," Whitman says today, "but I saw an opportunity to gain statewide exposure." Surprising the political pundits, she lost by only 2 percent.

Leadership Style

For the next three years she set out to establish herself as a viable candidate for the next gubernatorial election. She began hosting her own talk show, writing a column, forming a political action committee, and spearheading new programs such as the Neighborhood Leadership Initiative, which was designed to identify and train grassroots leaders. In the last months she donned blue jeans and sweatshirt, boarded a bus, and toured the state in an effort to meet the people. She beat the incumbent, Jim Florio, by 1 percent.[26]

It is difficult to determine the personality type of political figures, particularly when their staffs keep them from revealing too much about themselves. Determining Governor Whitman's personality type therefore became an investigative journey through biographies, articles, conversations with those involved in her campaign, and of course my own meeting with her. Every little bit helped.

Her childhood antics yielded the first clues. They pointed to the personality of Red Realists, who are free spirits from an early age. Cheerful and highly active, they bring laughter into any environment whether the humor is appropriate or not. From their youngest years they live by their own rules, finding the opinions of adults of little importance. They have a deep bond with animals of all types, hate being restricted, and are drawn to competitive activities. Today Christie recalls being attracted to politics at an early age. "Before I knew about issues," she says, "I knew it was competitive and fun."

Next I queried those who have worked for and with her. They emphasize her common sense and ability to gather facts and move quickly to a decision, always trusting her instincts. She has drive, they say, and an optimism that pulls others in. She is independent and plays the game by her own rules.

They also highlight her humor and sense of fun. Her biographer, Patricia Beard, describes a December day when the governor and her troopers pulled up at a discount lingerie store in Newark. She moved briskly past the displays of flimsy garments with cutouts in all the obvious places. "Remember your wives, fellows," she chirped cheerfully to the troopers as she headed straight for the hosiery bin to pick up a dozen pairs. Several years before that, friends speak of a birthday celebration during which she arrived at the office in a sweatshirt that said "40 and flawless."

She challenges everyone to keep up with her. The office joke is that after a couple of years of following her around, the troopers are in better physical shape than they were ever before.[27]

Of course, her love of sports and competition is well known. When her husband plays hockey at the hunt club, she comes to watch and yells if he makes a mistake. "I yell at all the family," she admits with a grin. "I yell to make them do more." She has no qualms about admitting that if he scores a point against her in tennis, all she wants to do is kill him on the court. "I swear under my breath, and then I hit him a hard one back."[28]

Several days each week are set aside as road days. She and the troopers set off, spending four or five hours in a car to talk to people around the state. "It keeps me in touch," she says. While in the car, she reads briefing papers, holds meetings on the phone, and periodically steps out of the car to play ball with the troopers. While she enjoys setting policy, it is clear that she is most energized when dealing with the public directly.

People mention her love of nature and animals. She has been known to join park rangers in freezing midwinter weather to look for bears to place ear tags on the newly born cubs. As the rangers tranquilize the mother, she cuddles the tiny cub inside her jacket.[29]

She is bold and not afraid of controversy. She has been known to don a bulletproof vest and go undercover with state troopers to see firsthand the life of drug dealing in urban communities. This helps her achieve a more focused urban perspective. At an earlier time she studied the recycling program by riding with truckers along their route.[30]

These characteristics speak of the Red Realists' shirtsleeve management style, which is easygoing, down to earth, and expedient. Their flexibility, spontaneity, and ability to relate to people make them successful in any job that demands persuasion, and politics is high on their list of satisfying occupations. More than any other type, they love risk and thrive in chaotic situations, moving in to bring order and focus. They love variety and action. Competition energizes them, and they bring fun, humor, and empathy into the lives of others.

Finally, on a humid August afternoon, I meet her in person. I am curious to see if my initial appraisal is correct. In the Trenton state-house I enter through a long corridor where secretaries and a uni-formed state trooper sit under the oil paintings of various governors. All the paintings are of men.

She is tall and elegant with short, dark blond hair, a Roman nose, large brown eyes, and a warm smile. Her conservative suit has a length that probably will hold for many fashion cycles to come. Most of all, she conveys a genuine interest in what you are doing, an ability to listen and be truly present.

I ask when she first knew what she wanted to do in life. "Early," she says. "At age 7, I finished cutting up worms and gave up wanting to be a surgeon. I have always found politics fascinating. It is so var-ied. You can never be bored in this business. The challenges change every minute. For all the aggravation and heartache you go through, you know it is worthwhile because you can have such a positive impact on other people's lives."

Which activities does she find energizing? "One is interfacing with people, hearing their concerns, and doing the challenging back-and-forth, always being on your toes. The second is working through knotty problems and building a consensus to support sensible solutions."

Then I ask her to define her style of leadership and strengths. "I like to set the goals but let others manage the process. I try not to micromanage. I say, 'Here is the framework. go ahead and take the risks to make it happen.' If they don't take risks, I view that as a neg-ative," she says. "My strength," she adds, "is that I don't have my ego on the line. I may want to go a certain way, but I can easily be per-suaded to change and not see it as a defeat. Also, I balance different competing interests and keep harmony. Sometimes people will call me brusque and determined. In a man this would be a positive, but for a woman it is usually not flattering. What it actually means is that I am independent and focused."

Asked about her ability to take criticism and deal with confrontation, she answers, "I look at the motivation of the person. If it is for political gain, then I get mad and fight back. If there is real concern, then I like to answer it. I like to get involved and stay in touch with what people are thinking."

Her comments confirm my earlier evaluation of her style. Like other Red Realists, she leads by keeping close to the grass roots, encouraging personal responsibility, seeking quick results, and focusing on practical goals. She is informal, action-oriented, and collaborative. Emergencies are viewed as an interesting challenge and not an intrusion. With her fun-loving, nervy, and nonconforming personality, she may go a long way toward challenging the staid conservative image that has dominated the Republican party for many years. She has already set new standards for women striving to reach the country's political pinnacle.

Advice to Others

"I would encourage others to go after what they want and be confident in their abilities. When I first took office I promised to cut taxes by 30 percent. Many people said there was no way I could do it, others said my husband was the 'brains' behind the plan. Well, I did cut taxes by 30 percent, it was my plan, and we did it ahead of schedule. The lesson is, if you believe you have the ability to do something charge ahead and get it done."

CATHERINE HUGHES
Chair
Radio One

On Thursday afternoon, May 6, 1999, Radio One founder and chair Cathy Hughes stood next to her son and watched in speechless amazement as the shares of her company soared some 44 percent in the first day of trading. It was the most money ever raised from an initial public offering of an African-American company. Within 3 months mother and son, who retain 71 percent of the shares between them, would see their personal stake increase to $285 million.

Few who knew her as a child in the housing projects of Omaha, Nebraska, would have guessed that at age 52 Catherine Liggins Hughes would become the first African-American woman in the U.S. to head a publicly traded company. Radio One is the nation's largest black-owned radio network. It has 27 stations in nine cities and grosses $85 million, a hefty sum for an organization that until a decade ago never showed a profit.

In earlier days Hughes slept in a sleeping bag at the one station they owned. She cooked on a hot plate, washed up in the office bathroom, and filled the airtime with her own talk show to save on salaries. She also walked from store to store selling advertising. She did it all, and she did it with passion. No sacrifice was too great for her company or her son. She groomed him to take over, and today Alfred C. Liggins III is at her side as CEO.

She was just 17 years old when he was born. His birth would forever alter the landscape of her ambition. "I could feel the energy exchange from the blood running through his veins and mine," she reminisces. "I knew then that I had to provide this child with a future. He would never, I vowed, become a black male statistic. And had he not been born, I probably would not have aspired to go into business for myself."

She attended classes at the University of Nebraska, carrying the baby in his tiny bassinet. Her mother had asked her to leave home after she refused to have an abortion. She worked during the day and attended classes in the evening. When the child started moving around and taking everybody's pencils, his presence in the classroom became a problem. Luckily, Howard University asked her to take over its ailing radio station. In 6 years she lifted its revenues tenfold to $3 million.

Energized by that success, she decided to purchase her own radio station. A black woman in 1980 raising funds, however, did not have promising prospects. It took her 2 years and 32 presentations to different sources of capital. She finally got a break from another woman, a Puerto Rican loan officer who had just started at Chemical Bank. It was a time of high interest rates (20 percent or more), and meeting monthly debt payments was almost impossible. She lost her car and house but kept creditors on her side by constantly writing notes explaining her problems and sending whatever she could. Finally, 7 years later, the company turned the corner.[31]

Over the next 6 years she would acquire 11 stations. In the process she developed Radio One into a major institution that would energize, inform, and entertain the African-American community.

Meanwhile, there was still a child to rear. "I made him part of my business," she says today. "He had his first tuxedo when he was 8 so he could be my date at all the social events I had to attend." Hughes picked up the child from school every day. He would do his homework, and then they would cook on the hot plate and sit down to have dinner together every night. He would watch television for an hour and snooze, and they would head home together at 9 or 10 P.M. The child also would go on business trips. Mom would pick up the assignments from school and do homework with him on the road.

Alfred went on to get an MBA from Wharton, and in 1995 his mother turned the day-to-day management over to him.

The relationship remains close; they are complementary in business. "She is compassionate about the company's contribution to the black community," says Liggins, now 34. "I don't think she went into business just for the money. I tend to be more focused on the business aspects of running Radio One."

Cathy Hughes is multifaceted. Some describe her as a motivational speaker who uses the microphone to raise political issues with polished passion. Others stress her philanthropic activities. Still others view her as a tough negotiator and business manager.[32]

When I interview her on the phone, her tone is chatty and conspiratorial, somewhat like a friend describing her dreams and aspirations.

Leadership Style

She describes her way of managing as direct and collegial, although with 700 employees, she admits that some structure is needed. "I love how the Japanese run companies," she says. "If you let people feel that their input is important and they are part of the solution, the outcome is always more productive. One of the reasons I started my own business is because I used to work in places where I dreaded coming in every morning. I felt like an outsider and did not feel productive."

The emphasis at Radio One is that all employees are part of the family and Hughes is the big mom. All the memos are addressed "To the Family." "I am always there for them personally and professionally," she says, "but I do not coddle them." Indeed, there are some interesting rules. For example, profanity is not allowed either on the premises or on the air. Hughes feels that profanity is counterproductive in a work environment. It intensifies the emotions surrounding the problem and kicks off a host of negative reactions.

This is a difficult rule for the radio group. "Black radio," she says, "is normally 'rootin', tootin' wild west. For these hip-hoppers, this is their standard vocabulary. So their reaction is, 'How can she tell me that?'" The managers explain that she can and she does.

A second rule involves pitching in and assisting when there is an overflow of work. Even though people have specific responsibilities, they are expected to stick around on Friday night if things need to be finished by another group. It is her way of cross-training. This can translate into promotions for the helpful ones.

Red Realists typically have an informal style with a strong commitment to keeping close to the grass roots. Highly results-oriented, they encourage collaboration and take pains to make everyone feel included. They are optimistic and always willing to try anything at least once. They decide quickly on the basis of what is realistic and doable now. Where possible, they bring others into the process.

Radio as a whole is highly energizing to her: "It is about the connection with people and the ability to make a difference in the community." She also enjoys problem solving, particularly in crisis situations. "I get this buzz going," she says, "and I literally have the energy of ten people. I don't even need to sleep. I can work around the clock."

The activities she finds stressful and boring are one and the same: meetings. "Regardless of the nature," she says, "everyone feels the need to express an opinion. I'm like, 'Didn't you just hear four other people say the same thing?' This is very challenging for me, because everyone watches my face, and they know I am not paying attention."

I ask about blind spots. Like many mothers, she admits to being overprotective: "Sometimes I decide things for my employees that they don't want to do. I may decide, for example, that someone should be a writer and he does not really want to write. So I have to back off."

Confrontation is less of a problem: "I deal with it rapidly and defuse it." Dealing with criticism, however, was a more difficult issue. In the old days she would be defensive, she admits. "Now," she says, "I see it as a communiqué from a higher source that I need to check out. Even if the criticism is wrong, I want to learn from it."

To what does she attribute her unusual success? "I think it is a combination," she reflects. "I work seven days a week, I solicit group participation, I never give up, and I have built a core group of listeners whom I continue to superservice. I think you succeed when people want you to succeed. Other people's desires play very much into your timing. When you establish your credibility, then there is a groundswell and you are pushed to the top."

Like many Realists, Hughes has created a work environment that is flexible and emphasizes customer service and attention to the staff. Once a month she asks all her general managers to send her a list of their direct reports with indications of what their functions are. "This way, wherever I meet them," she says, "I know what they do."

Today her goals are twofold. First, she wants the company to become one of the major players in the broadcasting industry. Second, she wants to increase the African-American portion of her staff to 1,000. This means increasing the number of employees to 1,400. "If I do this," she says thoughtfully, "it will mean that in my lifetime I will have given opportunities to 1,000 members of minority groups. And that will make me feel like a success. On that day I will turn off the machine and sign and cut each paycheck by hand!"

Advice to Others

"Acknowledge the power of God and accept the fact that being a woman is a special blessing from God, not a curse. Believe in yourself and never, ever allow anyone or anything to compromise what you know is the right thing to do."

COUNTESS EDITHA NEMES
Real Estate Broker

Ditha Nemes enjoys managing the unpredictable twists of her real estate business with experience gained from a life with many bizarre turns of fate.

At age 19 the countess was the bride of one of Hungary's richest aristocrats, but then the Communists moved in. On a blustery winter evening the family fled with the clothes on their backs and their jewelry wrapped in a piece of cloth fashioned into a belt. At the border she dropped the belt on the table, submitted to a search, and then calmly put the belt back on. The jewelry would support them on the torturous journey ahead. First there was a camp in Switzerland and then a slow boat trip to northern Africa.

Ultimately, she and her husband found themselves political exiles at the court of King Farouk of Egypt. Neither had been trained to earn a living. Their hostess, Princess Zeinab, admired her infant daughter's clothes, and Ditha opportunistically jumped into the fray. Within the month she had rented an apartment, found a cutter, hired a group of sewing girls, and proceeded to design children's clothes in the latest Parisian style. Once the king's three daughters appeared in her dresses, the "designing countess" became the rage of Cairo. For seven years life hummed. The Egyptian aristocracy flocked to her showrooms, and their children served as models at the annual fashion shows. Outfits were custom-designed for each prince and princess. Notes were kept in a tiny black book. Clients competed for the exclusive designs.

Then, on what is still known as "Black Saturday," political turmoil struck again. At his 550-room palace, King Farouk was receiving 600 guests for a feast of caviar and quail. Down the street the militants started marching. Thousands of religious fundamentalists, communists, and radical students began gathering. Within 24 hours many of the symbols that had given Cairo its glamour had been burned down.[33] Guests were thrown out of their windows at the Shepherd Hotel. Groppi, the famed patisserie where I collected my yogurt and cookies each day, was torched. Nightclubs and fashionable stores received the same treatment. From our window we could see the mobs pulling people out of their cars and stoning them to death. It is a memory that will remain with me forever. Ditha Nemes is my mother, and this is my story as well.

The king packed his 200 trunks; assembled his valets, doctors, tailors, barbers, and chambermaids; and retreated to Alexandria, a three-hour trip from Cairo. Alexandria was the summer retreat where the Montazah Palace loomed above the summer capital. There he lay back, smelled the jasmine, and luxuriated in the soft Mediterranean breeze. He checked his herd of a hundred gazelles that roamed free through the hundreds of acres. He consulted his aides-de-camp and came to the conclusion that the uprising was short-lived and could be managed.[34]

It was, however, a Nasser-inspired revolution. In a short time King Farouk was forced into exile, and Europeans took flight. Ditha finished her orders for the season, using the incoming cash to finance her family's exit from Cairo. Despite an advanced pregnancy, she made plans to come to the United States to give birth to an American citizen. She made it to Los Angeles an hour before the child was born.

Ditha Nemes is a Red, one of the superrealists who thrive because of their daring and ability to handle a crisis better than any other type can. They need variety, freedom, and opportunities to impress others with their tactical agility. They are superb negotiators and troubleshooters, excelling in careers in which each day presents a new and different type of opportunity. Reds are entrepreneurial and usually have their own businesses, where they can make the rules and change them as they choose.

Reds dislike abstract theories and predictable responsibilities. They live every day to the fullest. Their self-esteem is anchored in their ability to manage the unpredictable.

Ditha's Red qualities emerged again as she faced the reality of starting over in a new country. With the aid of the Folger family in San

Francisco, she held her first fashion show in the coffee magnate's living room, using 11-year-old Abigail Folger and her friends as models. A buyer from I. Magnin was encouraging, and once again the designer was up and running. Initially she had orders from one store; five years later she was serving 300 around the United States. An ongoing business, however, was no longer attractive. Unlike Golds, Reds prefer the excitement of a start-up and the flexibility of a small concern.

She found a new challenge in the real estate field, a career path that makes excellent use of her negotiating skills. Thirty years later she continues to succeed by managing the needs of opposing parties to bring difficult deals to a close. What to others is high stress is pure stimulation and joy to freewheeling Reds.

Leadership Style

She sees her strength as never giving up. If something does not go right, you try something else. Ditha finds the negotiating process the most energizing of her activities. It is a matter of finding a way to make the deal happen, to bring opposing parties together. Her goals are short-term. "I never plan into the future," she says. "I don't worry about tomorrow; I don't look back on yesterday. I just take it one day at a time."

Asked what she finds boring, she points to a pile of papers. "Details, keeping books," she says. "I really like to relax. Business is business, of course, but when it is not, I like to relax."

Advice to Others

"Do what you like to do. Never be afraid to change and get less money. Running your own business is a big advantage. You don't have to rely on a boss, and you work for yourself, so you probably achieve more. When you are on your own, you have to push. So you become successful.

"Also, learn languages. As many languages as you can speak, that many persons you are."

JUDY RESNICK

CEO, The Resnick Group
Author of *I've Been Rich. I've Been Poor. Rich Is Better.*

Judy Resnick grew up in the 1950s, having descended from a long line of women who were brought up to please men. Both parents were first-generation immigrants. "The overriding message was 'Stay thin, look good, find a man, get married, have children.' That was life. Who needed to think about education or a job?" she recalls. "Someone else would be there to watch over me."

Alternately protected and controlled, she never finished college, never made any significant decisions, and never had a full-time job until she was 41. By that time she had gone through a bad marriage, flirted with drugs, and lost her father, who had financially supported her and her two children. Shortly afterward she was diagnosed with cancer and lost both her mother and her sister in a plane crash.

Waking up in the hospital one morning after chemotherapy, she finally faced her life realistically. With a lack of alternatives, she purchased one good interview outfit and set out to persuade the brokerage industry to train and hire her. Most firms were not interested. "I was over 40 and had no college education and no job experience," she recalls. After a streak of luck she finally landed an interview with a manager at Drexel who said, "I don't know why, but I want to give you a chance." In a few years she made vice president and then senior vice president, a title reserved for the firm's hottest commodities.

Like many Realists, when push came to shove, Resnick tapped into her resiliency. When focused, this type can be among the most optimistic and opportunistic about finding new possibilities. Realists work well with a diverse group of people and motivate others with infectious enthusiasm and energy. Whatever their field, they are at their best when working in a freewheeling environment.

That attitude served her well in the culture of the trading group in which she had to work. It was one of Wall Street's hardest-hitting enclaves, the junk bond world of Michael Milken, who ran the most powerful operation at Drexel. Shortly afterward, however, he was indicted for securities fraud. What had been a testy environment before the investigation became singularly unpleasant. Once, she recalls she went into a meeting with traders after having been out for a day with the flu. "Sick?" one asked. "That is not an excuse unless you had your goddamn head stuck in a toilet." Still, she figures, she came out well. Later that day another trader threw a heavy metal disk at a colleague, nearly ripping out his eye.

Ultimately Resnick left and set up her own company, the Resnick Group, which was established in 1996 to provide investment advisory services for women.[35]

Leadership in business often is associated with building institutions that endure. That is the goal of Blues and Golds in particular. It is not a meaningful goal for most Reds. "Life is not about how much money you have; it is about using it wisely," says Resnick. "It means I can take care of other people in my life. It means I can give to charitable causes that I care about. It means that I have personal freedom." After an eventful life Judy Resnick is clearly energized by being in charge of her own destiny.

Advice to Others

"Get familiar with your inner self." She calls it the principle of holistic wealth. "You need to know who you are in order to handle your money because the various elements in your life—physical health, finances, and relationships—all connect."

"In my case," she continues, "therapy was the key. After all those terrible valleys in my life I needed to open up my psyche for inspection. Only then was I able to confront and meet my financial reality with intelligence." There are, of course, other techniques, such as meditation, yoga, running, and support groups. The key is to spend time with your inner self and get to know who you are."

14 The Greens

"Let's humanize it."

Empathetic, humanistic, and expressive, Greens represent 17 percent of the population.[36] Also, known as Intuitive Feelers, they often are found in human-interest areas but also excel in sales, marketing, and public relations. Any business that depends on these skills can benefit from Green management.

Whatever the work setting, however, Greens need harmony and authenticity. They look for an environment that is supportive and egalitarian. It also should provide variety and a chance to impact the lives of others.

Greens have an unusual ability to influence, which, along with their gift of drawing the best out of people, creates special characteristics.

Greens focus on relationships. They inherently value others. They have a never-ending interest in understanding the meaning of life, their own and that of family, friends, and associates.

They like being recognized for their uniqueness, that sometimes borders on the eccentric. Creative and expressive, they dwell in the world of metaphors, symbols, and fantasies, all fertile elements for creative expression: visual, verbal, and written.

Immature Greens may have difficulty dealing with the realities of every day life, time, energy, and financial resources.

Well-developed Greens are seen by others as sages with powerful insights who inspire others to heightened personal achievement. As skilled communicators, they express their thoughts with unusual imagery and sensitivity.

Summary of Core Characteristics

- Look for authenticity
- Need to have an impact on the world
- Enjoy being seen as unique and creative persons
- Require harmony and a tension-free environment
- Require the support of others
- Empathize with and have powerful insights into others
- Communicate skillfully both verbally and orally
- Focus on the future and the world of the abstract
- Coach, encourage, and develop others
- Take criticism personally
- Have well developed listening skills
- Value intangibles as part of their compensations: appreciation, making a difference, and the like
- Pay little attention to financial considerations
- Try to be tactful and diplomatic

Well-Known Greens

Oprah Winfrey
Eleanor Roosevelt
Diane Sawyer
Abraham Maslow
Jane Fonda
Mahatma Gandhi
Mikhail Gorbachev
Pope John Paul XXIII

Ann Morrow Lindbergh
Emily Dickinson
Shirley MacLaine
Carl Rogers
Wendy Wasserstein

MOST FULFILLING CAREERS

Greens are most productive in an environment that they find personally meaningful and satisfying. They want to feel that their work has an
impact on others. They like a harmonious and tension-free setting
without too many rules or procedures. They prefer working with people who have a personal interest in them and express appreciation.
Given a choice, they like to focus on finding creative ways of dealing
with issues related to human development.

They are found clustered in fields that deal with human development and market positioning. These fields include the following:

- Counseling of all sorts
- Teaching (upper levels)
- Family medicine
- Cause leading (human, ecological, and spiritual)
- Public relations
- Human resources/organization and development/training
- Psychology
- Art
- TV anchoring
- Writing
- Marketing and advertising
- Conference programming
- Motivational speaking
- Recruiting
- Consultative sales

Greens thrive in any field that allows an individual to work on a
variety of creative challenges in a casual and appreciative environ-

ment. They are, of course, also found in smaller numbers in areas more populated by other types, where they shine by establishing their own niches. Examples include strategic planning and money management.

CLUES TO RECOGNIZING GREENS

Greens exhibit many, though not necessarily all, of the following behaviors.

- Are charismatic communicators
- Express passionate views
- Use complicated sentence structure
- Write and speak in a colorful style
- Have a sense of humor
- Stress the big picture and forget about the details
- Speak about global implications
- Speak about future possibilities
- Are good at integrating different angles, aspects, and views
- Are adept at "reading" others
- Are warm and put people at ease
- Are at ease in social situations whether they are talkative or not
- Listen intently
- Look intently at the people they speak to
- Get visibly upset when there is a conflict
- Are not adept with mechanical objects
- Back causes involving human and ecological issues
- Are interested in cosmic and mystical issues
- Are informal
- Entertain readily and easily, even at the last minute
- Are good problem solvers
- Are always a little ahead of their time; favor new approaches
- Have many different types of interests
- Easily share resources; have a close network of allies
- Change careers more frequently than others do

15 The Mentors

Mentors combine preferences for intuition, the information-gathering process that favors abstract ideas, future possibilities, and connecting unrelated ideas to create new patterns; feeling, the decision-making process that emphasizes personal values and the impact of a decision on others; and judging, the lifestyle preference that stresses good schedules, structure, planning ahead, and settling matters as quickly as possible.

OVERALL

Intuition, foresight, and compassion drive Mentors, who excel at leading others to achieve their potential. They operate best in a people-focused environment, requiring the fellowship of a harmonious group.

Gifted communicators, they have an unusual ability to manage without appearing to do so, not by giving direct orders, but by influencing through their own passion and positive expectations. Mentors are very loyal to the individuals, causes, and institutions they admire. They expect a high degree of loyalty and support in return.

They enjoy areas that optimize their ability to exercise their considerable "emotional intelligence" and intuitive ability to project the trends and pitfalls of the future. Conscientious, goal-oriented, and orderly, they expect the same of others. Decisive and often in a hurry, they can be more than a little impatient with anyone who slows them down in achieving their goals.

Marketing, advertising, public relations, fund-raising, social services, human resources, education, organizational development, mediation and conflict resolution, sales, and client servicing are some of the fields favored by this group. They are also more than randomly represented among writers and editors. They lean toward careers that serve others with minimal interpersonal conflict and paperwork.

They are most irritated by people who are rude or bully others.

In relationships they are supportive and affirming, making others feel valued and liked. Conflicts are problematic and are ignored as long as possible.

In their leisure time Mentors enjoy attending cultural events and lectures and dining with friends and family members.

In the second half of life Mentors frequently develop greater objectivity and the realization that they do not need to always be at the forefront as "saviors of the world." It is their time to focus on personal needs.

Leadership Style

Offer a people-centered vision

Build consensus and cooperation; respect other opinions

Influence through persuasion rather than control

Inspire through a strong commitment to ideals

Are attuned to the needs of associates; support others through difficulties

Introduce structure and organization; initiate action to get things done

Get the best from others through appreciation, enthusiasm, and support

Are upbeat and optimistic; accept setbacks as new challenges

Work hard to convert ideals into reality

Optimal Working Environment

Is harmonious and has people who can be trusted

Has a work culture with strong values and a willingness to invest in the development of the staff

202 THE EIGHT LEADERSHIP STYLES

Produces products and services that contribute to the well-
being of society

Allows them to work with creative people in a variety of
activities

Makes the best use of their well-developed organizational
skills

Provides many opportunities for growth as an individual

Provides control of and responsibility for one's own projects

Is overtly appreciative of the staff's accomplishments

Least Preferred Working Environment

A tense, overly competitive, and highly political culture

Work or products that take advantage of clients and the staff

Impersonal working relationships

Approach to Change

Accept and welcome change as long as the goals of the
organization are balanced against those of the staff

Contribution to a Team

Understand and deal well with hidden conflicts among team
members

Are focused and results-oriented

Inspire people to put out their best efforts

Ensure that the team does not waste time and resources

Meet deadlines

Are generous with time and ideas

Decision-Making Style

Are quick

Emphasize how the decision will affect people

Potential Blind Spots

Take criticism too personally

Avoid conflicts, confrontations, and underlying problems

Base business decisions on personal likes and dislikes
Are slow to recognize underperformers
May irritate others by being moralistic
Idealize people and expect too much from them

How to Persuade a Mentor

Be yourself
Ask about her vision
Build the relationship; take an interest in a Mentor's family
    members. friends, associates, and pets
Stress points of agreement; give positive feedback
Be insightful
Stress innovative solutions
Stress the big picture; limit the use of factual information
Engage her imagination
Use colorful language; explain with anecdotes
Be organized and deliver on commitments

Strategies for Mentors to
Increase Leadership Effectiveness

Learn to manage conflict in a more productive way
Pay attention to details and the practical application of ideas
Invite feedback and accept criticism objectively
Learn to say no to people and projects
Slow down when pressing for a conclusion
Recognize that there are faults in the best people and causes
Schedule more free time and spontaneous activities
Analyze the factual data and hard evidence before
    embracing an idea

TWO TYPES OF MENTORS:
EXTRAVERTS AND INTROVERTS

Extraverted Mentors are outgoing, charismatic, and approachable, although they can be relentless about getting their own way. Their accepting friendliness puts others at ease. Outstanding communicators, they are particularly effective at motivating others.

Introverted Mentors are more reflective and meditative than their extraverted counterparts. They are complex personalities with a rich and imaginative inner life that is revealed only to close friends. Possessed of unusual insights into people, they inspire growth in others.

A Note of Caution

Since type does not explain many aspects that are important in defining an individual (intelligence, education, mental health, and individual life experiences, among others), no overall profile can describe all the variants in a personality. Invariably some of the traits described above will not ring true for you. If the majority do not ring true, however, it could mean that you belong to another group. In that case, go back and revisit your Leadership Q questionnaire. Check the columns where you have close scores. Try reading a profile that reflects the other combination of your close scores. Alternatively, show the profile detailed below to an individual who knows you well, such as a mate, boss, close friend, or team colleague, and ask for comments. If you are going through major life changes, try waiting until things have stabilized.

DEVELOPMENT EXERCISES FOR MENTORS

We may appear different in different situations. Over time we also grow and progress, but our basic preferences do not change. This has been proved by the large number of people who have retaken the Myers-Briggs Type Indicator in different periods of their lives and repeatedly come out with the same preferences. Thus, an abstract intuitive Thinker never really becomes a concrete sensing Thinker. A structured Judger never really becomes a flexible, go-with-the-flow Perceiver. A Green Mentor never becomes a dyed-in-the-wool-Gold Conservator.

People who succeed, however, instinctively or deliberately learn to develop their nonpreferences. This softens their blind spots and enables them to adapt to the demands of different people and situations. Listed below are exercises that will help you develop your non-preferences. Jung referred to this process as individuation.

Exercise 1. Giving Instructions

The strong intuitive mind-set of the Mentor often results in instructions that are vague and impressionistic. These instructions do not work well with Sensors (over 70 percent of the population), who need specific guidelines and a concrete plan of action. Poor instructions often lead to frustration, wasted time, and significant misunderstandings in the workplace.

Write your instructions or plan of action on a piece of paper. Check that the following conditions have been met.

- You have worked out the details in advance. Ask yourself when, where, what, how, and why.
- You are brief and specific about what needs to be done.
- You have demonstrated why the project makes sense, why it is needed, and what the practical applications are.
- If action is needed, give specific instructions; do not assume that others will read between the lines. For example, write "Materials need to go out before the end of the week," not "We should thing about sending materials."

The point is that other people take in information differently than you do. They cannot be productive unless that difference is honored.

Exercise 2. Handling Criticism

Ask someone who is blunt (a Thinker) to critique something of value to you: a project, an idea, an outfit, or a room decoration. Pay attention to your reactions to his or her comments. How do your intellect and feelings interact? What are your bodily reactions? Note them below. Can you sort out the facts you are hearing from your feelings about them?

- The critique:

- Facts:

- Feelings:

The point is that it is important to depersonalize criticism. It helps us grow, and it usually is not personal.

Exercise 3. Developing Spontaneity

You are goal-driven and outcome-oriented. These qualities have contributed to your success. Taken to an extreme they make you rigid and controlling. They also undermine your creativity.

Follow someone around for a few hours and just go with the flow. Do not suggest a schedule of activities. Note your reactions. Observe and appreciate their rhythm. At the end, write down what you have learned that you would not have learned under normal circumstances. Consider doing this once every couple of months.

The point is, spontaneity provides balance and stimulates creative thinking.

Exercise 4. Working with Other Types

You have been assigned to cohead a project with Mary, a well-regarded manager, who is considered to be on the fast track. She is a Red Realist. She differs from you in two major preferences. She is a Sensor (concrete, fact-driven, and sequential) and a Perceiver (spontaneous and adaptable).

This assignment is important to your career. Her impression of you will determine future assignments.

Read the Red Realist personality profile summary. Write down some of the key differences below.

Mary	Me
1.	1.
2.	2.
3.	3.
4.	4.

Read the section on how to persuade a Red Realist. Note the points below. Incorporate them into the presentation you will make at the initial meeting.

1.

2.

3.

Read through your blind spots. Note which of them will be most irritating to her. Devise a strategy.

My Blind Spot	Strategy
1.	1.
2.	2.

Now repeat this exercise with a real person you have to work with who is different from you. It can be a boss, colleague, or client. Look at the overall four color descriptions and the section on how to recognize each color group.

My Type _____   **His or Her Type** _____

How to Persuade

Blind Spots   **Strategy**

Photocopy your comments and keep them someplace where they are easily accessible.

The point is that if you do this exercise often enough, you not only will be more effective with that person but will learn to appreciate what he or she brings to the table. Soon you will expand that understanding to other people and become known for your skills in managing people. This is the path to leadership.

Exercise 5. How to Be a Better Leader

- Turn back to your leadership style summary.
- Choose one strategy for increased leadership effectiveness.
- Write it on an index card and develop three specific steps to achieve that strategy.
- Place the card someplace where you will see it frequently. Read it several times a day.
- After several weeks repeat the process with another strategy.

ALEXANDRA LEBENTHAL
President
Lebenthal & Company

Alexandra remembers coming to work at the age of 4. Her grand-mother, Sayra, looked imposing sitting at her large desk: "She would motion us forward and say, 'Now, dear, you know your Nana loves you very much, but now I am going to put you to work.' Then she would give us the task of putting reinforcers on the pages of her clients' account pages. After several hours of work she would pay us 25 cents." Today, at age 35, Alexandra Lebenthal is the youngest woman president of a Wall Street firm, with a magnificent twelfth-floor office in which "Nana's" desk still reigns supreme.

In the hard-charging world of Wall Street a woman running a firm is still an anomaly, yet Alexandra gets high marks from her peers. They acknowledge her skills as a communicator and the quality of her advertising and positioning. They also speak of her intuitive strength in understanding the trends of the business. "She has a very good long-term perspective," says Elaine LaRoche, managing director of the investment bank Morgan Stanley.

Running the firm was not always her goal. When Alexandra attended Princeton, she was a history major who dreamed of becom-ing an actress. One summer an injured knee prevented her from working as an intern in a summer theater group. She worked at Lebenthal instead, and she took that as an omen. After graduating in 1986, she went to work for Kidder, Peabody, a Wall Street firm.

Two years later she joined Lebenthal & Company, where her grandmother was still a dominant force. Sayra Lebenthal, a law school graduate in the 1920s, began the firm with her husband, Louis, in 1925. "She had the personality of a giant packed into a 4-foot, 10-inch frame," her granddaughter recalls today. "She was tough and car-ing and treated her clients like her family members, making sure they did what they were supposed to do." Sayra always worked even when she had small children, and in those days that was not done. Her son joined the firm in the mid-1960s. Jim Lebenthal made the family name a household word with memorable advertising such as "We treat you like family" and "Bonds are my babies." Alexandra was the only one of his three children who took an interest in the business.[37]

A year after she joined the firm she was assigned to work with her grandmother. She was 26, and Sayra was 91, still holding on to her clients despite the obvious signs of aging. Alexandra worked at a tiny desk at her grandmother's side. "It was emotionally a very stressful time," she recalls. "She was unwilling to give up control, and I thought I knew everything. There were many times I walked out of the office in tears." Did she ever think of quitting? "Never," she said. "I had a strong sense of loyalty and needed to think about what was right for the firm in the long term. That enabled me to stick it out." Again we see an example of how Mentors use personal values as a guide to run their professional lives.

A year after Sayra died, 31-year-old Alexandra discovered what it meant to run a firm with billions of dollars of other people's money. Her father kicked himself upstairs to chairman and made her president and CEO.

Leadership Style

We sit on her ice-blue velvet couch to discuss what she finds most energizing: "I like communicating with the people we recruit, trying to figure out what makes a person tick and how to make that person perform better." She defines her leadership style as being "very empathetic, very caring. I try to focus on the positive aspects of someone's skills and personality and use that as a motivating force." Like most Green Mentors, Alexandra is highly responsive to the needs of her staff. "I want the people who report to me," she says, "to feel that they are a meaningful part of shaping the company and shaping me as a leader." On the flip side, when someone "screws up and is unwilling or unable to change no matter how much effort I put in, I can let myself be taken advantage of," she adds realistically.

Also like other Mentors, she favors an open and participative management climate. That does not always work, she admits. "Some people want you to say, 'These are my expectations, and this is how you are going to get there, a, b, c.' I don't enjoy my relationships with those people as much as the ones with people with whom I can sit down and brainstorm and talk about theories and concepts." Brainstorming is a favorite activity of all Green leaders.

Other areas of strength include sales and client communication. She maintains her own book of clients, many of whom date back to her grandmother's days. "When I see the handwritings—both hers and mine—from years before, I have a wonderful sense of continuity," she says. "Several years ago, we positioned the firm by coming up with the commercial that said, 'I have a mission to make you a customer for life, and all I have to do is put your needs first.' Now I am forced to live up to that promise. Otherwise, it would be just commercial advertising hoopla, which would make me out to be someone false. That is something I very much care about."

Alexandra also enjoys creating the vision for the company and laying out the overall strategy, particularly with regard to the sales department. Despite the impressive office, she, like most extraverts, prefers to spend her time on the sales and trading floor, talking with people and getting a feel for the marketplace. Her current goal is to reinvigorate the company's client base by attracting a younger clientele, including women and those using the electronic superhighway. She is also taking the company, traditionally a bond house, into new areas such as mutual funds, estate planning, and insurance. Mentors are gifted in seeing the trends and potential pitfalls of the future, and this petite 1990s-style businesswoman is no exception.

The most stressful aspects of her position include dealing with risk management items and issues involving the firm's capital. While obviously strongly interested in profit and the bottom line, she assigns much of the analytic work to others.

She also admits to having put considerable effort into dealing with confrontation and criticism. "In earlier years I used to lash out. I can't stand criticism," she says emphatically. "Now I consciously try to depersonalize it and focus on the issue itself and what it is that I can get from the criticism. And when I need to confront someone, I fight my impulse to react immediately and end it. I try to stay balanced and listen to all sides."

Today she is also a mother of two children, ages 3 and 6. She works only until 6 P.M. and limits her after-work schedule to selected volunteer activities such as the Nightingale Bamford School, the United Jewish Appeal, and certain industry associations. "Otherwise," she says, "I live a very simple life with my husband and kids." There is an inner peace in Alexandra that is a refreshing change from the frenzied push that characterizes most of Wall Street, a focus that reflects her vision of becoming as she says, "powerful, profitable, and strong."

Advice to Others

Not surprisingly, she advises other young women to find themselves a mentor—male or female—and to pay their dues.

JOLENE SYKES
President
Fortune Magazine

On February 25, 1999, Time Inc. promoted Jolene Sykes to president of one of the country's foremost business publications. The move created a pronounced buzz in the staid halls of the U.S. business community. Today she is responsible for *Fortune* magazine's marketing, advertising, new business development, and circulation. *Fortune* has over $200 million in advertising revenues and a circulation of close to 1 million in the United States, Europe, and Asia, with sales of another 1.5 million newspaper supplements in Latin America.

Her circuitous road began in a small town in North Carolina. She had an older brother, a mother who was a bookkeeper at the local school, and a loving father who suffered from alcoholism. Her mother is now 80 and still works as a bookkeeper. She remains Sykes's most important role model.

Sykes attended college on a teaching fellowship, continued with a master's in education, and began work teaching middle-school farm children. It was frustrating, she recalls: "The kids had to be out on Friday to do the wash; when crop season came they did not turn up at all. Meanwhile, they could not do reading and math, but I was supposed to be teaching them world history." She was irritated by the system and went to graduate school to learn more about helping with those children's basic needs but ultimately wanted to work in a bigger pond.

Meanwhile, she had married someone she describes as hard-driving, competitive, and highly focused. "I became his little understudy," she recalls with a grin. She joined the insurance company he was working for and became a claims adjuster. Later, when he was transferred to another city, she studied for and took actuarial exams, ultimately landing a job as a policy rate analyst for the insurance commissioner in North Carolina. "I wanted my husband to admire and respect me as much as I admired his strength in business," she explains.

Two years later she gave birth to her daughter Kate and followed her husband, who was transferred again. Then the marriage began to fall apart, and she left. Sykes was on her own with a small child to support. "I was terrified," she admits, and soon was galvanized into action.

After a brief stint with an unethical broker, she joined a headhunter, hoping to parlay that experience into a better understanding of what was available in the workforce. Condé Nast offered her a job in advertising sales, and later she was recruited by *Time* magazine. "The beauty of sales," she notes, "is that they don't care if you are female."

Time provided the needed security, and she provided the magazine with hefty revenues. They moved her from Atlanta to Washington, D.C., and ultimately to New York. Time and Warner had just merged, and she became part of an elite hit squad of sales and marketing types who targeted big synergy deals.

By that time her daughter was in junior high, and Sykes realized she needed more time with her child. Getting on the train at 6 A.M. and returning home after 9 P.M. became a problem. She approached management, and they offered her the opportunity to open an office in Atlanta.

There have been many challenges along the way, but she recalls two in particular. "Being blond and Southern in those days meant people did not take you seriously or did not think you were smart enough. Also, as a divorced mother, there were always a million questions from prospective employers about my day care. I got testy and lost a couple of job opportunities. Later I learned to be more polite, but the juggling act was a challenge," she recalls. "I wanted to succeed in business and be a good mother." Doing it alone was not easy. She hired good household help and kept in touch through daily phone contact.

When Kate was a senior, *Fortune* offered Jolene the job of publisher. That meant working in New York. Not wanting to move Kate in her last year of school, she decided to turn it down. At dinner she told her daughter. Kate's reaction is etched in her memory. "Are you out of your mind?" said the child. "Next year I am going off to school, and you won't be able to take it. It will be easier for both of us if you go first." They worked it out. Jolene went to New York during the week and was home on weekends. Fortunately, she had built up a community of support in Atlanta: "You tend to meet people who are like you, and if you are there for them, they will turn around and support you when you need them." Besides the household help, she had the advantage of great friends to lean on.

Leadership Style

She describes her leadership style as being "soft lead." It is neither autocratic nor a matter of leadership by committee. "I am not afraid to step up to the plate," she says, "but I like to get everyone involved and on board with me." And if they don't buy in? "Then I say, 'Come work with me; let me explain it to you. I am open as to how else we can get there, but this is where we need to be. If, however you really don't want to be on this train, then let me help you find another train.' "

As with other Mentors who provide insights and take unusual approaches, what really energizes her is both the creative and people aspects of the business. It may be meeting clients and finding solutions to existing problems or coming up with new products and business solutions. "I love brainstorming and creating the vision," she says. "And in order to figure out how we are going to get there, I solicit a lot of input and feedback. I think it is really important that everyone be part of it."

Values also play an important part. "I have always said to my own bosses," she emphasizes, "that you don't pay me to not have an opinion, so I am going to keep hammering away with what I believe in. Of course, I have to carry out what they want to do. Fortunately, I have found good people to work for, so I have not had the problem of carrying out something I did not believe in."

She applies those skills to deal making. Associates speak highly of her abilities in the art of the deal. "I love making deals," she says, "that are win-win situations. Others may feel they win only when someone loses. That is not part of my psyche. A win is when everybody comes away from the table getting something better than he or she had originally hoped for."

On the flip side are the activities that she finds stressful. Paperwork is boring, and receiving negative feedback from others is stressful. "I am a self-flogger. I tend to see my own flaws and take them to heart. Sometimes if 1 out of 200 people writes a negative comment on my presentation, I take that to heart as well." Spending too much time worrying about the staff is another blind spot: "I so badly want to make it work for them that I may get overinvolved."

Dealing with confrontation used to be stressful but today is under control "In my younger days I would have stuck my head under the sofa, just hoping it would go away. I have taught myself to deal with it as soon as possible, which took until my late thirties. I was prompted mostly because I was a single mom. My daughter was 4; I was divorced. I had to get my career under way, and confrontation was part of the process."

Overall she finds her job highly satisfying. "I try not to kid myself that this is life-or-death stuff," she says, "but I do take great pride in bringing out something of value to the community."

Like the other Mentors profiled in this book, Jolene Sykes inspires change, leads through personal enthusiasm, and favors a participative approach to managing products and people. Mentors are global and like dealing with big picture issues. They are adept communicators with unusual sensitivity to nuances and have a highly developed capacity to understand other viewpoints. More than most other types, they are capable of assessing the organizational climate accurately.

Advice to Others

Her advice to young women is to define your values, take risks, learn from your mistakes, be true to yourself and others, and, most important, build strong relationships along the way. "At the end," she concludes, "life is all about relationships."

BARBARA CORCORAN
Chairman
The Corcoran Group

She exudes warmth and an almost kinetic energy and heads a Manhattan real estate agency that boasts 12 offices, a sales staff of 500 plus, and more than $2 billion in sales a year.

There is a cheerful bustle in the headquarters where I meet with her. Painted on the wall of the circular receiving area are the quotes of bygone visionaries: "The only credential the city asked was the boldness to dream" (Moss Hart, 1959) and "The great big city is a wondrous toy—we'll turn Manhattan into an isle of joy" (Lorenz Hart, 1925). These quotes speak of the optimism and imagination that are the hallmark of a Mentor's leadership style.

Leadership Style

Corcoran's special strength, as she sees it, is creating a working climate that brings out the best in all of her staff. She cites a number of examples: "When someone is not functioning well, I am able to back off and say to them, 'Okay, let's have another look.' Take Ron, for example. He was okay as a salesman, but never great. He rarely closed, but he was fabulous at attracting prospects and marketing himself. So I asked him to write a job description. He wrote that he wanted to teach people how to self-market. Well, that fit, so we put him in charge of training. Now staff members line up to meet with him. He is teaching everyone how to market themselves. I took his one asset and blew it into a job, and he is so ecstatic that he is actually a royal pain."

Another salesperson was not producing. Corcoran poked around until she got to the root of the problem. The woman flourished on loyalty, but it was a seller's market and clients tend to go with many brokers in order to get the best deal. Together they analyzed the situation, looking at all the customers to whom she had ever sold: how she met them and why they came to her. They concluded that every single client had come through a personal contact. "So I said to her," she announces with a grin, "'Stop showing up at work. I don't want to see you sitting at your computer or at the office at all. I want you out socializing, making your social front more prominent and more unique than every other broker in town.' Today she runs a string of ladies, parties that feature unique events, book signings and the like. People adore her parties, and she is now one of the top brokers."

Like many Mentors, Corcoran manages in a very personal way, concentrating on individuals rather than systems and abstract goals. She leads by encouragement and providing a great deal of positive feedback. Mentors understand the true meaning of coaching, which invariably translates into increasing profitability.

Where did all this passion and drive come from? Not from a promising start.

She was the second oldest of ten children. Her father held two jobs: plant manager at a printing company during the day and cleaning trucks at night. Her mother acknowledged the special talents of each child. Her younger sister took charge of the household chores, which she enjoyed, and Corcoran was designated as the entertainer of the family. This support of her creative abilities was particularly helpful, since she hated school: "I was sick to my stomach every day of my school years. I was terribly nearsighted and could not see the blackboard, and when I went to remedial reading class, I found myself with a mentally retarded child and an Italian boy who had just come off the boat and spoke no English at all. Now does that spell stupid or what? The turning point came in my college freshman year. The teacher, a hip Korean lady, took my essay and read it aloud. I cried as she was reading it because maybe there was a possibility, I thought, that I was not totally stupid. It was a life-changing experience."

She graduated but before hooking into the real estate world she had 21 jobs and was fired as a secretary twice. By age 22, "I was working as a receptionist for two builders," she reminisces, "when their son asked if I could help rent apartments during the weekend."

From there she never looked back. Two years later she had her own firm and a staff of two, subsidized by a $3,000 commission check. Within a year and a half, she had a staff of 18 and her company was on its way to becoming the largest real estate firm in Manhattan.

Greens excel at thinking "outside the box." Corcoran was the first real estate group to join the cyberspace crowd. It happened by accident, she admits: "First we decided to put apartments on videotape so that buyers could view them. I spent $70,000 and had 500 damn tapes sitting in my basement that no one was looking at. Then I heard about the Web and thought, Why not put them on a site." The rest is history. Today they sell more than one apartment from the Web each day, and her competitors have followed suit. Other innovations included being the first real estate firm to do brand marketing, to publicize brokers with full photographs, cobroker apartments, and publish statistics on the industry. "I had 11 apartments," she says mischievously. "I averaged them and came up with figures. *The New York Times* listed those averages on the front page of the business section. They never asked where they came from."

I am mesmerized by these stories. Another strength of Greens is their unusual ability to communicate in a colorful and persuasive style.

I break into her rapid flow of communication to ask about blind spots. "Oh yeah," she says, "I have a number of them. First, I am too quick to judge. If I like someone immediately, I ask very few questions. I don't get any hard data, I run entirely with my gut. I have been wrong, not so much on people but on projects. Of course, the reverse works as well. If I don't like a person in the first 30 seconds, they have a hard time convincing me with words or anything else." What about the financial side of things? I ask cautiously, mentally estimating the cost of 12 offices and the reputed overhead of more than $2 million a month. "I don't know how to read financial statements," she states without apology. So how does she sleep at night? "Oh, I never worry about it," she says. "Worrying wouldn't change anything. There are two choices in business. You either grow the business and throw overhead to the wind or you restrain yourself and watch every nickel and dime." Of course, Corcoran has a very good financial person in place who, she admits, "is a true worrywart."

How about confrontation? "I walk a mile to get away from it," she admits. "Eventually my need for order forces me to deal with it, but it is usually too late and much less direct than it should be."

None of these typical Mentor blind spots seem to dim the spirit of the office. Corcoran makes her own failures very public at sales meetings, and that provides inspiration for the staff.

Today she balances her life between a hectic business schedule and her 6-year-old son. She was 45 when she gave birth to him and acknowledges that had she had children earlier, she could not have built the business. "I was approaching the change, and as with everything else, I am good with deadlines," she says with a grin. "Earlier I lived life like a man. I was totally free to build the business. I married at 36. My husband is supportive. But still, when you have a child, you are emotionally tied to that child, so it is like sibling rivalry with the business."

Her vision for the future? "When I first started the business," she says, "my vision was to be the queen bee of real estate. It was so clear, I could touch it. Now my life vision is to be a happy person. I need to have fun in my life, within work and out of it. I believe the fun element is what makes my firm unique."

Advice to Others

Find your passion and be true to yourself.

IBOLYA DAVID
Minister of Justice
Hungary

The nondescript white building in the center of Budapest is known as the White House. In an earlier day its very name struck terror in the hearts of Hungarian citizens. This is where political prisoners were brought and tortured in the aftermath of the Hungarian revolution. Today, a decade after Communist rule ended, the atmosphere is benign. The sleepy young guard pokes diffidently around my briefcase. Madame Minister, he says with a yawn, will meet you in the party's meeting room.

A tall, elegant, blond, Ibolya David wields considerable power in the Byzantine politics of eastern Europe. Aside from being a member of the cabinet, she is president of her party, the Hungarian Democratic Forum coalition. Like other Mentors, she is positive and upbeat. "God was in his best spirit and smiling when I was born," she says when asked about her rise to power. "My life has been a series of good strokes." The facts, however, speak of a more twisted road.

Her grandfather owned a textile factory that was nationalized when the Communists took over in 1948. Her father started a small mill to produce folkloric textiles, clothing, and carpets under very stern and limiting socialist conditions. The whole family worked at the mill to make ends meet. In those days one could not hire outside employees. They lived in a small village in the southern part of Hungary, a town of 40,000 inhabitants that included minorities from neighboring countries: Serbs, Croats, and Germans. "We always knew," she says bemusedly, "which pubs not to enter."

She studied law. Her father tolerated her ambitions but was not particularly supportive. After she got her degree, he asked her to join him at the factory, which she did for 18 months. "One day, working at the weaving stand," she recalls, "I realized I needed to manage and be on a larger stage. I knew I had a mission to do something for society."

At 27 she moved to a nearby village, opened her own law practice, and took on all the work that came her way. In seven years she built up a practice in marital, child care, and inheritance disputes. She made a good living and established a presence in the village. In 1990, a year after communism ended in Hungary, Ibolya ran for parliament. She won and has never looked back since. Two years ago, when her party came to power, she was appointed to the cabinet, making her the only woman in the government.

She attributes her success to four ingredients. The first is her communication style. "I was never a diplomat or a bureaucrat," she points out. "I have a clear, transparent, and direct communication style." That statement speaks of the Mentor's desire to express ideas in a way that inspires and instructs others.

Second, she speaks of her ability to manage inter- and intraparty conflicts and find acceptable compromises: "Only those who have empathy can do this. You need to understand the opposition's way of doing things and rise above the heat of the political debate to find a compromise within the range of acceptable values." Finding mutually beneficial solutions while holding on to personal ethical standards is a key component of a Mentor's leadership style. Mentors also have an unusual ability to listen and hear not only what is being said but also what is not being said, providing them with effective conflict resolution skills.

A third ingredient is her participative management style. "I don't recognize or respect any hierarchy. I do have thoughts, objectives, and dreams, and I am looking for partners to assist me in realizing them. My staff works by request, not instruction. We discuss the job and the goal, and I ask my colleagues to give me the pros and cons. Then I make a decision. When people work in a more hierarchical way," she says, "their colleagues retreat into silence. They may see the traps and problems, but they don't mention them. Me, I don't like to be misinformed or ill prepared. So I give people a lot of freedom."

Fourth, Ibolya David is a change agent, a role of particular importance in light of the crossroads at which her country finds itself today. "The last few years have been a fantastic experience," she states with enthusiasm. "Imagine having the opportunity to assist in the development of so many new institutions: the constitution, the system of municipalities, the public accountancy system, the comptroller department, not to mention the whole process of converting a planned economy to a market economy system."

Contributing to that transformation is the aspect of her job that is most energizing. "My goals are crystal clear," she says fervently. "They are to see that this country remains a civilian and non-Communist state and that Hungary regains the national identity that it has lost over the last 40 years."

Leadership Style

Mentors enjoy leading teams by using primarily facilitative rather than management tactics. They have strong ideas of how organizations should treat people and typically handle people and projects in a collaborative way.

How does she deal with confrontation and criticism? "I am not a masochist," she says, "but I have taught myself to receive criticism and put it in the right place. I listen hard and interpret what that criticism is really saying. And as for confrontation, well, anyone who has a real opinion must face confrontation."

Like many successful women, Ibolya is backed by a supportive husband, a notary public and active parent to their two teenage children. "He always says," she states wryly, "that you are at the top of the ladder and you may fall, but at least you will always be welcome at home." Because evenings are unpredictable, the family makes a point of gathering each morning for breakfast. "We get up early, set a beautiful table, and enjoy a three-course breakfast. This is our time together," she says, "when all family issues are discussed."

Beyond that, she has used other techniques for helping her children cope with public scrutiny, rumors, and demands on her time. "Ten years ago, when they were 7 and 8, we spent the whole summer reading books by Dale Carnegie that focus on problem-solving techniques. We analyzed and practiced skills such as determining how much time should be devoted to specific problems, how to define them, how to put them in perspective, how to put each in the right drawer, and how to prioritize and deal with the more serious ones. Now," she says, "my children are independent. They know which problems they can take care of themselves and which they should bring to me."

Advice to Others

"Start at the local level to get an understanding of how the political process works. In politics you need luck and good alliances. Education is important, but mostly it is about making people believe in you, and that comes from your showing love and patience toward their problems."

MARIE WILSON
President
Ms. Foundation for Women

She started out participating in the civil rights movement and then realized she was about to have her fourth child in four years because she could not get good birth control. She said to herself that she was "still dealing with issues of being a woman, so I started focusing on family planning instead."

Today, as president of the Ms. Foundation for Women, she continues to work with programs that improve the well-being of women and young girls. Her initiatives include the development of Take Our Daughters to Work Day, in which some 53 million Americans participate each year, and the creation of the Women's Economic Development Collaborative Fund, which financially supports self-employment and job creation programs. Her current focus is the White House Project, which is designed to get Americans thinking about a female president and help women run in the elections to come.

Leadership Style

Wilson, a Green Mentor, describes herself as a social entrepreneur: "My primary responsibilities are to come up with the ideas that keep this organization in a good solid place, get those ideas funded, make sure those ideas are being communicated to the world, and keep them within a manageable framework." She works collaboratively by taking people's opinions and then attempting to incorporate these opinions into a working plan that is in sync with the foundation's goals.

Mentors are gifted communicators who exert influence through their own passion and positive expectations. They are loyal to institutions and causes they admire and expect a high degree of loyalty and support in return.

I asked Wilson what she thinks are the differences in leadership styles between men and women. "I think that women bring a different leadership style partly because they have been socialized differently. You get personalities that are conditioned by how they grew up. We still condition women to take care of the things in the workplace that need taking care of." She adds, "This does not mean that women are more caring, less hierarchical, or more cooperative when they get into positions of power. What really matters is having numerical balance and giving women power and opportunity. The rest will take care of itself."

Advice to Others

"Acknowledge and use your power well."

16 The Advocates

Advocates combine preferences for intuition, the information-gathering process that favors abstract ideas, future possibilities, and connecting unrelated ideas to create new patterns; feeling, the decision-making process that emphasizes personal values and the impact of a decision on others; and perceiving, the lifestyle preference that favors adaptability, flexibility, and keeping options open as long as possible.

OVERALL

Energized by new ideas, Advocates are drawn to the unusual and love to be acknowledged for their originality and unique contributions. Free spirits by nature, they are often unconventional and admire other nonconformists.

Sharp and penetrating observers, they have a strong sense of what motivates others. They see life as an unfolding cosmic pageant that presents infinite possibilities for people to grow and develop.

Adaptable and creative, they love a challenge, dislike routine, take life as it comes, and usually remain optimistic. They tend to change careers, projects, and goals more frequently than others.

Advocates are gifted in both verbal and written communications, and most take up writing or speaking at some point in their lives.

As big-picture thinkers, they are insightful and able to project the trends and pitfalls of the future. They are interested in many areas, focusing in particular on those which affect people and global concerns. They dislike bureaucracy, which they gleefully battle at every opportunity.

They are seen by others as warm and insightful. In relationships they establish rapport quickly by being genuine and nonjudgmental. They have a high need for empathetic relationships.

They are most irritated by people who are manipulative or controlling.

They are flexible and accommodating to work with. Marketing, public relations, consultative sales, psychology, writing, TV anchoring, organizational development, family medicine, and teaching are some of the areas where Advocates express a high level of satisfaction.

In their leisure time Advocates enjoy attending lectures, pursuing creative hobbies, and having in-depth discussions with friends and family members.

In the second half of life Advocates often develop a more objective and logical approach to projects and people.

Leadership Style

Create a humanistic vision which they communicate
persuasively to others
Understand what motivates others and draw the best out of
people
Encourage creativity and openness
Have extensive networks on which to draw
Motivate through positive and constructive feedback
Influence through a collegial style rather than control
See unique ways of solving problems
Inspire confidence that seemingly impossible goals are
reachable
Excel at facilitating groups

Optimal Working Environment

Is democratic and informal
Has a culture that places a high value on the well-being of
the staff and clients

Has a minimum of rules, restrictions, and procedures
Offers variety and change
Has an atmosphere of cooperation and trust
Is a place where humor is encouraged
Provides the opportunity to work with other creative people
Provides a chance to make a difference in the lives of others

Least Preferred Working Environment

Work with an emphasis on routine and details
Being micromanaged
A highly political atmosphere with power struggles

Approach to Change

Welcome it as long as the human element is given serious
consideration

Contribution to a Team

Create team identity
Synthesize the ideas of others
Bridge people and resources
Draw ideas from others
Excel at brainstorming
Put others at ease with warmth and humor

Decision-Making Style

Generate many options and delay making the decision as
long as is feasible
Factor in the impact on people

Potential Blind Spots

Have difficulty prioritizing; start too many projects and get
sidetracked
Take criticism personally
Use poor time management techniques
Do not prepare properly; rely on the ability to wing it

Ignore important details

Promise more than can be delivered

How to Persuade an Advocate

Be genuine and authentic

Stress the big picture; limit the details

Be on the same team, not selling a product

Develop the relationship

Build the relationship; take an interest in an Advocate's
family, friends, associates, and pets

Stress innovative solutions

Allow for nonsequential flow to the conversation

Engage her imagination; allow her to be part of the solution

Use colorful language; explain with anecdotes and personal
stories

Make it fun

Strategies for Advocates to Increase Leadership Effectiveness

Set daily priorities

Develop an action plan and a personal time management
system

Avoid starting new projects until old ones are complete,
passed on, or terminated

Check important details; factor in relevant facts before
moving ahead with a decision

Encourage critical feedback from others; look at criticism
objectively

Accept the fact that deadlines are important to others; meet
deadlines to enhance credibility

Give realistic feedback to others; be clear about what you
mean

Prepare when making presentations to others to ensure
focus and organization

TWO TYPES OF ADVOCATES: EXTRAVERTS AND INTROVERTS

Extraverted Advocates are lively, enthusiastic, openly affirming, and energetic. They are powerfully persuasive when drawing others into their areas of interest and tend to know everyone and everything that is going on.

Introverted Advocates may appear cool and detached, but they have strong private feelings and loyalties. Thoughtful and complex, they usually do not impose their views on others but are willing to share their insights with a select group of people they trust.

A Note of Caution

Since type does not explain many aspects that are important in defining an individual (intelligence, education, mental health, and individual life experiences, among others), no overall profile can describe all the variants in a personality. Invariably, some of the traits described above will not ring true for you. If the majority do not ring true, however, it could mean that you belong to another group. In that case, go back and revisit your Leadership Q questionnaire. Check the columns where you have close scores. Try reading a profile that reflects the other combination of your close scores. Alternatively, show the profile detailed below to an individual who knows you well, such as a mate, boss, close friend, or team colleague, and ask for comments. If you are going through major life changes, try waiting until things have stabilized.

DEVELOPMENT EXERCISES FOR ADVOCATES

We may appear different in different situations. Over time we also grow and progress, but our basic preferences do not change. This has been proved by the large number of people who have retaken the Myers-Briggs Type Indicator in different periods of their lives and repeatedly come out with the same preferences. Thus, an abstract intuitive Thinker never really becomes a concrete sensing Thinker. A structured Judger never really becomes a flexible, go-with-the-flow Perceiver. A Green Advocate never becomes a dyed-in-the-wool Gold Conservator.

People who succeed, however, instinctively or deliberately learn to develop their nonpreferences. This softens their blind spot and enables them to adapt to the demands of different people and situations. Listed below are exercises that will help you develop your nonpreferences. Jung referred to this process as individuation.

Exercise 1. Finishing Projects

Advocates are adaptable, flexible, and open to new options. They delay making decisions until the last minute. As a result, their world is filled with unfinished projects and many frustrated associates. This openness is part of their flexibility. If taken to an extreme, this flexibility is counterproductive and probably is the most important reason why this type derails.

- Identify a couple of partially completed projects. Try to determine why you were constantly pulled away from them. Identify and note those impulses. Were they boredom, the need to get more information, or not having the appropriate materials around.
- Set aside a block of time, say, three hours, in the most productive period of your day. Make sure you have all the information and materials you need. If you are an Extravert, ask a detail person to work with you. Finish one or all projects in the time allotted. Note how satisfying it feels to have them out of the way. Savor the moment. Enjoy the feeling of control. File this feeling in your memory for future recall.
- From here on, when making a to-do list each day, circle with a color felt pen the one or two items that need to be completed no matter what.

The point is that in a short time you will find that (1) you have a greater sense of control in your life, (2) you have the respect of more structured types around you, and (3) you have eliminated a lot of the clutter in your life. This is called "type development," which means softening your blind spots.

Exercise 2. Giving Instructions

The strong, intuitive mind-set of the Advocate often results in instructions that are vague and impressionistic. These instructions do not work well with Sensors (over 70 percent of the population), who need specific guidelines and a concrete plan of action. Poor instructions often lead to frustration, wasted time, and significant misunderstandings in the workplace.

Write your instructions or plan of action on a piece of paper. Check that the following conditions are met.

- You have worked out the details in advance. Ask yourself when, where, what, how, and why.
- You are brief and specific about what needs to be done.
- You have demonstrated why the project makes sense, why it is needed, and what the practical applications are.
- If action is needed, give specific instructions; do not assume that others will read between the lines. For example, write "Materials need to go out before the end of the week," not "We should thing about sending materials."

The point is that other people take in information differently than you do. They cannot be productive unless that difference is honored.

Exercise 3. Depersonalizing Criticism

Ask someone who is blunt (a Thinker) to critique something of value to you: a project, an idea, an outfit, a room decoration. Pay attention to your reactions to his or her comments. How do your intellect and feelings interact? What are your bodily reactions? Note them below.

Can you sort out the facts you are hearing from your feelings about them?

- The critique:

- Facts:

- Feelings:

The point is that it is important to depersonalize criticism. It helps us grow and usually is not personal.

Exercise 4. Working with Other Types

You have been assigned to cohead a project with Joan R., a well-regarded manager who is considered to be on the fast track. She is a Gold Conservator. She differs from you in two major preferences. She is a Sensor (concrete, fact-driven, and sequential) and a Judger (structured and goal-oriented).

This assignment is important to your career. Her impression of you will determine future assignments.

Read the Gold Conservator personality profile summary. Write down some of the key differences below.

Joan R.   **Me**

1.   1.

2.   2.

3.   3.

4.   4.

    Read the section on how to persuade a Gold Conservator. Note the points below. Incorporate them into the presentation you will make at your initial meeting.

1.

2.

3.

    Read through your blind spots. Note which of them will be most irritating to her. Devise a strategy.

My Blind Spot   **Strategy**

1.   1.

2.   2.

Now repeat this exercise with a real person you have to work with who is different from you. It can be a boss, colleague, or client. Look at the overall four color descriptions and the section on how to recognize each color group.

My Type _____   **His or Her Type** _____

How to Persuade:

Blind Spots   **Strategy**

Photocopy your comments and keep them someplace where they are easily accessible.

The point is that if you do this exercise often enough, you not only will be more effective with that person but will learn to appreciate what he or she brings to the table. Soon you will expand that understanding to other people and become known for your skills in managing people. This is the path to leadership.

Exercise 5. How to Be a Better Leader

- Turn back to your leadership style summary.
- Choose one strategy for increased leadership effectiveness.
- Write it on an index card and develop three specific steps to achieve that strategy.
- Place the card someplace where you will see it frequently. Read it several times a day.
- After several weeks repeat the process with another strategy.

DIANE SAWYER
Journalist
ABC News

It is the afternoon of Diane Sawyer's birthday, and we meet in her dressing room. She has just returned from a celebratory lunch and in less than 90 minutes will be poised for the cameras, picture perfect as always. But at this moment she is, well, slightly rumpled, endearingly so given the fabled natural beauty and the dazzling smile with which she greets us.

She has been up well before the first light of dawn on this chilly December day. She arrived, as she does each working day, at 4:15 A.M. and will stay till well past 9 in the evening. In addition to her biweekly duties as coanchor of *20/20,* she is currently the cohost of *Good Morning America.* By all the standards of the business that is a full schedule.

Striving for excellence started early for Sawyer, who grew up in Louisville, Kentucky, the younger of two girls. Her father, a gentle and introspective man, was a judge who composed country music in his free time. Her mother, an elementary school teacher, took Diane to every type of lesson possible: piano, fencing, classical guitar, children's theater, tap, ballet, voice, and horseback riding.

For most of her early adolescence she recalls being a nonconformist, klutzy, and "tediously serious." She and her friends would go off to a creek to read Emerson and Thoreau. They called themselves the "reincarnated transcendentalists." "My sister was the elegant one," she recalls. "I was the one who kept falling down the stairs."

Others remember it differently. They remember that she was class vice president and a cheerleader. They also remember her entering and winning the U.S. Junior Miss pageant. The victory had its price, however, including having to wear her crown and sash at all times, even on planes. It also had its rewards, the most important being an $11,000 scholarship that was applied to Wellesley College the next year.

After graduating from Wellesley in 1967, she put in three years as weathergirl and news reporter in Louisville. The experience was marred by her 20/400 vision. Prevented from wearing glasses on camera, she could not see the weather map. She made up for it in other ways, such as sprinkling her reports with quotes from Emily Dickinson.

In 1971 she moved to Washington, D.C., and became part of the Nixon White House, initially as an assistant to the press secretary, Ron Ziegler. Her job was hectic, and she did not furnish her apartment, opting instead to sleep on a mattress on the floor for three years. She first met Nixon while heading for the photocopying room with scissors in hand. She knocked him over. The Secret Service grabbed her, and thus began an enduring relationship. "You could get hurt that way," Nixon cheerfully said to her.

A year later she became the President's staff assistant. When Nixon resigned in the wake of the Watergate scandal, she joined a small band of aides who, under the glare of a frenzied press, boarded the plane with him to return to San Clemente. It was 1974. She expected to stay for four months but remained for four years, helping him write his memoirs. She also created a flowchart that traced the events and players of Watergate and the links between them.

Many who knew Sawyer derided her decision to join the disgraced President. Today she says, "I am by nature loyal. I worked for this man; he had been good to me, and now he was asking something of me. I have never regretted the decision."[38]

In time the memoirs were finished, and she returned to Washington, D.C. CBS hired her, but the heavy hitters there—Dan Rather among them—were initially very vocal about having someone tainted by Watergate hovering in their tent. In a short time they capitulated. They were in awe of her stamina; during the Iranian hostage crisis she spent a week parked at the State Department, often sleeping no more than an hour a day, propped up on two chairs. They also were disarmed by her charm and ability to let her ego go for the sake of the story.

In 1981 she was promoted to the *CBS Morning News* show, and 3 years later she was chosen to be the first female correspondent on the prestigious team at *60 Minutes,* the most popular show in the history of television. In the next 5 years she would handle 82 stories for the show, jetting worldwide some 200,000 miles per year.

It was during a transatlantic flight that she met her future husband, the noted film and stage director Mike Nichols. "I tried to hide from him," she recalls. "My skin was broken out, and my hair was a mess." Fate intervened. They met on the plane and had several subsequent meetings in New York to discuss a profile for *60 Minutes*. The interview never took place, but the marriage, did a year later at a friend's house on Martha's Vineyard. Today the two circulate between homes in New York, Connecticut, and Los Angeles, but Diane's tastes remain simple. "Give me a room, a bed, a chair, a TV, and my books and I am happy," she notes with a grin, referring to her famed lack of domesticity.

By that time her interviewing skills were much talked about. A CBS producer was reported to say, "She has the skills of a surgeon, except that she gets under the skin of her subject without drawing blood."[39] She attributes this ability to being prepared—reading the extra book or making the additional phone calls; others, however, say it is an intuitive touch. People like Diane and open themselves to her without even being aware of it.

In 1989 ABC wooed her away to coanchor the news magazine *Prime Time Live,* which has since been merged with *20/20.*

There are many polarities to Diane Sawyer. She is at once aloof and warm, earnest and irreverent, intense and funny, authoritative and vulnerable. She is known as an intellectual who also excels at portraying glitz and froth. Most of all she is both intensely private and genuinely interested in people.

Such seeming contradictions are best explained by examining the special traits of her personality group. Green Advocates are insightful and original thinkers who are genuine idealists. They find their deepest calling in creating a better world. To that end, they use whatever avenues are available to them—work, volunteer activities, and contacts—in a myriad of often hidden ways.

Rarely do they choose to head an organization or manage extensive resources. Instead, they rely on their almost psychic ability to understand the motivations of others. Their management style is caring and participative. They dislike rules and procedures and avoid structures that curtail their freedom. Most of all they crave variety and change; to that end they will pursue an almost overwhelming array of new ideas and activities.

Advocates are also intensely loyal, focusing their loyalty on individuals rather than institutions. Introverted Advocates such as Sawyer also prefer quality to quantity in relationships. They need large blocks of time alone and use solitude to recharge their internal batteries and create new ideas. It is these moments of privacy that provide the energy needed to meet the demands of a highly public life.

They are flexible and easy until someone steps on one of their values. Then a toughness comes to the fore that usually takes others by surprise.

Leadership Style

Sawyer defines her goal as "to keep finding something that matters. All your difficult decisions can be triangulated if you go where your greatest joy meets the world's need. Of course, today you have to be ready to sail in a different way, but it is still about seeing something that excites you and that will excite others. Staying connected to that joy is what changes the world faster than anything else."

What energizes her the most? "Thinking about the story," she replies, "and figuring out how to tell it so that it moves people."

On the flip side, stressful activities include "the appearance stuff," having to worry about hair and makeup. "I should be on radio," she notes disarmingly.

Asked what she finds boring, she points to the mounds of paperwork and reading needed to crack "the nut" of a story. When you cover five to six stories each morning and also do work for *20/20* in the afternoon, that is a lot of nuts to crack, "and getting there does get tedious," she admits.

Sawyer describes her leadership strengths as seeing the big picture and how people fit into it. "I love writing scripts," she says, "but I like to capture the overall structure first, then, with others, fill in the small factual details. So my first drafts often say blah blah blah (details of early life), then something profound." She gives a sheepish grin.

"To me," she continues, "it is still about finding the sweet spot, and that is the point where the thing you care about meets and joins with what matters most to others. When you do find it you actually launch an idea into the world and make people think in new ways. And that is very satisfying."

Others call her relentless, but to Sawyer it is mostly about pursuing something that "is so beautiful that you just have to get there, no matter what."

The challenge is to stay at the "edge of competence," as she calls it. It is the place where "everything is still new and you are awake for it all. I always wanted to move on as soon as it got familiar and comfortable."

Thoughtful and complex, Advocates lead by offering penetrating insights to others. They judge issues by inner ideals and values. They value authenticity and are genuinely committed to the growth of the people around them, whether the staff or the public at large. Driven by an inner moral compass, they rarely care about how others judge them.

Advocates are also gifted communicators. They have an elegant and almost lyrical writing style. With some training they can become powerful public speakers, capturing their audiences with the intensity of their convictions. They listen closely and provide an abundance of verbal and nonverbal feedback. It is their great gift, and it makes the receivers feel understood and valued.

Advice to Others

Sawyer is reluctant to give advice, feeling that most people find their own way. "All I know," she says, "is to be brave and laugh a lot." Still, she comments on the many who come in for interviews who are so polished and trained for cameras and presentations. "I always ask them," she says thoughtfully, "'What is it you want to tell people?' And they look at me like I just spoke in Urdu. They haven't asked themselves that. After all, it is the teleprompter that's supposed to tell you what to say."

Of course, it helps that the numbers speak in women's favor these days, she admits. The self-confidence issues are different when you are one of 40 as opposed to having a lot of women around. Still, the basics remain. "Connect to what you care deeply about" is Sawyer's only piece of advice.

LAURA ZISKIN
Film Producer
Laura Ziskin Productions

In today's Hollywood women form alliances, throw each other baby showers, and make blockbuster movies. In a move that surprised many in the industry, Laura Ziskin stepped away from a position as president of Fox 2000 to return to what she loves best: producing films.

She used to head a division at 20th-Century Fox that was mandated to make six to ten feature films a year. It was a business that had been started from scratch with the objective of creating a unit run by a woman to tap into the female market more effectively.

She signed on for other reasons. From almost the beginning of her 20-year career Ziskin has balanced work against complicated family demands. First there were several stepchildren from a previous marriage and then the responsibility of being a single parent for her daughter, Julia. Ziskin was a highly regarded producer for 12 years with credits that include *Pretty Woman, No Way Out, The Doctor, As Good As It Gets,* and *What About Bob?* In 1990 she was about to start working on *To Die For,* which entailed moving to Canada for five months. Her 10-year-old daughter said she would not go and started to cry. "We had never been separated," she recalls. "We always got tutors, and she traveled with me on location." This was a turning point, and Ziskin realized that her life would have to change.

Shortly afterward she accepted the position at Fox. As a highly respected producer, she did not want to become a "suit." It was a difficult compromise for her. She still thinks of herself as more of a "creative talent" than a manager: "I took it because of personal reasons, and even then because it was a start-up where I could have some impact."

Leadership in business usually means building institutions, which is a natural goal for Golds and Blues but not for Green Advocates. They prefer leading small creative organizations that downplay hierarchy and rules and promote originality and fun.

Having an impact in the world of films, however, is a high priority, and Ziskin has grappled with that issue. "I think women still tend not to be heard as clearly as men," she says. "I used to think it was the timbre of the voice, so I would repeat things. Then, 20 minutes later, a man would say, 'What about . . .' and all the men in the room would sit up and pay attention to the very point you had made earlier. Ideas are power, but not unless someone listens to them."

Today people are listening. To bring movies to fruition she deals with writers, directors, actors and actresses, accountants, and distributors. Her goal is to try to create something of significance while making money. "The most difficult thing about this culture," she says, "is that the main value is greed. My daily quest is to find things that will stimulate, excite, and keep people engaged while still providing the necessary profits."

Ziskin, the middle child of two psychologists, originally aspired to be an actress. It was a single-minded interest from an early age that was not supported by her parents. While still a student in the drama department of the University of Southern California School of Cinema, she found that another girl was getting the parts she wanted. Pragmatically, she changed dreams and decided to learn how to run the entire show instead. She became a producer, ultimately teaming up with the likes of Sally Field, Disney, and Sony.

She feels women excel in producing. "They are better able to marshal and nurture people," she notes, "particularly in an industry governed by the egos and insecurities of the artists."

Leadership Style

Ziskin describes her style as "laissez-faire." "I am very good about seeing the whole picture and trying to keep everyone focused on it," she says. The rest is mostly about choosing the right team.

She is most energized by the creative aspects of film production: putting the elements together, solving script problems, and editing. The stressful parts of the job include having to say no to movie ideas. "I never feel comfortable saying to people that their work is not good enough. In fact, I hope they prove me wrong," she says, "and I'll be among the first to go out and buy a ticket." Like other Green Advocates, "I am intolerant of conflict," she says, "and not interested in mediating it. It makes me uncomfortable. If people can't work it out, then they have to go."

She says about the financial aspects of filmmaking, "I look at it as an algebra problem. I like the deal-making part, which is creative. The rest I can't get too excited about." The day-to-day management of expenses gets delegated to others.

Ziskin understands her strengths and plays to them. "Power is the ability to accomplish what you want to accomplish," she says. "And for me that means coming up with fresh ideas, being an architect and builder rather than just bidding on existing properties."

Advocates need to believe in the value of their work and find creative ways to express themselves. Intuitive and complex, they can be very persuasive in getting others to support their ideas without feeling the need to impose their views on others. They enjoy novelty and despite a generally easygoing manner often challenge the status quo. They dislike conflict, avoid confrontation where possible, and have trouble dealing with criticism. Making money and dealing with budgets, while a necessary part of their endeavors, are rarely a priority. Having fun and making a difference usually are.

Advice to Others

"Have patience and perseverance. If you believe in something and stick to it, you will succeed."

WENDY WASSERSTEIN

Playwright, Pulitzer Prize Winner
The Heidi Chronicles, An American Daughter,
The Sisters Rosensweig

At first she actually wanted to be normal. She applied to law school and then to business school and at one point thought about medical school. In between she fielded calls from her mother, Lola, who checked in daily for a progress report on the marriage front. At the end, Wendy Wasserstein took a different route; she opted to become extraordinary.[40]

She was born in Brooklyn, New York, the youngest of four siblings. All the children became superachievers, including brother Bruce, a wheeler-dealer investment banker and cofounder of Wasserstein Perrella & Co. Her mother was original and flamboyant. She believed that all her children were destined for greatness and pushed them in every direction possible. This included having the three girls attend the Helena Rubinstein Charm School just in case.

From an early age Wasserstein put on plays with her stuffed animals. "I always knew I was funny," she says today. "Even at 7 I would look at a sitcom and think to myself, I can do better than that. I just never thought you could make a career out of the theater."

She attended Mount Holyoke College in Massachusetts. Later she would say, "I figured if I attended one of the seven sister colleges, my parents would stop trying to get me married." After graduating with a degree in history, she studied creative writing at the City University of New York. Shortly afterward her first play, *Any Woman Can't,* was produced off Broadway in 1973. She was 27 years old. The success of that production prompted her to enter Yale University's school of drama. She earned a master's in 1976, and a year later her first major success, *Uncommon Women and Others,* opened as a full-sscale off-Broadway production in New York. In this play as in others she explored the large changes in the lives of women over the last generation. Her plays are comical and full of one-liners, but they have serious undertones, often viewed through the lens of her own experience of choosing personal satisfaction over traditional roles.

In the mid-1980s she began work on her most notable play, *The Heidi Chronicles,* which went on to win both a Tony award and the Pulitzer Prize. The success of that production brought to an end the many years of doubt. She knew that the unconventional road had been the right choice.

Fast-forward to December 1999. At age 49, Wasserstein has just given birth to her first child, Lucy Jane, father not yet announced. The birth was a production in itself. The baby was born three months premature. A famous costume designer decorated the hospital room, and a disguised Meryl Streep (Wasserstein's friend from Yale Drama School) sneaked in to see the baby. Wasserstein was her usual humorous self. She referred to the neonatal intensive care unit where Lucy Jane had just spent three months as a "Jewish boarding school with a heavy emphasis on the sciences." In reality she had been debating having the child for many years. On her fortieth birthday to-do list, she noted, "Write a play, lose weight, have a baby." The process just took a little longer than expected.

Today, at this significant moment of her life, she encapsulates many of the aspirations of her generation of women: being feminine, having children, and gaining power and money. The question is how to do it all and how to do it well.[41]

Leadership Style

There are many sides to Wasserstein; she is caustic, gently funny, and serious. Leadership for a writer, she notes, means something different. "As opposed to figuring out what people want to hear," she says, "I have to honestly try to figure out what it is I am hearing." In the world of theater it is also about establishing and nurturing a community. "People come together and laugh and cry together," she continues. "You can't talk down to them." Of course, putting on a play is both thrilling and terrifying, she admits. She finds the collaboration involved in making a play happen one of the many energizing aspects of being involved with the theater: "Other people further your vision and expand your work."

Asked what she finds stressful, she says, "When you can't fix it or you know that you have hit your limitation." Dealing with criticism also can be stressful, she admits. A bad review can mean that a play is not going to run, and so opening night can be tense. Also, the criticism is relative and depends on many circumstances. For example, she points to an earlier play, *An American Daughter*, that opened to mixed reviews two years ago. Now there is new interest, and it will be produced for television. That makes up for a lot of the earlier stress.

In her free time she and her friends take high school students to plays, courtesy of a special fund set up for young New Yorkers. It is her way to introduce the next generation to the field that has brought her so much satisfaction.

Wasserstein is an introverted Advocate, deep and full of contradictions. Serious, fun, flexible, and insightful, she has many layers that she does not reveal. Telling a good story, however, is one way of communicating her values, sense of fairness, and aspirations for the world. Like others in her color group, she uses her profession to further the cause of human development.

Advice to Others

"Keep writing. It is very easy to negate and undermine yourself. Also, beware of temptations such as the lure of Los Angeles and the large amounts of money you can earn writing in a group. The danger is that you lose your voice."

PEGGY DULANY
President
Synergos Institute

She was always considered one of the more unorthodox of the younger Rockefellers, so much so that Oliver Tambo, president of the African National Congress, made a point of admonishing her not to get arrested outside the South African embassy. "We have enough people who can do that," he told her. "What we do need is someone with your business connections." With that a new seed was planted; the notion that there was a way of, as Peggy articulates it, "using resources specifically to help people bridge gaps." Bringing that idea to full fruition, however, took another 20 years.[42]

Bridging business and philanthropic interests is of special interest to many Advocate leaders, for whom the traditional model of creating wealth is rarely the point. For them, money serves other purposes, including self-development and sustaining the development of others. Peggy Rockefeller is a prime example. Her nonprofit company, Synergos Institute, focuses on promoting entrepreneurial activities at the grassroots level of developing countries. For example, Synergos set out to develop "village tourism" in western Zimbabwe by connecting local organizations to international businesses and agencies. It also helped set up a foundation in Ecuador which funded the training of 1,200 women who make "panama hats." The women ultimately formed a cooperative, eliminated the middlemen, found their own source of straw, and developed markets in Europe. To achieve those goals she used her considerable family and business connections with the unabashed finesse of a born deal maker.

She is the great-grandchild of John D. Rockefeller, Sr., founder of Standard Oil, and the daughter of David Rockefeller, former chairman of Chase Manhattan Bank, the fourth of his six children. The family wealth is legendary. Their estate, Pontico Hills, is a 3000-acre enclave 30 miles north of New York City dotted with sculptures by

Picasso, Maillol, and Henry Moore. So impressed was playwright George Kaufman when he visited that he was overheard to mutter, "This is what God would do if he had had the money." To be born into this privileged world is to be born to unimaginable security. It is also, however, to be born into a class confined by the very possessions that create its distinction. For many people it is a road to nowhere.[43]

Not for Peggy. Through introspection and work experience, she has tapped into the innermost fibers of her style. It is her personal philosophy of "bridging leaders" that gives new meaning to the Advocate leadership profile.

We met in her New York City town house in a pleasant book-lined space that encompasses living room, dining room, and kitchen. The 14-foot ceilings accentuate the architectural openness favored by this group. She is unpretentious to the extreme, dressed in casual slacks and a sweater with no makeup, a personal style shared by many in this group. "Have you had lunch," she asked solicitously. Peggy belongs to the more reflective type of Advocates. She is warm but not gregarious. Her low-key demeanor, however, belies the force of her vision. At 51 she is clearly entering a new phase in her life.

Her interest in social change began at age 19, when she was invited by a family friend to visit Brazil. She went but insisted on spending the summer in the type of squatter community known as a favela. That experience revolutionized her views. She had planned to be a writer, but after that summer she turned to the social sciences. Ultimately, she got a doctorate in education from Harvard and ran an alternative high school for troubled adolescents in a lower-middle-class community in Boston. The enduring lesson of that period was, she recalls, that you always have many interest groups around a problem. The key is to bridge them.

After six years she moved to New York with her two-year-old son, realizing that she needed a larger and more global stage.

In 1986 she began exploring ways to start her own venture, focusing on the vision of an organization that would engage in partnerships with local communities in third world countries. How and under what form were unclear. She set out on an international tour and began the search for financial resources. "That took a lot of time, many seven-day weeks," she recalls, "because the idea was so different and I talked a language that was not always clear to the business community whose financial backing I was seeking. I used words like *empowerment* and *fulfillment*. Those benefits were not selling points for them." They wanted to hear about actionable results, bottom-line applications, and economic growth. Like many advocates, Peggy is a gifted communicator, but initially her natural language was not appropriate for every audience.

Aware of the gap, she soon came to understand the need for a director who would complement her vision by providing analytic and administrative skills. She chose Bruce Schearer, a focused strategic thinker. Their values had always been in sync, but they battled when it came to goals and approaches. An example was his determination that the organization be more aggressive in taking credit for what it accomplished. "I understood what he was saying," she notes, "because in a sense it is true. You cannot sell if you don't emphasize what you have accomplished. But in my view this was violating some of the things we wanted to do, or at least some of the things we stood for."

Still, she gave him free rein. "I could see early on that his style was more convincing with some of the people we wanted to get to."

Leadership Style

Like many Greens, Peggy runs an organization in which people have a great deal of autonomy and individual differences are honored. She allows the contributions of others to surface. Esprit de corps, enthusiasm, and cooperation are encouraged, and the Synergos staff members frequently comment that the human needs of the organization receive conscientious attention. As is the case with other well-developed Advocates, her style is marked by a finely tuned ability to see the possibilities of both the institution and the people with whom she works.

The leadership style she aspires to is that of a "bridging leader," a new paradigm that has been evolving in both her verbal and her written presentations; and that she hopes will rebalance the world in a way that women will be key in helping to create. "As the world shifts from independence to interdependence, from control to connection, from competition to collaboration, and from tightly linked geopolitical alliances to loosely coupled global networks," she ruminates, "we need to encourage both bridging leaders and bridging institutions. Bridging leaders seek out and develop connections to groups other than just the ones with which they are affiliated. By joining forces across sectors, disciplines, and beliefs, we extend like a chain of trust across seemingly unbridgeable gaps." Few have summarized the Advocate ideal as eloquently.

Peggy also understands her own liabilities and blind spots: "I am not a detail person, and I am not very fond of staff meetings, particularly when they involve detailed planning. I have also been accused of overpersonalizing things. I know what people are saying, but one must view this trait in a larger framework. When we first go into a country, we identify our partnerships through individuals. At the onset at least, that relationship is the partnership, so personalizing it is not a bad thing. Later, of course, the partner becomes a group—local or governmental—so it requires a different approach." Dealing with confrontation, she admits, is also somewhat problematic. "I defuse rather than engage in it," she says somewhat sheepishly.

Peggy's leadership style is based on an enthusiastic commitment to the cause she leads. She has always understood at a gut level that Synergos must not be known only as a Rockefeller-funded organization, otherwise people will not contribute to it. "They'll think to themselves," she says, "that we don't need the money." While she has contributed substantially, the total is less than 10 percent of the yearly budget. Foundations, Fortune 500 companies, and supporters make up the balance, yet at the end of the day it is her charisma that pulls many in. This was evidenced at a recent fund-raising dinner attended by many of New York's most powerful in commerce, politics, and Wall Street. The room was palpably hushed during her presentation. The power brokers were moved, and that evening they gave more generously than usual, many without understanding why.

Advice to Others

"Being a bridger is a different form of leadership that is often not recognized as much. Hence, it takes a certain degree of self-confidence to recognize you are on to something that can work. If you have the natural inclination to bring people together to solve problems, don't give up! Keep working to do it more effectively. You can make a difference. But don't look to get all the credit. Joint work means shared credit, and it is more important to achieve the goal than to get credit for getting it done."

ABIGAIL DISNEY
President
The Daphne Foundation

She grew up in a small town near Burbank, California. As the grand-niece of the visionary Walt Disney, she led a sheltered existence in a society and age known for surfeit and affluence. It was the 1970s, and while her classmates developed cocaine fingers and came of age in designer clothes, Roy Disney kept his brood of four on a tight leash. Weekends were spent at family outings. "In our community," she remembers with a chuckle, "we always had the least: secondhand cars and down-to-earth clothes. We resented it then and appreciate it now. Once I asked my mother to what class we belonged. "'Middle,' she answered, and then paused for a moment. 'Well, maybe upper middle.'"

Still by most standards it was a privileged life. The Disneys lived in a large Art Deco house formerly owned by Norman McLeod, director of the Marx Brothers. Abigail went to Yale, where she first became conscious of what it means to carry a globally recognized name. "It was embarrassing both socially and politically. People point at you," she recalls. "They treat you differently; they cut you more slack and have a need to be near you. Of course, they are also quick to criticize and remember that you had spinach between your teeth. And that is the story that gets told over and over again." Like many young Advocates with substantial wealth, Abigail was embarrassed by her family's economic and social advantages.

"I had to teach myself how to get used to it," she says, but that would take many more years. First she took a year to work as an au pair in Ireland, responding to a need to do menial work and compensate for her unearned privilege. Later there was more academic work, attending Stanford to earn a master's. She moved to New York, married, and became actively involved in philanthropic circuits.

"At first," she recalls, "I did not understand how much money I had and what I could do with it. So I got involved in a settlement house program and started doing laundry for poor families. It was important for me that the work be as physical as possible and that I give the maximum of my time. Soon I was involved with other volunteers, spending 40 hours a week organizing others, which is not my strength to begin with." Disney refers to this as her "pretzel-thinking" years, coming to terms with the burdens of her inheritance.

Shortly afterwards Disney started a doctorate in English at Columbia. Advocates pursue knowledge for its own sake and, when circumstances permit, earn advanced degrees. She simultaneously immersed herself in the dynamics of grant making and the intricacies of funding a private foundation.

Fortuitously, she met Helen Hunt, a noted philanthropist of the Hunt family who had fought her brothers to gain control over her money. It was an immediate click and would prove to be a turning point in Disney's life: "Helen's experience showed me that I was reacting in a predictable way, the way many women with trust funds do. The tendency is to downplay any display of affluence, dress shabbily, and live in lower-level apartments."

"This is a dicey relationship" she points out, illustrating her type's need for participative management. "The power is all on one side. Donors typically do not acknowledge the reality of that power. They don't see that the executive directors of the foundation who receive the money cannot be straight with them. The directors cannot tell you that they need a salary increase or that they are working too many hours and jumping through enormous hoops to get things done."

Her sensitivity to these issues prompted her to form her own foundation while in her mid-thirties, earlier than most philanthropists take this step. Her goal was to provide a source of reliable support year in and year out for the staff working at the grassroots level. They would not need to beg for annual funding. In typical nonconformist fashion she also decided to support lesser known groups ignored by other, more status-driven donors.

Today, true to her Advocate's need for constant change and variety, she has added a new interest: the world of publishing. Hoping to start her own firm, at 38 she is back in school, sandwiching publishing courses between raising four children under the age of 9.

"I think publishing is altruistic," she notes. "Otherwise, I would not consider doing it. It contributes to the culture by bringing fine works to the world." The lure is precisely that she is in a position to set up a firm that can afford to back riskier works.

While to other groups these convictions may appear somewhat Pollyanna-ish, to Advocates they are real. Greens are among the most idealistic of all the types. They view the world through the lenses of human development, theirs and others. They see possibilities in people. They need to lead a life that has personal meaning and contributes to the well-being of others.

Leadership Style

"I try to emphasize consensus," she says, "and to always go the extra mile to get it." Advocates are particularly sensitive to the interpersonal atmosphere; they bring harmony to groups and suffer more than others from conflict and discord. Disney admits it readily. "I am not good at conflict. I had to train myself to stay in the room. Before that I used to break out in a sweat and sometimes even suffered from nosebleeds when my anxiety was extreme. I have taught myself to recognize the response, to name it and to manage myself. I say to myself: 'This is a conflict. You are having a reaction; take a deep breath and stay with it.'"

Criticism is another problem area for most Greens "It is my biggest flaw," admits Abigail. "Often I do not even recognize my inability to deal with it. In fact, I have been in situations where I took a position I didn't even believe in because I felt threatened."

Advice to Others

"Know yourself well, particularly the unconscious motivations that may not be as good as they should be. Don't let fashion hold you back from doing things that feel right. Always mention the elephants (hidden agendas) in the room. Most people are relieved when you do."

JANET THUESEN
Managing Partner
Otto Kroeger Associates

In the late 1970s, Janet Thuesen worked at the White House. It was Jimmy Carter's era, and she was hired for a new unit that would provide organizational development services to the administration and Congress. "I did a lot of work on the Hill with congressional offices, trying to open up some paths of communication," she says, remembering the chaos of that period. "It was heady and painful. There was constant change and turmoil."

A colleague suggested that she meet Otto Kroeger, the noted Myers-Briggs consultant. It did not happen for 2 years, but when they finally got together, they hit it off. "He proposed and then turned around and said to me, 'My business is a mess. If you can straighten it out, you can have it.'" Thuesen took on the challenge. She went through his briefcase—which was his office—and found piles of bills, checks, and invoices. After sorting through them for several days, she decided the main part of the business was organizational development with a focus on using psychological types. From there, the husband-wife team began developing workshops to help people understand the Myers-Briggs personality model. Now, in addition to having their own training and conference center, they have 7 full-time administrative staff members and 17 training associates. They do training in Kuwait, India, the United Kingdom, Germany, Australia, and Nigeria. Together have coauthored *Type Talk, Type Talk at Work,* and *16 Ways to Love Your Lover.*

It was a long road from Michigan, where Thuesen grew up, the only child of Danish immigrants. Her parents owned a bakery, where she first learned to be an entrepreneur. "I worked at everything from cleaning the pans to helping my father bake," she recalls with a wry smile. Marriage, three children, a divorce, and a master's in counseling and organizational development followed. "I never knew what I wanted to do," she says, "but I always believed that if you do your best, keep learning, and keep your eyes open, something interesting always pops up." This is a refrain heard from many Advocate leaders, who change professions more frequently than do any other personality groups.

Leadership Style

"My style of leadership is one of risk taking and adventure," she says, "but I always keep one foot anchored to the ground." Her strengths include a positive belief in the individuals with whom she works. For the most part, she notes, they rise to the occasion and do their best.

What activities are most inspiring to her? "I love the training," she says in a passionate tone. "When Otto and I are training together, it's fun. We bounce off each other, and the interaction with the group is always great." Others recognize this passion. "People often tell me that I am very affirming and sensitive to people's needs."

Asked what she finds stressful and boring, she quickly highlights taxes, finances, and organizing training schedules. These are things that need to be done but that she does not particularly enjoy. Thuesen's blind spots come from trusting too much. "We have been ripped off by former staff members three times," she says. "Last time it was to the tune of $300,000." She was the company's finance person and was in charge of all the accounts. It took many months to uncover the fraud. Thuesen recognizes that because of her trust and her lack of interest in financial issues, things like this can happen.

Advice to Others

"Always keep your eyes and ears open for anything that all of the sudden lights a spark in you. Be willing to work very hard and do whatever it takes to make your effort a success."

ROSEMARY JORDANO
CEO
ChildrenFirst, Inc.

At a low child's table the lawyer sits between his pint-sized daughters. His Hermes tie is flipped over his shoulder for protection against the jelly drippings of the sandwich the 4-year-old directs toward his mouth. John, as we shall call him, is taking time out away from his high-powered practice for a visit to the ChildrenFirst backup child care center in Boston. His wife is bedridden, suffering from severe back pain. Fortunately, his firm provides and pays for emergency day care, a fast-growing benefit for busy parents.

He can thank Rosemary Jordano, founder and CEO, who started the company with personal and credit card debts. The oldest of three children, she was the first in her family to go to college. Her father was an independent painting contractor who most enjoyed painting church steeples and altars. Her mother, a homemaker and sometime secretary, was the valedictorian of her high school class but shortly afterward went to work to help pay for her brothers' college tuition.

Jordano graduated magna cum laude with degrees in economics and psychology from Wellesley. She went on to get a master's in developmental psychology from Oxford in England and an MBA from Stanford. In between she worked as an investment banker for Merrill Lynch.

While she was at Stanford, her mother was diagnosed with breast cancer. Jordano traveled every weekend from San Francisco to Boston to be with her. During the weekends the two would spend many hours talking. "She made me think through the goals of my life," she says, recalling the intensity of that period. "She stressed the importance of doing things that touch your heart and honor your soul. But she also would ask me whether I was ready for the stress and financial risks that starting my own company would entail." Her mother passed away that year, but she remains the principal inspiration behind the culture of the firm.

At age 30, Jordano sent a business plan to her professor at Stanford. His comment was that the plan outlined a social service, not a business. She was initially devastated but then worked with him to think it through and convert it into a business model. He suggested that she offer the service to a consortium of companies. They would offer backup child care services to their employees at a reasonable cost to both the company and the employee. Each year Jordano returns to the professor's class when he presents her company as a case study. She always enjoys hearing the words "she proved me wrong."

She started the company by managing the on-site child care services provided by Wall Street firms. Two years later she made her first pitch to venture capitalists. The $3 million they provided, developed the business, providing the capital to build new centers. Today, 7 years later, the company serves roughly 200 businesses and has 20 centers caring for more than 20,000 children throughout the United States. This makes it the nation's largest provider of corporate-sponsored backup child care.

Advocates run firms in a very personal way, with a genuine commitment to the development of the staff and clients. They typically do not like to run large companies, preferring small creative groups that operate in a culture that reflects their values. While other types may view these goals as unrealistic, Advocates succeed because of their enthusiasm, deeply felt commitment, and ability to articulate their message.

Leadership Style

"I am collaborative, inclusive, passionate, and communicative," says Jordano. "I believe in leading with the heart. The rational side needs to be present, but a leader has to inspire." The difference between management and leadership, she notes, is that managers oversee the different functions that keep a business healthy, while leaders move others to follow them. This is particularly important today, when people work longer hours and do not live near their families. The workplace needs to be a community: "We need to nurture each other within the company the same way we expect our teachers to nurture the children."

The activities she finds most energizing are sales, client service, public relations, and all the culture-building aspects of the business. "I like to make sure," she says, "that the culture of the company is as crisp as it was the day we founded it."

When asked what she finds stressful and boring, she lists investor relations, raising money, and board meetings. "I understand finance," she notes, "but it is not what is satisfying to me. I let others do it."

Running effective board meetings, however, is important and is something she is working on actively. She recalls her first board meeting four years ago, attended by high-profile financial backers. "It was brutal," she says, wincing. "One of them came in and tore up the agenda despite the fact that I had vetted it with the entire board." Later the light bulb went on. "They were figuring out their roles to each other," she says. "It was not about me." It is still difficult, she admits, to understand what the expectations are and how honest one is expected to be.

As to blind spots, she admits to giving people the benefit of the doubt longer than is appropriate. Handling criticism and confrontation is still difficult. "I get flustered and do not hear what is being said to me," she says, "so I have learned to pause, breathe deeply, and calm myself. Then I look at the person and say, 'I think I heard you say this.'" This clarifies the issues.

Being true to oneself is the hallmark of an Advocate's leadership style. Advocates have a people-centered vision and excel at inspiring, motivating, and pulling others in behind them. They encourage openness, have extensive networks to draw on, and find unique ways of solving problems that are not evident to others. The flip side is that they respond very personally to criticism and confrontation.

Advice to Others

"Be authentic," she says. "Everyone wants to do business with people who have similar values, and the quicker you show who you are, the faster you build the relationships." Not that there is anything wrong with good public relations, she is quick to note, but you need to know when you are embellishing. "Don't fool yourself as well."

NADYA
Designer

She works in two very different worlds: in Bali, Indonesia, where the fabrics are made and fashioned into one-of-kind outfits, and in the United States, where the clothing is sold through special exhibitions. The clothes cannot be found in stores. Customers learn about the showings by word of mouth. Yet she dresses many prominent people and calls them her special community. It is an nontraditional approach to the competitive world of fashion, but it seems to work.

In Bali, where she designs and produces the clothes, she has a staff that, she says, "manage each other. I don't have to be a boss in that system. We are a collaborative team." She gives vague guidelines on her vision of the fabric and trusts the team to interpret them and turn them into a marketable product. The styles may be repeated, but the fabric combination always changes. She does not keep an inventory of the fabric or the finished product. She makes only two or three sizes of each design. She packs them in duffel bags and then ships them by the thousands to the United States four times a year. This unusual management style has inspired numerous collections that are sold in key cities in the United States.

Leadership Style

Nadya believes that she leads through her designs. "My clothes are designed to be inspirational," she says. "They should help people develop and express themselves. And in the process we create a community of shared values." Many of her clients are from the arts, the film industry, broadcasting, and the community of Jungian therapists.

Creating these communities and connecting her customers to each other are what energizes her the most. Bookkeeping and paperwork are stressful, and so she does practically none of that. An associate in the United States does the mailings. Asked how she deals with confrontation, she says she doesn't. That is why she has chosen to live in Bali. In Asia direct confrontation is not encouraged.

Nadya is a pronounced Advocate with an attitude that anything can be achieved through collaboration and humanistic goals. Authenticity and the ability to help others develop and express themselves are her top priorities. Her unusual business model enables her to put those ideals into practice.

Advice to Others

"Be true to yourself and follow your dream."

PART

3 Putting It All Together

17 Sag Factors: Career Derailment Spot Check

Dr. Bonnie Kellen

You have identified your leadership type and done your exercises. The results reveal that you have leadership qualities and potential. Why, then, is it not happening? Why have you not achieved to the extent you would like?

In my counseling practice I have noticed that there are often personality features, cutting across type, that limit the maximization of leadership potential. People are often unaware of what I term "sag factors," which cause motivation to droop and languish. We may think of the leadership profiles as having a stainless-steel quality, with leaders who are undaunted, consistent, self-disciplined, and highly motivated. What you need to remember is that these are descriptions of highly developed examples of particular leadership types. In your quest to develop your own leadership style, you may need to work through some sag factors while maintaining a vision of your peak performance.

There are different degrees of sag factors. Often people are unaware that they are projecting their inner landscapes onto the outer world. Many people can be highly functional and still be limited by these traits. Insight is the first step toward positive change. Keeping an open mind about the relevance of some of these sag factors in your life will give you an opportunity for growth. To help you further, this discussion culminates in a spot-check survey that will allow you to determine the extent to which your sag factors need to be addressed.

SELF-MANAGEMENT

Are you affected by fluctuations in your mood? Many highly functional people do not realize their thinking is tainted by depression or by anxiety and its close relative, fear. This does not fit the self-image of a confident and self-reliant leader, yet to a certain degree and in some circumstances many people are afflicted by doubt, negativity, and fear. Is it possible that someone who is a leader can be prone to feelings of discouragement, a sense of hopelessness, low energy, loss of pleasure, and a lowered ability to concentrate and make decisions—a negative cognitive, emotional state that will get a person stuck in a leadership fog? It is the management of this shadow side that frees you to pursue and attain your ideals.

For our ancestors, fear was associated with survival. The modern descendant of fear is worry. Perhaps that is why it is often a very strong reaction. For many people, however, the worry and anxiety to which they are subject far outweigh their usefulness. In fact, they hinder decision making and engender ambivalence and stress after decisions are made. Anxiety is experienced as "the dread that something bad will happen," whether to one's plans, one's children, one's money, or the world at large. Some people even believe that worrying prevents bad outcomes. At its worst a person beset by anxiety may be unable to act in the midst of uncertainty or ambiguity. A worried leader can create a culture of worry that inhibits optimism and the belief in the creative potential of others that is necessary for effective leadership. This rules out the possibility of the leader giving people the benefit of the doubt, trusting and empowering them to show initiative.

SELF-ESTEEM

Put simply, your self-esteem is related to the view you harbor of yourself: bright, dull, pretty, fat, competent, don't have what it takes. It's not that these terms are at the surface of your mind but that they subconsciously form a collective representation of your assets and liabilities. Self-esteem is inextricably linked to how you perceive yourself in comparison to others. It's important to remember that a sense of self-esteem has different degrees of objectivity. Some people always come out higher when they compare themselves to others; there is no one they would rather be than themselves. This is a measure of high self-esteem and becomes an automatic trigger for self-confidence and initiative.

TWO FEET IN THE DOOR/ COMMITMENT TO THE MOMENT

Have you noticed that some people are 100 percent present whatever they are doing? I call this commitment to the moment having both feet in the door. By contrast, many people hold back, are preoccupied, are not fully there. Our minds are elsewhere, perhaps because we are reserving our energy for the perfect moment, which is elusive. We have one foot out the door. Reserving our energy in this way deflects our commitment to decisions and drains our purposefulness.

DECISIVENESS QUOTIENT

A leader must be able to make a decision, determine a strategy, and request and obtain the resources necessary to get results. A leader is a doer as well as a planner. Part of the drag on some leadership decisions occurs when the leader has not resolved her predecision stresses. This is related to the ability to set specific goals as opposed to remaining ambivalent. If ambivalence continues after a decision is made or a goal is set, it interferes with the leader's strength of purpose. Decision making is a way to resolve ambiguity. An effective leader is able to contain, for herself and others, the anxiety and confusion engendered by the decision-making process. She is not threatened by the finality of a decision.

According to the executive coach Linda Seale, insisting on the resources necessary for implementation is as important as the decision itself. This empowers the people who have to put the decision into effect.

APPROACH, AVOID, ATTACK

In understanding what motivates you, how you characteristically respond to emotional challenges, the "approach, avoid, attack" framework can be instructive. There is a level of automatic response that people often bring to situations. However, this is not as simple as it appears. You can be physically there and feel and look like you are in the approach mode but still retain huge elements of avoid and attack motivation.

For effective leadership, the approach mode is essential. Behaviors associated with this mode are those of encouraging, cooperating, and guiding as well as setting protective limits. A person who can approach is confident that problems can be solved. She crosses bridges when she comes to them. She is not disposed to be guarded or suspicious. She is calm and open.

The avoid reaction, which can be hidden, is compounded of anger and fear. Rejection, withdrawal, and manipulation are all avoidance behaviors. The anger involved in avoidance can shade into attack. Retaliation, threats, and coercion appear in the attack mode.

Be aware of how complex your characteristic responses may be. This framework of approach, avoid, attack is used by Dr. Steven Stosney[44] to train compassionate parents. It is no accident that many of the problems you have to deal with in the workplace have deep elements of the reenactment of family dynamics.

SUPERCOUPLE SYNDROME

The pressure of being a female leader as well as a mother and wife can be overwhelming. As Wayne and Mary Sotile outline it in *Supercouple Syndrome*,[45] the new myth is that of the "Big Life." The superachieving couples of today have high expectations for fulfillment in family, career, and self. We must be superpeople with extraordinary coping abilities despite incredible stress. We used to have Ozzie and Harriet as our ideal family; now "having it all," the Big Life, is what we strive for. This new myth is as unrealistic as the old one. The sag factor here is believing that the hard-charging Type A traits appropriate to our careers (being competitive, striving for excellence, being in control, moving fast) can be just as effective in our personal lives. As the Sotiles warn, this "ready, set, go" lifestyle can lead to burnout and divorce.

I recommend developing a new balancing act which combines an understanding of your own and your family types, your work and leadership goals, and your unique needs and a program to reconcile these often competing areas and fight stress. In the absence of such a program, your leadership performance will be affected by a depletion of energy resulting from a downward spiral in your personal life. Ideally, couples can develop a lifestyle committed to using their relationship as a sanctuary from the pressures of the outside world, setting strict boundaries, and taking time to have fun and appreciate each other.

Many of the leaders profiled here have found it possible to combine career success with motherhood. These women seek highly competent caretakers with whom to share their children's upbringing. This is not as easy as it sounds. Subconsciously, many mothers want to be the "mother-in-chief" and therefore have caretakers who are somewhat lacking. This keeps the mother tied to the home.

There is another factor here with which successful women have to contend. For both men and women, self-esteem rises with success at work. While men's self-esteem continues to rise, that of women can peak and drop because of the guilt associated with the pull to be a first-class nurturer.

Women who are successful leaders are able to draw strict boundaries to protect quality time with their families. Having two feet in the door at home allows them to have two feet in the door at work. This is not to deny that they suffer conflict between work and children, but they are able to handle this conflict in a way that maximizes their efficiency in both spheres.

DEALING WITH SETBACKS

The ability to deal with setbacks in a positive way is a critical leadership quality. No matter what cards are dealt, the leader holds her own and plays the hand as well as she can. Her optimism and self-esteem buoy her ability to create new opportunities and move on. This scrappy, "can't be stopped" quality allows the leader to find stepping-stones and new directions where others would give up.

Many of the leaders described situations in their lives where they assessed that they could not win. They were able to make plans to move on. Change is not easy, and the sag factor here is that many people stay in ruts, deny the reality of the situation, and are more afraid of the risk of change than of stagnation. Leaders can move. What is important here is that both of these factors have to do with conquering fear and anxiety while maintaining a positive perspective. The sag factor is not being able to meet setbacks in an effective manner.

AT THE END OF THE DAY

No one is perfect. Give yourself a pat on the back for taking the time to learn about leadership and perhaps commit yourself to lifelong growth as a value. Many small steps consistently taken over time are the way to significant change.

KNOW YOURSELF!

Know who you are. Understanding your preferences and style is a good start, and finding the environment that will allow you to be your best self is the key. Understanding other types will make you fluent in connecting and establishing relationships with others.

After you know your type, know your own psychology: your strengths, defenses, fears, and values. Do you make the same mistakes again and again? Understand the impact your nuclear family has had on your development. Are remnants of your past blocking your present and future?

Learn about office politics, refine your timing, and decide what prizes are essential to you. We are not all born politically savvy, but establishing work relationships and trust is essential to leadership. Use whatever opportunities there are for developing this skill.

SEEK BALANCE IN YOUR LIFE

You do not have to sacrifice one area for another, but learn to set boundaries and limits that work. Variety tends to reenergize you when you droop in one area and prevents burnout.

Realize that life is long and that at different stages you may have different priorities. Enjoy each stage to the fullest but also give yourself the leeway to change at different junctions. Don't get stuck in ruts.

YOU DON'T HAVE TO DO IT ALONE

Nowadays individuals don't have to suffer through trouble spots alone, although unfortunately, many do. There are therapists, coaches, entrepreneurial networks, and courses. Create your own support group that works for you.

It's your life. Take ownership of it.

SAG FACTORS: ARE THEY HOLDING YOU BACK?

Read each statement and circle the description that most applies to you.

1. I dwell on times when I believe I was unfairly treated. Rarely (0) Often (1) Usually (2)

2. I often find myself dwelling on the what-ifs. Rarely (0) Often (1) Usually (2)

3. When I take on a project, I find doing harder than planning. Rarely (0) Often (1) Usually (2)

4. When I am having a rough time, I tend to question my self-worth. Rarely (0) Often (1) Usually (2)

5. I find myself preoccupied rather than being 100 percent in the moment. Rarely (0) Often (1) Usually (2)

6. I am more negative than I would like to be. Rarely (0) Often (1) Usually (2)

7. I feel it is dangerous to feel confident. Rarely (0) Often (1) Usually (2)

8. The hassles of daily life tend to ruffle me. Rarely (0) Often (1) Usually (2)

9. I find it difficult to set goals. Rarely (0) Often (1) Usually (2)

10. If I make a mistake or fail to achieve a goal I tend to become self-critical. Rarely (0) Often (1) Usually (2)

11. As I look back on my career, I find that I often have been outmaneuvered by others. Rarely (0) Often (1) Usually (2)

12. When I am under stress, I tend to

    a. Avoid (I want to withdraw from the situation).   Rarely (0)   Often (1)   Usually (2)

    b. Attack (I want to devalue or manipulate those involved).   Rarely (0)   Often (1)   Usually (2)

Note the reverse number value below.

    c. Approach (I try to understand the situation).   Rarely (2)   Often (1)   Usually (0)

13. When facing a job–threatening setback, I tend to look for new opportunities.   Rarely (2)   Often (1)   Usually (0)

14. I feel a sense of mission at work, a purpose larger than a paycheck.   Rarely (2)   Often (1)   Usually (0)

15. When I compare myself to others, I usually come out as follows.   Less than (2) Equal to (1) Better (0)

16. I usually appreciate the contributions of others.   Rarely (2)   Often (1)   Usually (0)

Add each column for a subtotal (note the change after item 12b).   _____   _____   _____

Add the three columns.   _____

SAG SCORE INTERPRETATION

The minimum score is 0. If you scored 0, you are a supremely effective potential leader—keep going!

The maximum score is 36. If you scored 36, it is good you have discovered your potential derailment weak spots early in the game. Now it is time to do something about them.

The implications of your scores are as follows:

0–9	You are in excellent condition to go forward.
10–18	You are on your way but could use a tune-up.
19–27	You have tendencies toward sag that should be addressed if you want to achieve your goals. You might consider reading some of the books listed below, attending a workshop, or consulting a professional.
28–36	Danger zone. If your sag score is this high, you need to pay serious attention. It may be useful to consult with a professional or a career counselor. The books listed below will be helpful. This level of sag will keep you from achieving your goals.

SOME HELPFUL RESOURCES

Dubrin, Andrew. *Winning Office Politics.* Englewood Cliffs, NJ: Prentice-Hall, 1990.

Hallowell, Edward. *Worry.* New York: Ballantine, 1997.

Mundis, Jerrold. *Earn What You Deserve: How to Stop Underearning and Start Thriving.* New York: Bantam, 1995.

Sotile, Wayne, and Sotile, Mary. *Supercouple Syndrome.* New York: Wiley, 1998.

YapKo, Michael. *Breaking the Patterns of Depression.* New York: Doubleday, 1997.

18 The Dinner Party

On a wet November evening a group meets for dinner at an apartment in the Upper East Side of Manhattan. It is a gathering of past and present board members of the Financial Women's Association. The FWA is a network that helps women steer their way through the financial community. These are some of the brightest trailblazers in New York. They make no apologies for their competence and ambition; they are women who know themselves well and make use of those insights to guide their careers.

Tonight they reminisce, remembering past obstacles and the self-management tools they used to overcome them. Claire Irving heads Investigative Consultants International, a white-collar investigation firm that serves the business and legal communities worldwide. She recalls a painful period 15 years ago when she was enticed to join a financial services firm with the promise of being made a partner within 12 months. She was brought in to help another partner set up an international mergers and acquisitions unit. "It is clear now," she says, "that he only went along to get my contacts. Soon he was taking my clients out to dinner without me and cutting me out of internal meetings." He also started spreading rumors. The atmosphere became ugly, and within three years Irving left the firm. No longer enthusiastic about investment banking, she decided to lock up her Rolodex of contacts in the bottom drawer and get creative about her next career move. Irving is a Blue Strategist with a strong need to find new ways to solve problems. For four months she read about different fields and called people up for short information meetings. One day someone offered her a job in a major investigative firm. She signed on, stayed for six years, and then left to start her own company. She enjoys the field, which demands strong problem-solving abilities. Like most Strategists, Irving likes to be in charge of her own show.

Sarabeth Wizen, a Gold Conservator, recalls the credibility issues involved in her role as the president of a small Wall Street brokerage. It was a firm where everyone from the chairman down answered his or her own phone. "I was 35 years old, and I had a young voice," she recalls. "As a result, everyone would call and say, 'Can I talk to your boss?' I would say, 'I am the boss,' and they wouldn't believe me." Conservators have a strong feeling preference and do not like to confront people. As a result, rather than making an issue of the problem, she started answering the phone, "Sarabeth Wizen, President. May I help you?" The clients responded accordingly. "Interestingly," she says "this continuous affirmation served also to increase my self-confidence. I began to feel that I really belonged in this position, which was not normally open to women in the industry at that time."

Individuals who are comfortable with themselves handle obstacles with greater ease than do those who are not. A poignant example is the story of Lenore Albom, a vice president at the Chase Manhattan Bank. Several years ago things were humming for her. She had a full life that included a job she enjoyed and was looking forward to serving as president of the FWA in the year to come. Suddenly she was diagnosed with cancer. The illness, she was told, was serious and would require intense treatment. "I had seen numerous doctors in that one week," she says, recalling the anguish of the moment, "and I was sitting in my office in shock and had no idea what would come next."

While recovering, she had time to evaluate how she viewed her career and the direction she wanted it to take. "Things got clear and focused," she recalls. "I had a lot of time to think about the kind of impact I wanted to make in the business world." Since that time she has come a long way and is now part of Chase's e-commerce business. "I used to sweat the small stuff," she says. "Now I have a unique perspective on the importance of developing good leadership skills and building successful relationships in business."

Norma Niehoff, a financial consultant and a Green Mentor, speaks about an earlier battle with the executives at a prestigious money management firm. Paid on a commission basis, she excitedly announced that she was about to introduce a very major new account to the firm, one that would increase their earnings 50 percent. Suddenly all the senior guys at the firm started moving in on it. They would go through her files, set up meetings in her name, and then not tell her about the place and time. It became increasingly difficult to prove that it was her account and get her share of the commissions. She contemplated suing the firm but knew that in the early 1980s that would have meant the end of her career in finance. Ultimately she decided that a hostile environment was not one that played to the strengths of her Green Mentor style. She enjoyed persuading and working with a team of cooperative people. Coincident with assuming the presidency of the FWA, Niehoff moved to a major insurance company that allowed her to do what she does best: bring in new business. "Sometimes the best way to deal with an obstacle," she says, "is to know when to walk away from it."

For Jeannette Hobson, a principal at Gateway Consulting, walking away was not an option, although she tried. She was a vice president at the Bank of New York who wanted her own business. She found a partner, and in 1990 they formed a small firm that would be the first to provide marketing database services. Their arrangement was that he would provide the technological expertise and she would market it. Suddenly he died of a heart attack. Almost overnight the clients and staff disappeared, realizing that she did not have the technological knowledge to carry the project through. For six months

Hobson lost her self-confidence and could not function. Then she took a hard look at herself. In typical Blue Strategist fashion, she sat down and analyzed the qualities that had contributed to her success at the bank and why she had left a promising career to move out on her own. Suddenly she realized that she had had a vision and that the vision was still attainable. She would find a different way to get there. Today she works as a coach to CEOs and consults on strategic planning and implementation. The variety of problems and people provides the intellectual stimulation and challenge needed by this personality group.

For Mina Baker Knoll, a partner at Deloitte and Touche, the challenge was more self-directed. After 18 years of working with corporate clients, she wanted to pursue a long-standing dream of going into public service. Granted a leave of absence, she moved back to Pennsylvania to run for the position of state treasurer. With little money up-front this meant doing it all: fund-raising, canvassing voters, setting up an office, managing the staff, dealing with the press, and strategizing to win. The race was close; she lost by only 2 percent. But as a Red Tactician, Knoll found the experience energizing. It played to her unique leadership strengths, which include the ability to embrace risk, persuade others, take charge, negotiate, find compromises and handle pressure with grace and skill. "It was fun," she recalls, still relishing her memories of the race. "I loved the excitement and challenge of persuading people to support me." Today she is back at Deloitte and Touche with a new perspective that enables her to work on cutting-edge projects. Someday she will be in politics again. "And this time," she says with a grin. "I will win."

Debra Flanz, a leading marketing consultant in the financial industry, is another Gold Trustee. Her obstacle was less dramatic but equally important. "I didn't have an MBA," she says, "and after several years of working in a family firm in the Midwest, I set my sights on developing my career in New York." After doing some research she realized that the fastest track into management for a woman without an MBA was sales. She joined a large financial services firm and found herself making at least 30 cold calls a day. "It was a painful experience," she says. "I'd come home brain-dead every night. But it was the best thing I could have learned. Business is about persuasion. Being an effective manager is about persuasion. As a result, my career has evolved into marketing highly sophisticated services to the most senior executives, including the CEOs of Fortune 500 companies. I don't hesitate to call anybody to suggest a business idea. I know the worst thing they can say to me is no, and I know that no can change to yes tomorrow or the day after." The lesson learned for a Gold Trustee is that if you focus on and stick to your plan, you ultimately will succeed.

In looking at these women and the others profiled in this book, one draws some promising conclusions. They can be themselves and still achieve their goals. The glass ceiling is slowly receding. Linda Seale, a Manhattan-based executive coach who specializes in senior executive women, believes the trend toward women succeeding in top leadership roles is skyrocketing. "Women are demonstrating out-standing leadership performance in a broad scope of industry sectors," she says. "The business landscape offers diverse role models to learn from, and women in power are changing the rules for success. In this new century women have more support to help them succeed than ever before."

A persistent refrain weaves its way through many of these interviews: If they had to redo it, they would spend more time understanding themselves. They would explore with greater depth the nature of their unique strengths and whether those strengths were in sync with the demands of their chosen professions.

Ultimately, the quest for leadership is an inner journey. Our best tool is still ourselves. Understanding that tool is a bit like peeling an onion. The more you peel, the closer you get to the core of who you are. Confidence is not obtained without struggling and overcoming personal doubts. Self-knowledge leads to self-management, which leads to confidence and accomplishment, which produce self-esteem and ultimately the ability to lead and influence others. Master the formula well. It is your passport to success.

BUILDING BLOCKS OF LEADERSHIP

Leadership

⇧

Self-Esteem

⇧

Accomplishment

⇧

Self-Confidence

⇧

Self-Management

⇧

Self-Knowledge

APPENDIX

A When You Have Close Scores

If you are undecided about your preferences or feel that your profile does not fit your personality, read through the following statements. Insert the appropriate letter in your color code combination.

If you want the most thorough possible evaluation of your personality type, contact Consulting Psychologists Press in Palo Alto, California, for the name of a Myers-Briggs counselor.

If you have close scores between A and B, choose one of the following:

I am interested in the world right now. I am realistic. I get impatient with people who focus on theories and abstractions. I think it is important to first have the facts and then to move on to the possibilities. I like working on projects that have tangible results. I am admired as a practical thinker.

I am an A

I usually look at future possibilities. I see the big picture more than I see the facts. I like to be with imaginative people. I get impatient with too many details and prefer discussing ideas and theories. I always look for new patterns and relationships among ideas. I am admired as a conceptual thinker.

I am a B

If you have close scores between 1 and 2, choose one of the following:

Reason is very important to me. I base decisions on rational data. I think it is very important to be objective and fair. If asked for my opinion, I offer constructive criticism first. Logic rules my life. I am good at analyzing plans and situations. I quickly see cause and effect. At my most extreme people may view me as cold.

I am a 1

When I make a decision, I take into account my personal values and the impact of the decision on others. I think it is very important to be compassionate. I am empathetic and quick to understand the motivations and needs of others. If asked for my opinion, I usually give a compliment before offering criticism. At my most extreme people may view me as soft.

I am a 2

If you have close scores between □ and ∇ choose one of the following:

I set goals and follow my schedule. I am always punctual and sometimes early. I like things to be settled in advance. I make and complete lists every day. I am decisive. When possible, I like to be in control; then I know things will be done properly. At my most extreme people call me rigid and controlling.

I am a □

I am spontaneous and adaptable. I like to go with the flow and stay open to new options. I normally meet deadlines at the last minute. Too much planning takes the fun out of things. I handle problems as they arise. I am easygoing. I like surprises. At my most extreme people call me disorganized and flaky.

I am a ∇

If you have close scores between ee and ii, choose one of the following:

I prefer face-to-face interaction to the written word. I tend to have a broad circle of friends and a broad range of interests. I enjoy meeting new people and usually am energized by people and activities.

I am an ee

I prefer e-mail or the written word to meeting people face-to-face. I tend to have a few close friends. Although I like people, I am reenergized by my time alone. I normally reflect before I speak or act. Meeting too many new people tires me.

I am an ii

B Leadership Revisited

Dr. Bonnie Kellen

The concept of who is a leader, who needs leadership skills, and what leadership competencies are has evolved dramatically. Indeed, the whole context of work has changed drastically and continues to change at an accelerated rate. As we have moved from an agricultural economy, through the industrial revolution and industrialization, to the information age and now into the era of the knowledge worker of the twenty-first century, leadership has moved with us. This evolution has not been uniform, however. The developing world has lagged behind the industrialized world and may exhibit some of the features of earlier stages of development. If you do not understand these historical and generational differences, you will be at a great disadvantage in a global, interconnected world. As a leader you will be expected to deal with all these nuances as you interact with representatives of different cultures.

Our country was founded on the radical belief that leaders do not have to be kings or their descendants. In spite of the political revolution, attitudes were slow to change. During the industrial era workers were accustomed to relationships at work that were formal and hier-archical; they were fearful of dismissal and were obedient. Leadership styles were accordingly hierarchical and remained so through the nineteenth century and well into the twentieth. In the generations after World War I shifts began to be apparent.

As the generations changed, certain features of workplace culture also changed in concert with the wider historical changes that were shaping society. Workplace issues were addressed differently in each generation and leadership styles changed accordingly. New develop-ments in technology led to entirely new work situations for which fresh leadership solutions had to be found. The following chart syn-thesizes some aspects of the flow and interdependence of historical developments, workplace culture and practices, and the development of leadership frontiers, which both influenced and responded to these developments.

THE NEW WORKPLACE

We have all witnessed jobs being rendered obsolete by the thousands. Organizations are eliminating many layers of the hierarchy, and decentralization, speed, and flexibility are valued. The wish for cradle-to-grave employment is now unrealistic. Loyalty on either side is ten-uous. Through downsizing or by choice, more individuals are finding themselves entrepreneurs and on their own. Even those who are lucky enough to keep full-time employment constantly shift around to get the job done. Specific job descriptions will not be practical for the companies of the future.

Does this sound like science fiction? Handy[46] describes today's "virtual organization" as 20/80, with only 20 percent of people employed full-time. The rest are dispersed, becoming subcontractors, the products of outsourcing, who work on a contractual, part-time, temporary, or project basis.

The globalization of the world economy that followed the cold war has added a new dimension. This globalization involves an inter-meshing of markets, finance, and technology. The world is shrinking.

This is a period of connectedness, which is both facilitated and symbolized by the Internet, where no one is in charge.

THE E-ECONOMY

The question that is arising is whether a new leadership paradigm will emerge on the high-tech frontier of the Internet. The driving force of the new high-tech companies is engineers and "technogeeks" rather than traditional managers. This is a culture that values youth, nonconformity, a casual and restless style, entrepreneurship, brains, and money. Since the whole world is the potential marketplace for e-commerce, the twenty-first century may well be marked by a gold rush mentality. There is intense pressure across the whole spectrum of business to stake out territory. What will this new phenomenon do to leadership?

CAREER SURVIVAL IN THE TWENTY-FIRST CENTURY

The new reality is that individuals work for themselves first and for organizations second. According to management guru Peter Drucker, the new societal demand to "manage oneself" is no less than a revolution in modern society.[47] It demands that each knowledge worker think and behave as a chief executive officer on her own behalf. Drucker discerns two new realities: (1) Workers will outlive organizations, and (2) the knowledge worker of the twenty-first century will have high mobility. He emphasizes that knowing and developing your strengths and placing yourself where those strengths can produce performance results are the key. Knowledge about how you perform and get things done as compared with how others perform is also essential. Drucker stresses the importance of being aware of your values.

For Barbara Moses, career intelligence means becoming a career activist, defining yourself independently from your organization. In developing your portfolio of skills and competencies you must play to your strengths and preferences and take charge of your career strategy.[48] Career power in the twenty-first century as well as self-leadership skills will include global thinking, career lattices rather than ladders, sensitive communication and feedback ability, and the ability to build trust. Reputation will become all-important and will be available to others on the Internet.

INCLUSION: DIVERSITY IN THE TWENTY-FIRST CENTURY

A diverse workforce is a simplistic definition of the global workforce of the twenty-first century. Diversity has been understood as the attempt to include minority groups, women, gays, older workers, and the disabled. Magnify this a hundred times in the global market, where one is dealing with multiple cultures that wish to retain their identities or those have different business customs. They may also individually be evolving through the same or different generations of leadership at their own pace. In most countries establishing a relationship is a prerequisite for doing business. The diplomatic leader of the twenty-first century will have to connect and communicate with all kinds of people.

THE DIPLOMATIC LEADERSHIP IN THE TWENTY-FIRST CENTURY

The new leaders of the twenty-first century must adapt to a new world. These renaissance leaders must be agile competitors who can thrive in a world of virtual enterprising, dynamic teaming, and knowledge networking, all in a global context.

The diplomatic leader must be flexible and responsive, able to play different roles at different times—whether as team leader, project coordinator, or facilitator—or be part of distributed leadership within a group. She will be in the middle rather than on top. She must be able to transcend boundaries and forge links between organizations. She must have the emotional strength to manage her own and others' anxieties in this fast-paced milieu.

Generation	Historical background	Workplace culture	Flow of leadership/management styles	
Silent generation 1925–1942	Depression and World War I	Formality Respect for seniority and age Hierarchy Obedience Top-down authority Few employee rights One person, one boss	1900s	Scientific management Efficiency and Industrial engineering
			1940s	Operations research Quantitative Solutions
Boomers 1943–1964	Rock 'n' roll Me generation Women's movement	Self-interest Teamwork Questioning of authority Management development	1950s 1960s 1970s	Organization man Loyalty to organization
Yuppies	Birth control Universal education		1960s 1970s	Human relations Motivation, participation
Information age	Equal employment opportunity laws End of cold war Credit cards Television Globalization Divorce	Legal rights Diversity Materialism Downsizing Free agents Computers	1950s 1960s 1970s 1980s	Strategic planning Cognitive management Japanese management Quality assurance and novel approaches

Generation	Characteristics		Era	Management/Leadership
Generation X 1965–1981	Globalization	Casual workplace	1990s	Matrix management
	Materialism	Loyalty to self		Project management
	Downsizing	Distrust of hierarchy		
MTV generation	Dual-career families	Portable careers		Team building
	Computer as a friend	Balance of work and play		Organizational development
Knowledge workers	Credit card debt	Cutting-edge technology		
	Competition	Not wanting to pay dues		Situational leadership
	Cross-functional teams	Entitlements		Leadership style adapts to situation
	Knowledge networking	Adapting to change		
	Free agents	Lifelong learning	2000+	New forms of information networking
	Decentralization	Entrepreneurs/intrapreneurs		
		Understaffing		Diplomatic leadership
				Inclusion

Leadership is still about getting things done through people, and a diplomatic leader must generate feelings of inclusion and connectedness and, most important, of being valued and appreciated.

THE IMPENDING LEADERSHIP SHORTAGE

With many baby boomers taking early retirement, there will be a leadership shortage, especially in light of the drop in the birthrate after that generation. This will be intensified by the need for everyone to be her own leader and manage her own career.

Women leaders will have greater opportunities in the next generation especially since there is evidence that younger women prefer to work for a female boss. In a 1993 Gallup Poll, 61 percent of generation X women answered that they preferred to work for a woman, compared with 26 percent of older women.[49]

GOOD NEWS

Leadership skills can be learned and developed. Keep in mind this short legacy and how you can adapt your leadership style to an ever-changing context. The profiles in this book will sharpen your image of what is involved in effective leadership. Being aware of the experience of the past will help prepare you to succeed in your own leadership adventure.

NOTES

1. MBTI and Myers-Briggs Type Indicator are registered trademarks of Consulting Psychologists Press, Inc. For further information, contact the publisher at Consulting Psychologists Press, 3803 East Bayshore Road, Palo Alto, CA 94030, (800) 624-1765.

2. Howard Gardner, *Leading Minds.* New York: HarperCollins, 1995, p. 6.

3. Deborah Blum, *Sex on the Brain,* New York: Penguin USA, 1999, pp. 44–46.

4. Thinking/feeling ratios among women have ranged from 40 percent/60 percent to 25 percent/75 percent depending on the sample used. Surveys from my seminars reflect a split of 65 percent/35 percent and may indicate greater freedom among women in today's workforce to express their thinking preference.

5. Statistics on the four preferences taken from Isabel Briggs Myers, Mary H. McCaulley, Naomi Quenk, and Allen Hammer, *MBTI Manual,* 3d ed. Palo Alto, CA: Consulting Psychologists Press, 1998, p. 298, and data collected at seminars.

6. *MBTI Manual,* p. 298.

7. Mary Lord, "A Sharecropper's Daughter Revives Labor's Grass Roots," *U.S. News & World Report,* December 25, 1995, p. 95.

8. Betsy Morris, "It's Her Job Too," *Fortune,* February 2, 1998, p. 65.

9. *MBTI Manual,* p. 298.

10. Cindy McDaniel, "Mixing Medicine and the Media: Dr. Nancy Snyderman," *Arthritis Today,* January 1991, p. 27.

11. Roger Morris, *Partners in Power.* New York: Henry Holt & Company, 1996, p. 113.

12. Evan Thomas, "Bill and Hillary's Long, Hot Summer," *Newsweek,* October 19, 1998, p. 38.

13 Ibid., p. 41

14. James Bennet, "The Next Clinton," *New York Times,* May 30, 1999, p. 26.

15. David Keirsey and Ray Choiniere, *Presidential Temperament.* Del Mar, CA: Prometheus Nemesis, 1999, appendix.

16. Lucinda Franks, "The Intimate Hillary," *Talk,* September 1999, p. 174.

17. Myrna Blyth, "Hillary Speaks Out," *Ladies Home Journal,* November 1998, p. 140.

18. Daniel LeDuc, "Kathleen Kennedy Townsend," *Washington Post,* November 28, 1999, p. W6.

19. Rory Ross, "Countess Albina du Boisrouvray," *Tatler,* September 1999, pp. 186–188.

20. Marlin Fitzwater, *Call the Briefing.* New York: New York Times Books, 1995, p 82.

21. Ibid., p. 92.

22. Facts and quotes culled from her autobiography, *Front Row at the White House.* New York: Scribner's, 1999.

23. Patricia Sellers, "The Toughest Babe in Business," *Fortune,* September 8, 1997, pp. 63–66.

24. Alison Frankel, "Skadden's Queen of Torts," *American Lawyer,* June 1991, pp. 81–83.

25. Sandy McClure, *Christie Whitman for the People.* Amherst, NY: Prometheus, 1996, pp. 16–18.

26. Antonia Felix, *Christie Todd Whitman.* New York: Kensington, 1996, p. 198–202.

27. Patricia Beard, *Growing Up Republican.* New York: HarperCollins, 1996, pp. 196–197.

28. McClure, op. cit. p. 234.

29. Lisa Belkin, "Keeping to the Center Lane," *New York Times,* May 5, 1996, p. 50.

30. Felix, op. cit. p. 166.

31. Chandrani Ghosh, "The Comeback Queen," *Forbes,* September 20, 1999, p. 86.

32. Keith Alexander, "Quiet Storm," *Emerge,* September 1999, p. 44.

33. William Stadiem, *Too Rich.* New York: Carroll & Graf, 1991, p. 3.

34. Ibid., pp. 4–5.

35. Material culled from her autobiography, Judy Resnick and Gene Stone,

I've Been Rich. I've Been Poor. Rich Is Better. New York: Golden Books, 1999.

36. *MBIT Manual,* p. 298.

37. P. S. Henley, "Alexandra Lebenthal: Yours for Life," *Lifestyles,* vol. 26, 1998, p. 22.

38. Rose Blue and Joanne Bernstein, *Contemporary Women's Series: Diane Sawyer.* Hillsdale, NJ: Enslow, p. 41.

39. Ibid., p. 77.

40. Kim Hubbard, "Wendy Wasserstein," *People,* June 25, 1990, p. 99.

41. Dinitia Smith, "The Newest Wasserstein Creation Comes Home," *New York Times,* December 23, 1999, p. E1.

42. Elisabeth Bumiller, "Out of the Shadows of a Noted Family," *New York Times,* May 28, 1998, p. B2.

43. Peter Colliers, *The Rockefellers.* New York: Holt Rinehart & Winston, 1976, p. 29.

44. Dr. Steven Stosney, Director of Compassion Power, 16220 Frederick Road, Gaithersburg, MD 20870.

45. Wayne Sotile and Mary Sotile, *Supercouple Syndrome.* New York: Wiley, 1998.

46. Charles Handy, "The New Language of Organizing and Its Implication for Leaders," in The Drucker Foundation, *The Leader of the Future.* San Francisco: Jossey-Bass, 1996, p. 6.

47. Peter Drucker, "Managing Oneself," *Management Challenges for the 21st Century.* New York: Harper Business, 1999, pp. 163–195.

48. Barbara Moses, "Career Intelligence: The 12 New Rules, *The Futurist,* August/September 1999, p. 28.

49. Gallup Monthly Poll, 1993.

RESOURCES

GENERAL INFORMATION BOOKS

Beard, Patricia. *Growing Up Republican*. New York: HarperCollins, 1996.

Blue, Rose, and Bernstein, Joanne. *Diane Sawyer: Super Newswoman*. Hillside, NJ: Enslow, 1990.

Blum, Deborah, *Sex on the Brain: The Biological Differences between Men and Women*. New York: Penguin USA, 1999.

Drucker, Peter. "Managing Oneself," in *Management Challenges for the 21st Century*. New York: Harper Business, 1999.

Felix, Antonia. *Christie Todd Whitman*. New York: Kensington, 1996.

Fitzwater, Marlin. *Call the Briefing*. New York: New York Times Books, 1995.

Gardner, Howard. *Leading Minds*. New York: HarperCollins, 1995.

Handy, Charles. "The New Language of Organizing and Its Implication for Leaders" in the Drucker Foundation, *The Leader of the Future*. San Francisco, Jossey-Bass, 1996.

Jupiter, Marlene. *Savvy Investing for Women: Strategies from a Self-Made Wall Street Millionaire*. Paramus, NJ: Prentice-Hall Press, , 1998

McClure, Sandy. *Christie Whitman for the People*. Amherst, NY: Prometheus, 1996.

Morris, Roger. *Partners in Power*. NY: Henry Holt, 1996.

Resnick, Judy and, Stone, Gene (contributor). *I've Been Rich. I've Been Poor. Rich Is Better*. New York: Golden Books, 1999.

Stadiem, William. *Too Rich*, New York: Carroll & Graf, 1991.

Thomas, Helen. *Front Row at the White House*. New York: Scribner's, 1999.

BOOKS ON TYPES

Barger, Nancy, and Kirby, Linda. *Challenge of Change in Organizations*. Palo Alto, CA.: Consulting Psychologists Press, 1995.

Baron, Renee. *What Type Am I*. New York: Penguin, 1998.

Barr, Lee, and Barr, Norma. *Leadership Development*. Austin, TX: Eakin Press, 1994.

Berens, Linda V. *Understanding Yourself and Others*. Huntington Beach, CA: Telos Publications, 1998.

Berens, Linda V., and Nardi, Dario. *Description for Self-Discovery* and *Character* and *Personality Type*. Huntington Beach, CA: Telus Publications, 1999.

Bridges, William. *The Character of the Organizations: Using Jungian Types in Organizational Development*. Palo Alto, CA: Consulting Psychologist Press, 1992.

Brock, Susan. *Using Type in Selling*, Palo Alto, CA: Consulting Psychologist Press, 1994.

Brownsword, Alan W. *It Takes All Types*. Nicasio, CA: HRM Press, 1987.

Campbell, Joseph. *The Portable Jung*. New York: Viking Press, 1971.

Delunas, Eve. *Survival Games Personalities Play*. Carmel, CA: Sunflower Ink, 1992.

Fitzgerald, Catherine, and Kirby, Linda, eds. *Developing Leaders*. Palo Alto, CA: Davies-Black Publishing, 1997.

Giovannoni, Louise, Berens, Linda, and Cooper, Sue. *Introduction to Temperament*. Huntington Beach, CA: Cooper, Berens, 1986.

Golden, Bonnie. *Self-Esteem and Psychological Type*. Gainesville, FL: Center for Applications of Psychological Type, 1994.

Hirsh, Sandra, with Kise, Jane. *Work It Out: Clues for Solving People Problems at Work*. Palo Alto, CA: Davies-Black, 1996.

Hirsh, Sandra, and Kummerow, Jean. *Introduction to Type in Organizations*. Palo Alto, CA: Consulting Psychologist Press, 1990.

Isachsen, Olaf, and Berens, Linda. *Working Together*. Coronado, CA: Neworld Management Press, 1988.

Keirsey, David W., and Bates, Marilyn. *Please Understand Me* and *Please Understand Me II*. Del Mar, CA: Prometheus Nemesis, 1978, 1998.

Keirsey, David, and Choiniere, Ray. *Presidential Temperament*. Del Mar, CA: Prometheus Nemesis, 1999.

Kroeger, Otto, and Thuesen, Janet. *Type Talk, Type Talk at Work* and *16 Ways to Love Your Lover*. New York: Dell, 1988, 1993, 1994.

Lawrence, Gordon. *People Types and Tiger Stripes*. Gainesville, FL: Center for Applications of Psychological Type, 1979, 1993.

Murray, William. *Give Yourself the Unfair Advantage*. Gladwyne, PA: Type & Temperament, 1995.

Murphy, Elizabeth. *The Developing Child: Using Jungian Type to Understand Children*. Palo Alto, CA: Consulting Psychologists Press, 1992.

Myers, Isabel Briggs, with Myers, Peter. *Gifts Differing*. Palo Alto, CA: Consulting Psychologist Press, 1980.

Myers, Isabel Briggs, McCaulley, Mary H, Quenk, Naomi, and Hammer, Allen. *MBTI Manual*, 3d ed. Palo Alto, CA: Consulting Psychologist Press, 1998.

Myers, Katharine D., and Kirby, Linda K. *Introduction to Type Dynamics and Development*. Palo Alto, CA: Consulting Psychologist Press, 1994.

Pearman, Roger. *Hardwired Leadership*. Palo Alto, CA: Consulting Psychologist Press, 1999.

Provost, Judith, and Anchors, Scott. *Applications for the Myers-Briggs Type Indicator in Higher Education*. Palo Alto, CA: Consulting Psychologist Press, 1987.

Quenk, Naomi. *Besides Ourselves: Our Hidden Personality in Everyday Life*. Palo Alto, CA: Consulting Psychologist Press, 1993.

RoBards, Martine, and RoBards, Michael. *Type-Temperament Trainers Resources*. Louisville, KY.

Rogers, Jenny. *Sixteen Personality Types*. Cambridge Management Center, London, UK, 1997.

Tieger, Paul D., and Barron–Tieger, Barbara. *Do What You Are: The Art of Speed-Reading People*. Boston: Little, Brown, 1995, 1998.

PROFESSIONAL DEVELOPMENT RESOURCES

Jeannette Hobson
Gateway Consulting
300 Winston Towers, 407
Cliffside Park, NJ 07010
(201) 886-1311
www.gcgresults.com
Provides strategic planning, implementation and leadership coaching for small and medium size companies.

Dr. Bonnie Kellen
Licensed Psychologist
150 East 58th Street, 27th Floor
New York, NY 10155
(212) 888-7887; fax (212) 588-9721
Provides individual and couple therapy, personality and career assessments, and counseling and training and development (including Myers-Briggs).

Linda C. Seale
The Seale Group
575 Madison Avenue, Suite 1006
New York, NY
(212) 605-0440; fax (212) 308-9834
Provides executive coaching for senior management and high potential executives.

Leadership Q and Investment Q
Zichy & Associates
340 East 64th Street
New York, NY 10021
(212) 755-2849; fax (212) 355-0637
www.leadershipQ.com
Provides private consultation and seminars on leadership development, team building, and the psychology of investing.

U.S.-BASED TYPE AND TEMPERAMENT ORGANIZATIONS AND RESOURCES

Association for Psychological Type (APT)
4700 West Lake Avenue
Glenview, IL 60025-1485
(847) 375-4717; fax (847) 375-6317
www.aptcentral.org
An international membership organization open to all people interested in personality types. Sponsors conferences, workshops, and local chapter activities.

Center for Application of Psychological Type (CAPT)
2720 Northwest Sixth Street
Gainesville, FL 32609
1-800-777-2278
www.capt.org
Produces the CAPT bibliography, a semiannual listing of more than 1700 research papers, articles, dissertations, and books related to personality types. Also provides qualification training programs, publishes type-related books, and maintains the Isabel Briggs Myers Memorial Library.

Consulting Psychologist Press
3803 East Bayshore Road
Palo Alto, CA 94303
(800) 624-1765
www.cpp-db.com
Exclusive publisher of the Myers-Briggs Type Indicator, parent of Davies-Black Publishing.

Leadership Dimension
Louisville, KY
(502) 473-1931
www.insightsystem.com
Provides consultation and training related to personality types.

Otto Kroeger Associates
3605 Chain Bridge Road
Fairfax, VA 22030
(703) 591-6284; fax (703) 591-8338
www.typetalk.com
Provides qualification training programs in the Myers–Briggs Type Indicator
and distributes books and type-related materials.

Prometheus Nemesis Book Company
Box 2748,
Del Mar, CA 92014
(800) 754-0039 or (760) 632-1575
www.keirsey.com
Produces books and videos on David Keirsey's temperament model.

The Temperament Research Institute
16152 Beach Boulevard, Suite 179
Huntington Beach, CA 92647
(800) 700-4TRI; fax (714) 841-0312
www.tri-network.com
Provides training and certification by facilitators, consultants, and coaches in
the TRI methodology as well as qualifications in the MBTI.

Type Resources
101 Chestnut Street, H-135
Gaithersburg, MD 20877-6284
(310) 840-8575
Provides qualification training in the Myers–Briggs Type Indicator.

Type and Temperament
Box 200
Gladwyne, PA 19035-0200
(800) 447-8973
Publishes and distributes books and materials related to personality types.

INTERNATIONAL TYPE AND TEMPERAMENT ORGANIZATIONS AND RESOURCES

Anima-Reason Consultants
Budapest, Hungary
(361) 210-7095; fax (361) 210-2854
www.anima-racio.hu

Association Française des Types Psychologiques (AFTP)
Paris, France
(33) 1-48.83-14-56; fax (33) 1-48-83-22-10

Association for Psychological Type, Singapore (APTSing)
PA Consulting Group, Singapore
(65) 296-4066; fax (65) 285-5266

Australian Association for Psychological Type (AAPT)
Queensland 4145, Australia
(617) 3394-2807
cbm@bigpond.com; aapt@aapt.org.au

British Association for Psychological Type (BAPT)
Devon, United Kingdom
(44) 1404-851-255
cornerstones@compuserve.com

New Zealand Association for Psychological Type (NZAPT)
Wellington, New Zealand
(64) 4-472-0430 and (64) 4-472-0430
leggat@actrix.gen.nz

Association for Psychological Type Canada
Canada Harrowsmith, ON KDH IVD
(613) 372-2313
Lynda@kingston.net

South Africa Association for Psychological Type (SAAPT)
Betty's Bay, South Africa
riavn@iafrica.com

LEADERS PROFILED IN THE BOOK

Sherry Barrat is president and CEO of the Northern Trust Bank of California, a subsidiary of the Northern Trust Company. She is a Blue Strategist.

Jessica M. Bibliowicz is president and CEO of National Financial Partners, a group designed to acquire investment advisory firms with high-net-worth clients. The group owns 63 independent advisers and has another 250 deals in the pipeline, and plans to go public within five years. She is a Red Tactician.

Sheila Birnbaum is considered one of the top female lawyers in the country. A senior partner at Skadden, Arps, Slate, Meagher, & Flom, she heads the firm's mass tort and insurance group, managing 70 lawyers and a practice in excess of $30 million a year. She is a Red Tactician.

Countess Albina du Boisrouvray founded the Association François-Zavier Bagnoud—a global relief foundation—in memory of a son killed in a plane crash. She is also a film producer with 22 films to her credit and has been vice president of the Cannes Film Festival jury. She is a Blue Innovator.

Linda Chavez-Thomson is the executive vice president of the AFL-CIO, the highest-ranking woman in a labor federation of over 13 million members. She is a Gold Conservator.

Ellen Chesler is a senior fellow and program director at George Soros's Open Society Institute. An international foundation, the institute supports social-policy change programs. She is a Gold Trustee.

Hillary Clinton was part of the impeachment inquiry staff that investigated Richard Nixon. She has been a top lawyer and First Lady of the United States as well as a senatorial candidate in New York. She is a Blue Strategist.

Barbara Corcoran founded the Corcoran Group, a Manhattan real estate agency. Today the group, which she chairs, has 12 offices, a sales staff of 500, and more than $2 billion in sales per year. She is a Green Mentor.

Ibolya David is Hungary's minister of justice, the only woman in Hungary's current government. She is also president of her party, the Hungarian Democratic Forum coalition. She is a Green Mentor.

Abigail Disney, a longtime philanthropist, started The Daphne Foundation to provide reliable annual support to grassroots philanthropic projects. She is a Green Advocate.

Peggy Dulany is the founder and president of the Synergos Institute, a nonprofit organization that promotes grassroots entrepreneurial activities in developing countries. She is a Green Advocate.

Lisa Egbuonu-Davis complemented her medical degree with an MBA in health care management. She is vice president of global outcomes research and medical services for Pfizer Pharmaceuticals Group. She is a Blue Strategist.

Jean Hamilton is executive vice president of the Prudential Insurance Company of America and CEO of the institutional unit. She is a Blue Strategist.

Catherine Hughes founded and chairs Radio One, the nation's largest black-owned radio network, with twenty-seven stations and gross revenues of $85 million. She is a Red Realist.

Kay Bailey Hutchison is a Republican senator for Texas, the first woman to hold that post. She is a Gold Trustee.

Rosemary Jordano is founder and CEO of ChildrenFirst, Inc., the nation's largest provider of corporate-sponsored backup child care. She is a Green Advocate.

Marlene Jupiter was a senior vice president at the brokerage house Donaldson, Lufkin & Jenrette before becoming an independent financial consultant and money manager. Her first book, *Savvy Investing for Women,* was published in 1998 and is now in paperback. She is a Gold Conservator.

Sheila Keohane, a former model, is the principal of the Barbizon Modeling School. She is a Gold Trustee.

Alexandra Lebenthal started working for her grand-mother, the famed Wall Street investor Sayra Lebenthal, at age 4. She is president and CEO of Lebenthal & Company and is the youngest woman on Wall Street heading a firm. She is a Green Mentor.

Darla Moore is president of Rainwater, Inc., a private investment firm. She is a Red Tactician.

Barbara Munder, a senior vice president at The McGraw-Hill Companies, is responsible for developing ecommerce strategy for the company's operating units. She is a Blue Strategist.

Nadya designs fabric and clothing. She is a Green Advocate.

Countess Editha Nemes fled the communist government in Hungary for Egypt, where she designed clothes for the children of Egyptian aristocrats. She then moved to the United States, where her designs have been carried by hundreds of stores. Eager for new challenges, she left the fashion business and now works in real estate. She is a Red Realist.

Kim Polese is CEO and cofounder of Marimba, Inc., a $31.1 million software business. In 1997, *Time* magazine named her one of the 25 most influential Americans. She is a Blue Innovator.

Judy Resnick chairs the Resnick Group, which she established in 1996 to provide investment advisory services for women. She drew on her investment experience to write *I've Been Rich. I've Been Poor: Rich is Better* (1998), a book showing women how to take control of their money and their lives. She is a Red Realist.

Diane Sawyer began as a weathergirl and news reporter in Louisville; later she worked as President Richard Nixon's staff assistant. She was the first female correspondent on the *60 Minutes* team. She is a journalist for ABC News. She is a Green Advocate.

Nancy Snyderman is both an active surgeon and a medical correspondent for ABC television. She is a Blue Strategist.

Sonia Sotomayor is a judge in the U.S. Court of Appeals, the nation's second highest court. She is a Gold Trustee.

Candace Straight was Merck's director of investments before leaving to become vice chair of the New Jersey Sports and Exposition Authority and president of WISH List, a Republican group dedicated to electing women to Congress. She is a Blue Innovator.

Jolene Sykes was promoted to president of *Fortune* magazine in 1999. She is a Green Mentor.

Helen Thomas was a Journalist and White House correspondent for United Press International for more than 30 years. She is a Red Tactician.

Janet Thuesen a former White House OD specialist provides qualifying programs for the Myers-Briggs Type Indicator. She is a Green Advocate.

Kathleen Kennedy Townsend was elected lieutenant governor of Maryland in 1994. She is responsible for 15,000 employees and manages a budget of over $1 billion. She is a Blue Innovator.

Wendy Wasserstein, a playwright, has won both a Tony Award and the Pulitzer Prize. Her plays include *The Heidi Chronicles, An American Daughter,* and *The Sisters Rosensweig.* She is a Green Advocate.

Lorna Wendt founded and heads The Institute for Equality in Marriage. She is a Gold Conservator.

Christie Todd Whitman has been governor of New Jersey since 1994, the first woman to be elected to that office. She is a Red Realist.

Marie Wilson is president of the Ms. Foundation for Women. Her initiatives include the development of Take Our Daughters to Work Day and the Women's Economic Development Collaborative Fund, which supports self-employment and job creation programs. Her White House Project is designed to encourage women to run in upcoming elections, with the ultimate goal of electing a woman president of the United States. She is a Green Mentor.

Laura Ziskin has produced numerous films, including *Pretty Woman* and *As Good As It Gets.* After a stint as president of Fox 2000, a division of 20th-Century Fox, she resigned to return to producing full-time. She is a Green Advocate.

INDEX

ABOUT THE AUTHORS

Shoya Zichy heads a New York City based consulting firm specializing in executive coaching and management development seminars based on the Myers-Briggs Type Indicator® and related personality models. She is also a behavioral finance specialist, having developed and implemented programs on the impact of personality on risk tolerance and investment style. Her clients include Con Edison, Standard & Poor's, The Harris Bank, The Northern Trust Bank, and Deloitte & Touche.

Her work been featured in *Fortune* Magazine, on CNN TV, and as the cover story of *Plan Sponsor* magazine. Ms. Zichy's innovative proprietary research on investment behavior serves as a cornerstone of both Peter Tanous' book *The Wealth Equation* and of several Web based investment coaching programs designed for 401(k) participants and high net worth individuals.

Her background includes 15 years in international private banking and journalism at major financial institutions including Institutional Investor, Merrill Lynch, Rothschild Inc, and American Express Bank. Her business experiences, including overseas assignments and a proven track record penetrating new markets, provide a real-world focus to her training programs. In 1990, she tapped into a long-standing interest in psychology and became qualified to administer and interpret the Myers-Briggs Type Indicator®. She has served on the regional board of the Association for Psychological Type and is a past Board member of the Financial Women's Association of New York.

Educated in the United States and Europe, Ms. Zichy holds a masters degree in Education and Counseling from Boston University and is fluent in French and German. She is also an exhibited artist whose paintings hang in numerous private collections. Additional information on Ms. Zichy may be found on her website www.LeadershipQ.com.

Dr. Bonnie Kellen has a Ph.D. in Industrial/Organizational Psychology and a Post-Doctoral Respecialization in Clinical Psychology from Teachers College, Columbia University, where she taught. In addition she has a masters in Vocational Rehabilitation counseling from New York University. In her Manhattan practice she covers a wide range of counseling issues. She works with individuals and couples on personal and professional development using individual psychotherapy, short-term, solutions-based therapy, personality assessment, career counseling and testing, and executive coaching. She also creates and presents training programs for corporations, nonprofits and professional organizations. Dr. Kellen is certified in the Myers-Briggs Type Indicator®.

She has researched and lectured extensively on cross-cultural work practices and perspectives. This involved a comparative understanding of hiring, firing, training, promotion, motivation, management styles, and family and gender issues in such diverse cultures as Japan, the People's Republic of China, and Saudi Arabia. For eight years she was cochair of the International Training Group of the American society for Trainers and Developers and was a member of the Society's executive board.

Another area of interest to Dr. Kellen is "our psychological relationship to money." She cowrote a chapter on "Debtors Anonymous and Psychotherapy" for the book *I Shop, Therefore I Am* edited by Dr. April Lane Benson, Dr. Kellen can be contacted at: (212) 888-7887.